BEYOND DISRUPTION

A collaborative work

by Jean-Marie Dru

and business partners

BEYOND DISRUPTION

CHANGING THE RULES IN THE MARKETPLACE

An Adweek Book

JOHN WILEY & SONS, INC.

This publication is designed to provide accurate and authoritative
information in regard to the subject matter covered. It is sold
with the understanding that the publisher is not engaged in
rendering professional services. If professional advice or other
expert assistance is required, the services of a competent
professional person should be sought.

0-471-21899-5

Printed in the United States of America.

10 9 8 7 6 5 4 3 2

To:
MV,
PM,
FM,
N,
C,
M.

Adweek Books is designed to present interesting, insightful books for the general business reader and for professionals in the worlds of media, marketing, and advertising.

These are innovative, creative books that address the challenges and opportunities of these industries, written by leaders in the business. Some of our writers head their own companies, others have worked their way up to the top of their field in large multinationals. But they share a knowledge of their craft and a desire to enlighten others.

We hope readers will find these books as helpful and inspiring as *Adweek, Brandweek,* and *Mediaweek* magazines.

Published

Disruption: Overturning Conventions and Shaking Up the Marketplace, Jean-Marie Dru

Under the Radar: Talking to Today's Cynical Consumer, Jonathan Bond and Richard Kirshenbaum

Truth, Lies and Advertising: The Art of Account Planning, Jon Steel

Hey, Whipple, Squeeze This: A Guide to Creating Great Ads, Luke Sullivan

Eating the Big Fish: How Challenger Brands Can Compete Against Brand Leaders, Adam Morgan

Warp-Speed Branding: The Impact of Technology on Marketing, Agnieszka Winkler

Creative Company: How St. Luke's Became "the Ad Agency to End All Ad Agencies," Andy Law

Another One Bites the Grass: Making Sense of International Advertising, Simon Anholt

Attention! How to Interrupt, Yell, Whisper and Touch Consumers, Ken Sacharin

The Peaceable Kingdom: Building a Company Without Factionalism, Fiefdoms, Fear, and Other Staples of Modern Business, Stan Richards with David Culp

Getting the Bugs Out: The Rise, Fall, and Comeback of Volkswagen in America, David Kiley

The Do-It-Yourself Lobotomy: Open Your Mind to Greater Creative Thinking, Tom Monahan

Forthcoming:

And Now a Few Laughs From Our Sponsor, Larry Oakner

"When the rate of change
inside an institution
becomes slower than
the rate of change outside,
the end is in sight.
The only question is when."

JACK WELCH

Changing the Rules in the Marketplace

BEYOND

DISRUPTION

A collaborative work by Jean-Marie Dru and business partners.

DISRUPT\ON

It's more than a noun.
It's more than a book.
It's more than a process.
It's a way of thinking.

It's a way to look at our clients' business and find opportunity.

It's a way of defining how brands should act.

It's a lens through which the world should view our network.

It's how each of our agencies should do business every day.

Think boldly.
Sell brave ideas.
Create dramatic business results for our clients.

Disruption means dismantling of the status quo
and replacing it with something bold and new.

It can be the most powerful thing we sell.
It can be what the world expects us to do.
It can define who we are.

Clow

Disruption began in the early 1990s.

The method was initially developed by our advertising agency. It was designed to help produce more intrusive advertising strategies, and to give brands more substance and weight, by making a clean break with the status quo, by creating a "disruption."

Disruption soon proved to be much bigger than we had initially imagined, bigger than advertising. It turned out to be relevant for business in general — not just for brands, but also for companies. It gradually evolved into a way of thinking that encouraged companies to create and manage change at all levels of their organization.

Our original source of inspiration came from the success stories of businesses that had achieved exponential brand growth in an established, yet stagnant, climate. We discovered that all these cases shared certain characteristics. They all overturned convention in some way by means of product innovation, marketing stance, and/or advertising. And they all had a clear idea of the direction they were taking.

Disruption was thus designed as a means of questioning the established order, of challenging tried-and-true approaches. Our first book, *Disruption: Overturning Conventions and Shaking Up the Marketplace* (Wiley, 1996), explained the principles of the methodology. This sequel is about Disruption at work, Disruption in action. The years that separate the two books have proven the efficacy of the method. By seeing how the idea has evolved in practice, you can begin to apply Disruption in your own business, no matter what business you are in.

From the outset, Disruption was built on a three-step process: ⬜ Convention, 📐 Disruption, and ◯ Vision.

You start by identifying the Conventions that restrict the thought process, and then you challenge them through a Disruption, a radically new and unexpected idea. This is all done with a very definite sense of Vision — of where you are going, of the ground you want to cover from today to tomorrow.

This is the way the format of the methodology was designed some years ago. You will see throughout this book how Disruption has developed a life and a culture of its own. Some of the best-known international examples of Disruption at work are companies such as Absolut, Apple, Nissan in the United States, Sony PlayStation in Europe and the United States, McDonald's, TAG Heuer, and Danone in Europe. Details of these case histories appear in the section entitled "Seven Disruption Stories."

Here, however, are a few words about each of these brands.

Absolut vodka has embodied Disruption from the start by positioning itself as a fashion brand, rather than a spirits brand. It resisted the conventional approach of relying on the product's provenance and heritage. Twenty years on, hundreds of ads later, and as many public relations events, such as sponsorship of the arts, Absolut has become one of the top-selling brands in the world. Its average price is 20 percent higher than its competitors' prices.

Apple is a company that makes "tools for creative minds." This strategy was embodied in the "Think different" campaign featuring Picasso, Einstein, John Lennon, Martin Luther King, Gandhi, Muhammad Ali, Richard Branson — great creators of the twentieth century. These people, as the voice-over says, "...are not fond of rules and they have no respect for the status quo." They are the ones who changed the world.

The Apple ads defy convention and, at the same time, they champion the challenging of convention; they are different themselves and, at the same time, they encourage us all to be different. They aim high and, at the same time, urge us to raise our sights. "Think different" would have been a great motto for the concept of Disruption.

Nissan, again poised to be the most brilliant car brand coming from Japan, has pioneered an exclusive campaign format in the United States, which has subsequently been exported to Japan and Europe. The launch campaign for each new model is preceded by a phase in which one of the head designers — Jerry Hirshberg in the U.S., Shiro Nakamura in Japan, or Steven Schwartz in Europe — talks personally on TV about the car. These designers have gradually helped this recently faceless company to achieve a voice of its own. In two years, Nissan's image has been reinvigorated. Its new models have become a "cure for the common car." This is a case history in the making.

PlayStation was third into its market, after Sega and Nintendo. By overturning the convention that computer games are for kids and geeks, Sony declared that PlayStation was not just a game, but a totally new experience, a way of life for teens and young adults. Sony captures the intensity of the whole gaming experience, with no age limits. PlayStation is now market leader with 82 million units sold worldwide. As the advertisements say: Do not underestimate the power of PlayStation!

In France, **McDonald's** has decided not to communicate exclusively on a commercial level. It now also communicates at a corporate level. Since 1999, McDonald's advertising has focused on the nutritional value of its food for children (after the mad cow disease and the foot-and-mouth disease crises), and, more recently, it has addressed criticism of the "exploitation" and "victimization" of young employees in a so-called overly competitive system. This approach marks a rupture with McDonald's customary reserve, founded on the principle that nowadays, it is impossible to create a deep relationship with customers by isolating company issues from the brand. For McDonald's in France, this idea marked a turning point.

Initially a trendy sports watch, **TAG Heuer** has become a luxury brand. TAG has shifted from applauding physical effort to advocating mental strength, embodying the power of the mind. The brand image has been upgraded to such a degree that the price for an average model has more than doubled, impacting profits considerably, as you can well imagine.

Danone in France is the same company as Dannon in America. No one conducts more research into the relationship between food and health than Danone. At the agency's recommendation, they created the Danone Institute, as a means of providing tangible evidence of the company's commitment to health. Danone has since become the most popular brand in France, all product categories considered. It has provided its parent company with a name. In the same way that the Minnesota Valley Canning Company became Green Giant, BSN, the former name of the company, has become Danone, a brand now synonymous with health all over Europe.

In each of these cases there has been a distinct rupture with convention.

Creating new market spaces creates greater wealth. A study by the *Financial Times* revealed that, out of 100 new business launches, 86 percent were "me-too" launches, or incremental improvements. However, these generated only 62 percent of launch revenues and

39 percent of profits. By contrast, the remaining 14 percent of launches — those that created new markets or recreated existing ones — generated 38 percent of revenues and a whopping 61 percent of profits.

It was with this in mind that we designed the Disruption methodology. Its goal is to reframe, restage, and reshape, by rejecting the obvious.

Our aim is to identify the conventions that surround clients' businesses. We look at the established practices and specific characteristics of the sector or industry in question. We examine the conventional approach to marketing its products and services. We explore the consumer's anticipated attitudes and behavior. We inspect how similar the approaches of various agencies are. We try to expose deep-seated cultural prejudices.

We often use one particular metaphor to illustrate what we mean by challenging convention. This is the "Fosbury Flop," the back-to-front high-jumping style introduced by Dick Fosbury at the Mexico City Olympic Games in 1968. Fosbury disrupted the conventional approach to jumping, which held that the only way to go over the bar was on your front. It also made all other techniques obsolete. Within a few years, virtually all competitors were forced to adopt this style, and those who could not had to retire. Fosbury had challenged sporting convention with total success.

Once the imagination is fully prepared, we move on to the next stage. By challenging the way things are done, by developing new hypotheses and unexpected scenarios, by searching for unprecedented angles of attack, we help our clients create visions that represent a distinctive point of view, visions that have the power to transform markets.

The more powerful the vision, the more it vitalizes the brand. Consider Apple and "Think different," or Danone and "Entreprendre pour la Santé" ("Taking a stand on health"), Sony and "Do not underestimate the power of PlayStation," IBM and "Solutions for a small planet," CNN, The Body Shop, MTV, Häagen-Dazs, BMW,

Intel, and Absolut, a brand we have been handling for 20 years. All these brands have clear visions; they stand out from the crowd. They have greater value, in both senses of the word — image and financial.

Our company is the result of numerous mergers that brought together a lot of local, entrepreneurial agencies that shared parallel views on our business. In fact, all of them have always believed in the underlying principle that formed the bedrock of Disruption: strategies that are creative.

These agencies were often praised for their creativity and showered with prizes at award ceremonies. As a result, they were too quickly categorized as "creative," which, in a simplistic, Manichean world, meant "nonstrategic." This is absurd. The force of the campaigns for Apple, Absolut, Danone, and Sony PlayStation resides not only in the quality of the creative expression and the executional talent of the people involved, but also in their strategic insights, their courage to think big, to aim high. The people who work on these brands do not under-leverage them. On the contrary, they build them a "larger share of the future," as evidenced by the advertising.

"The Tyranny of the Or"

The book *Built to Last*, by James C. Collins and Jerry I. Porras (HarperCollins, 1994), devotes a chapter, called "The Tyranny of the Or," to the problems that arise from "categorization," or putting things in boxes. Conventional thinking says it is impossible to be two things at the same time: You have to choose. It is either, or... That star striker in soccer cannot also be a great defender, even if he can tackle well. The authors explain how conditioned we are by this way of thinking, and they recommend that we transcend it. You should never accept being creative to the detriment of being strategic. You should be both. And this is what Disruption is all about.

The years pass. Our agencies have become bigger everywhere, in all our activities. Disruption has become our common language, which has created communities of thought that transcend borders. Disruption structures our network, at every level. An account executive in Seoul can have a conversation with his/her counterpart in San Francisco, each understanding without spelling things out, using the same references, sharing the same discomfort with Convention. Disruption has become a shared mental model, our cultural glue.

Our internal tools have grown in number and sophistication. Their goal is to address the three stages of the process: Convention/Disruption/Vision. A toolbox, called Disruption Central, has been created. Each tool has its own particular purpose and its own mode of operation, and each indicates the name of the most appropriate expert to contact in the network. There are numerous open-ended, revolutionary tools in this toolbox. In a library, you choose a book depending on your current mood. Here, you choose a tool relying on your intuition. The tool you choose and the way you use it are in themselves creative acts.

I am wary of tools that are formatted to such an extent that they restrict the thought processes, clip the wings of imagination. These tools are flexible; they can be modified, enriched by your own personal experience; you can use one for a particular job, then a different one for another.

However, at the same time, a minimum of process is needed. As Peter Drucker said, "Creative destruction needs to be an ongoing process, and it has to be organized." No company can rely solely on its existing resources. It must find a way to build on them. In our case, our process helps each employee develop a capacity for nonlinear thinking.

You can gain a great deal from bringing clients into the process and tapping the potential of their imagination. We created Disruption Days, which have gradually developed into highly structured workshops with a very specific format. Their objective is to identify new markets, develop new products, revamp brands, invent new organizations, trigger cultural changes, suggest new distribution channels, and so on. The outcome of a recent workshop in South Africa was a complete reexamination of the customer segmentation of the Standard Bank, the second-largest bank in the country. The result was a fundamental change in the way their branches were run.

The vast majority of clients who have taken part in these sessions subsequently ask us the same question when we are in strategic discussions: "Where's the disruption?" Disruption now also forms an integral part of their thought processes, their logical reasoning. As somebody once said, "A mind that is stretched to a new idea never returns to its original dimensions." It keeps us on our toes.

A collective book

It is in this spirit that we decided to publish a new book, a collective book, written by partners from many countries, in order to demonstrate how Disruption can energize brands all over the world.

This book consists of 19 chapters divided into four parts.

The first part, **"Disruption Context,"** describes the business environment in which Disruption happens. It begins logically with the United States, the land of opportunity, in "America, the Disruptive Brand" (Chapter 1). It is followed by "Disruptive Organizations," an analysis of companies renowned for their disruptive approaches (Chapter 2). "Disrupting Marketing Conventions" shows that marketing is a discipline burdened by outdated practices (Chapter 3).

The second part, **"Disruption at Work,"** explains how to practice Disruption. "First Impressions" (Chapter 4) was written by the most recent arrival to our company. He gives us his impressions on Disruption in action. "State of the Art," the core chapter of the book, shows how Disruption can completely reshape an agency and redefine the way we think about our clients' brands (Chapter 5).

Our clients make an appearance in "Workshops," which explains the procedures of the Disruption Workshop (Chapter 6). In "Tools," the tools underpinning the Disruption process are explained (Chapter 7).

The third part, **"Disruption Scope," takes us through a wide array of applications**, from one communication discipline to another. This part demonstrates that Disruption applies to all fields of communication (Chapter 8, "Disruption across Disciplines"), that great Disruptions can be at street level (Chapter 9, "Street-Level Disruptions"), that certain types of Disruption can be very concrete, even tactile to some extent (Chapter 10, "Tactile Disruptions"). Moving from the real world to the virtual world, we then show that Interactivity and Disruption make excellent bedfellows (Chapter 11, "Disruption On-line"), and that Disruption can inspire ideas for permission marketing (Chapter 12, "Disruption, Interruption, Permission"). When it comes to media planning, this science becomes an art when thinking is allowed to be unconventional (Chapter 13, "Disruptive Media Planning"). Our journey leads us to England, where Tony Blair, together with our agency, has successfully questioned a considerable number of political advertising conventions (Chapter 14, "Disruption in Political Advertising"). We then fly to emerging countries, where there is little or nothing to disrupt (Chapter 15, "Disruption in Emerging Markets"). We return to the West. "The Luxury of Disruption" urges us to regard mass-marketed products as if they were premium brands (Chapter 16).

The final part, **"Disruption Tomorrow," outlines where the methodology is heading.** "Insights" looks at contemporary consumer insights, the human truths that should inspire our thinking (Chapter 17). "Connections" describes a discipline that seeks to identify and optimize every point of contact between a consumer and a brand in a continual bid to enrich the brand experience. Our competitive edge will come increasingly from the marriage of

Disruption and Connections, the act of uniting the idea behind the brand with its public manifestation (Chapter 18). This all leads to the development of a new business model for our own company, which forms the subject of the last chapter, "A New Business Model" (Chapter 19).

This, then, is a summary of the subjects addressed in this book. Each chapter shows what can be gained for each communications discipline by being "disruptive."

The idea that change has become discontinuous, and therefore no longer a predictable process, is, we admit, not totally original. However, it is less of a cliché to say that this has always been the case. The only thing that has changed is that, before, the rate of change was sufficiently slow and straightforward to create the illusion of predictability.

Tomorrow is full of surprises that are coming faster and faster. In *Lessons from the Future* (Capstone, 2001), Stan Davis explains that the age of information that we are still trying to come to grips with, will, in fact, draw to a close very soon. It will be replaced by the age of biotechnology. In 20 years' time, we will be able to palpably reproduce various types of human characteristics such as smell, taste, touch — even intuition and imagination.

Every day, applied sciences are modifying our lives at an accelerating speed. Gone is the time when companies could react quietly by just managing their assets. Gone is the time when the success of the future was modeled on the past.

In a world that is much more complicated than it was 20 years ago, time that is lost cannot be regained.

Disruption is a way of unearthing new opportunities.

It means being nonconformist, unorthodox, rebellious.

It means always trying to change the rules.

It means believing that a company can transform its future through the sheer power of an idea.

Absolut

The Swedish brand Absolut has embodied Disruption from the word go. In the case of a premium brand like this, the conventional course of action for consolidating this position would have been to embrace a strategy based on heritage and provenance. Just as whiskey brands had been selling their Scottish or Irish provenance, Stolichnaya had been selling imperial Russia. For Absolut, we avoided building brand legitimacy in this conventional way. The idea was to treat Absolut as a fashion brand, not a spirits brand. We based our campaign on Absolut's two most unique product attributes: its name and its crystal-clear bottle unmarred by paper labels.

Ads featuring memorable images of the bottle swiftly became an advertising phenomenon, creating the iconoclastic status of the brand. Absolut's perennial success relies on careful management of the campaign and other forms of communication to maintain a perfect blend of intimacy and inaccessibility. Absolut is now the world's fourth-best-selling brand of liquor and, on average, its price is 20 percent higher than that of other vodka brands.

Convention The premium quality of a spirit brand lies in its provenance.

Vision Absolut is a fashion brand.

Disruption Transform the bottle into an icon, and build a territory around who drinks it and where.

Apple

A recent Harvard Business Review poll found that 80 percent of CEOs felt that the biggest challenge they faced was the need to create new business space. Few people embody this burning desire to generate new market space like Steve Jobs. Our agency in Los Angeles has always sought to translate his penetrating market insights into punchy, hard-hitting advertising: "On January 24, 1984, Apple launches Macintosh. And you will see why 1984 won't be like *1984*," said the voice-over for the commercial that launched Macintosh. This allusion to George Orwell's novel made this commercial highly memorable. Macintosh was about to change everything, so the advertising agency had to create advertising that would do the same.

The vision then was that people no longer had to adapt to machines, but the reverse. Macintosh freed people from machines. Nearly 15 years later, "Think different" would launch the new vision shaped by Steve Jobs. In this, Apple's caretaker CEO stressed his conviction that the brand "is not about bytes and boxes, it is about values." With the concomitant launch of the iMac, Apple redefined itself as the company making "tools for creative minds." The "Think different" campaign has served both as a creative platform enabling each country to pay tribute to its own creative heroes and as a solid foundation for the Apple products themselves.

Apple will soon be at the heart of the digital lifestyle. This will again involve breaking with tradition on a grand scale, something that is never unexpected on the part of its CEO, who is always seeking to create new market spaces.

Convention In high technology products, communication must revolve around product features.

Disruption "Apple is not about bytes and boxes, it is about values." (Steve Jobs)

Vision Apple is the tool for creative minds.

Danone

Danone is another of our agency's case histories. In order to raise public awareness of the company's concern with health, we recommended the creation of the Danone Institute, an organization bringing together scientists, doctors, and Danone researchers to sponsor and publish studies of the relationship between health and food. The institute has become the vehicle for a mass-market image-building campaign, drawing its inspiration from the Hippocratic idea that diet is the best medicine.

In one of the many commercials on the subject, a young boy is crawling up the stairs leading to the terrace of a garden. There, two men — his father and grandfather — are looking at a third man sitting in front of an easel. The painter is the boy's great-grandfather. The voice-over says: "Today, people can expect to live 20 years longer than a century ago. Improved nutrition has helped make the difference. Tomorrow, thanks to research, our diet will be our primary defense. We will have a better chance of being around to see how the latest newborn resembles his great-grandfather." Several similar commercials have followed.

Not only have Danone market shares risen steadily, but Danone is the only dairy brand to have successfully resisted the rise of store-brand labels. Surveys carried out among the general public showed that Danone had become the preferred brand in France, all categories combined. Danone is now more than just the sum of its products. The strategy of the Danone brand even inspired the parent company, BSN, to adopt the Danone name. By doing so, CEO Antoine Riboud was highlighting the key role played by the Danone Institute in the brand's institutionalization.

Vision Health is a major concern for Danone.

Convention Marketing spending should be allocated product by product.

Disruption Founded the Danone Institute for Health to back the brand vision with an umbrella campaign.

McDonald's

No opinion is more entrenched than the view that McDonald's offers average-quality food and is too hard on its employees who are part of an overcompetitive system. Recently, in France, we mounted a frontal attack on these prejudices. This was an indirect response to Naomi Klein, who made McDonald's a prime target in her book *No Logo* (Picador, 2000). In her opinion, economic power means the power to control minds; the more brands grow and broaden to become an experience, the more they curtail the consumers' choice. An eloquent reply was printed in the September 2001 issue of *The Economist*, completely overturning the No Logo thesis. In "Prologo," *The Economist* explained that, far from being instruments of oppression, brands made firms more accountable to the consumer. Recent actions give credence to this point of view.

When McDonald's had to face the mad cow disease crisis, we took the time and money to explain precisely and in technical (and unsexy) detail what McDonald's was intending to do to reduce the risks. We even invited French people to visit everyone involved in creating the McDonald's experience, from the abattoirs to the restaurants, from McCain's potato fields in northeastern France to the agency.

This bold move worked; it altered many people's perception of the company. The experience led us to believe that such communication was not just good crisis management. It added an invaluable ingredient to the communications mix; you cannot create a meaningful brand relationship with people by divorcing the brand from corporate issues. In subsequent TV campaigns, McDonald's has publicly addressed the subject of the nutritional value of its food for children, responding to the prevailing fear of importing the problem of child obesity into France. More recently, advertising has tackled the issue of McDonald's as an employer of young people, counteracting the precon-ception that the company only offers McJobs.

This last subject had to be dealt with sensitively. Young people frequent McDonald's on both sides of the counter, and we needed to speak to them on their level. Instead of showing the target audience, we decided to show where they lived. In a typical student apartment, a subjective camera scans all the stuff that makes up their lives — from studying, to listening to music, to going out with friends. In a voice-over, the McDonald's brand expressed an intimate understanding of young people, as well as providing a concrete commitment as an employer to responding to their needs and aspirations.

"They want a job or better still a profession. They want to get ahead, but they don't always know how....They are our customers and our employees."

"... Today we are offering jobs that will give them a start and a chance to grow and live in line with their aspirations. Because life is meant to be lived to the full."

McDonald's is now very quick to adopt an institutional position and disarm the prejudices people have toward the company. The company has decided to make the public sit up and take notice of its brand vision. This has an impact on the company's performance. In France, it enjoys some of the highest profit levels and is gradually winning the respect of authorities and opinion leaders.

Convention People will never love the company; you need to distract them with the fun of the brand.

Vision McDonald's is accountable to its customers; if they have concerns, the company has a responsibility to be straight with them.

Disruption Make public McDonald's stance on issues such as nutrition and McJobs, through TV commercials.

Nissan

Disruption can also result from a more unexpected approach. Nissan's sales in the United States have shown a strong upward trend over the past two years. The brand image has asserted itself, making it possible to drastically cut back on customer incentives. Discounts inherently cut company and dealer profits, and work to erode the brand image.

The company's renewed success is mainly the result of a new model line and a much more sharply focused marketing strategy. But we also played our part. In terms of publicity, the campaign format and the related allocation of resources were highly innovative. Each model campaign was preceded by what we call a Product Vision campaign. Around 15 percent of the investment for each model was earmarked for these short but densely packed campaigns that lasted two to three weeks. In each, a key designer — in this case, Jerry Hirshberg in the United States — gave us some insight into the forthcoming model and the supporting campaign.

He told us things like this: "We took a fresh look at truck guys and found, 'Hey, truck guys actually have friends and families. They are not the lonesome cowboys we used to think they were.' Truck guys have friends, we need doors for the friends. The idea of putting four proper doors on a compact pickup is really a no-brainer. Our brain just got there first." Or, "When we set out to design the new Sentra, we had this very simple philosophy, we never called it compact. As a result there was no 'compact' thinking." Or, "We begin each project the way Method actors work. We become the buyer, we become minivan drivers." Or, "There's a kind of directness about the people we met at trailheads, on beaches, who were sometimes not even using SUVs but kept creating them as they went along. Duct tape, bungee cords everywhere to hold their monster load of gear. They needed help."

Each time, Jerry gave us a slant, an opinion, a fresh take on what we were going to see within two weeks. It was very effective. This approach, which put everything into perspective, sent the campaigns, and the models, into orbit. It worked as a teaser, but a specific teaser, with a great deal of institutional content. The Nissan dealers saw these campaigns as actual launch campaigns, and so did we. But we also saw them from a brand image point of view.

Jerry spoke on television for several days, disappeared, then came back three months later to talk about another upcoming model, and so on. The cumulative effect of these campaigns, which ran for two weeks four times per year, for example, was to form a de facto image campaign. This had two main advantages: The campaigns did not wear out their welcome (or hardly at all), and our dealers did not perceive them as costly corporate brand campaigns, which do not drive sales. Rather, the performance of the model launch campaigns was improved. Everyone was a winner: the products and the brand.

This campaign format is very important. An automobile brand can only be built by its models, but this takes time. The aim of these Product Visions was to accelerate the process in order to remedy Nissan's faceless image as quickly as possible. In this case, the campaign format equaled Disruption.

"Every product has a soul. But the biggest soul of all belongs to our automobiles; they are our offices, our decompression chambers. Americans love cars and we have a passion for making cars which have a soul under the skin," Jerry Hirshberg tells us. Now Nissan has a soul, and the public is becoming increasingly aware of this. We have exported the format to Japan and Europe. In Japan, the senior vice president in charge of design, Shiro Nakamura, has become the company's spokesperson in the advertising.

It is a well-known fact in Detroit and Tokyo that Carlos Ghosn, the new CEO at Nissan, is spearheading a remarkable recovery. In a year, the company has gone from losing $20 billion to realizing a profit of $2.69 billion. We are proud to be involved, even from a distance, in what will probably become a historic case history. Carlos Ghosn recently said, "If you are coming from hell, then purgatory does not look too bad." In other words, there is still a great deal to do, even if remarkable progress has already been made.

Convention In automotive advertising, nothing is more effective than pure product advertising.

Disruption Create Product Vision campaigns to accelerate brand building.

Vision Nissan designs cars to anticipate individual needs and desires.

Sony PlayStation

Building a brand is a tough challenge when the market is monopolized by two superbrands that share more than 90 percent of it. This is exactly what Sony Computer Entertainment faced in its 1995 launch against Nintendo and Sega. Sony was forced to approach the market differently.

The element that overturned convention was that of positioning. PlayStation decided to upgrade to an older age group. To do this, they needed to make their product socially acceptable for teenagers and young adults. Before PlayStation, it was thought that computer games were used by kid brothers or geeks — they had no place in teen culture. We gave the advertising a new role. We decided not to showcase the entertainment value of characters like Super Mario anymore, but to capture the intensity of the whole gaming experience, one with no age limit.

This positioning, as described in the following Disruption format, has enabled Sony PlayStation to become the number one game brand worldwide.

Convention Computer games are for kids and geeks.

Disruption Capture the spirit of gaming as an intense lifestyle experience.

Vision PlayStation is not just a game.

This Disruptive positioning has been epitomized in Europe by a brand commercial called "Double Life." In the commercial, people talk about the secret life they have when they play with Sony PlayStation. About 15 people, looking straight at the camera, deliver a text, a type of poem, which has been edited in a deliberately fragmented style: "For years, I have lived a double life. In the day I do my job, I ride the bus, roll up my sleeves with the hoi polloi. But at night I live a life of exhilaration, of missed heartbeats and adrenaline. And, if the truth be known, a life of dubious virtue. I won't deny, I have been engaged in violence, even indulged in it. I have maimed and killed adversaries and not merely in self-defense. I have exhibited disregard for life, limb, and property and savored every moment. You may not think it to look at me but I have commanded armies and conquered worlds. And though in achieving these things, I have set morality aside, I have no regrets. For though I have lived a double life at least I can say, I have lived." The tag line is: "Do not underestimate the power of PlayStation."

With the "Double Life" commercial, the culture of gaming acquired street cred. Sony gave people who do not play a better understanding of those who do. Sony is not just about kid's entertainment, it is about a completely new experience. In the United States the challenge was different; the market was mature and the established game platforms had a following among older teenagers. Being the most intense gaming experience, Sony dared teenagers to play. The "UR not E" (you are not ready) campaign threw down the gauntlet. To existing gamers, there are computer games and then there is Sony PlayStation. Be it in Europe or the United States, Sony has forever changed the gaming experience.

TAG Heuer

Successful advertising campaigns can be the catalyst for broader change within a company. Following the success of our worldwide TAG Heuer campaigns, the watch manufacturer completely upgraded its design policy. Since TAG Heuer was considered a sports watch, not a luxury brand, we tried to enhance the prestige of sport in a bid to enhance the brand's prestige. "Don't crack under pressure" was our first campaign, followed by the renowned "Success is a mind game." By celebrating the power of the mind, TAG Heuer bridged the gulf between sport and luxury goods. Sales grew fast and, at the same time, the average price of a watch more than doubled, turning what used to be a sports brand into a luxury brand. Since then, the company continually invests in its design, constantly upgrades the look of its styles, and is quick to capitalize on the talents of designers such as Mijat, Edd Schopfer, and Jorg Ysek, not to mention photographers like Mondino and Les Guzman. The advertising was the trigger: It opened our client's eyes to the brand's potential.

Convention Luxury brands need to use identifiers like wealth and status to symbolize prestige.

Disruption Enhance the prestige of sports to enhance the status of the brand.

Vision With TAG Heuer, sports prestige is a question of mental strength.

"Evolved individuals know that people who are not intuitive can be dangerous to work with, since they are guided solely by the present appearance of things that are, in reality, changing. Evolved individuals seek out others who have intuition and vision — a form of intelligence that comes from cultivating their instinct, observing the direction of change, and apprehending changing ideas."

LAO-TZU, 3,000 YEARS AGO,
IN HIS CLASSIC TAO TE CHING

DISRUPTION

CONTEXT

The first part of this book is devoted to the context — the overall business environment — in which Disruption exists. The challenging nature of the chapters will put you into a disruptive frame of mind and eventually lead you to question your own business and marketing practices. Is your company governed by outmoded conventions?

It begins in America, the land of entrepreneurs. **Tom Carroll**, head of our American operations, joins forces with **Cindy Scott**, our business strategist in Los Angeles, to show how all major American companies have disrupted, in one way or another, the conventional ideas of their period. They go on to enumerate seven Disruption triggers, characteristics, or moments within a company's lifetime, that, when identified, signal the need for reinvention. These characteristics or moments happen far more frequently than we might expect.

Each year, U.S. business magazines publish the rankings of foreign countries in terms of their investments in the domestic United States. If we accumulate investments over a century, the United Kingdom ranks first. Holland, with only 15 million inhabitants, ranks second, before Japan. This is why I felt it was appropriate to ask **Anne Charbonneau**, our head of planning in Holland, to lend us her insights into disruptive companies from different countries. She describes what they have in common. This serves to highlight the difference between change and Disruption.

Moving from a country level to a company level, we proceed to tackle the world of marketing in Chapter 3. **David Hackworthy**, head of our planning department in New York, together with his senior planner, **Ian Leslie**, look at disrupting marketing conventions. They reveal that many of our views on marketing are preconceived and demonstrate how we can open up new horizons by challenging accepted ideas.

1. AMERICA, THE DISRUPTIVE BRAND

"…French and American attitudes are complete opposites. And advertising reflects this. On the European side of the Atlantic, the commercial act remains suspect. People rarely trust a salesperson. This leads to very staged commercials and to indirect, almost oblique arguments. Advertising in France is very theatrical. Not so in the United States. Nobody there is shocked by a hard sell. Americans do not fear deadly competition. They cherish brutal pragmatism …

…These differences result from each country's respective traditions and the contrasting attitudes toward business and profit they engender…" Jean-Marie Dru, *Disruption*

American attitudes toward business are deeply rooted in our history and psyche. Disruption is part of America's DNA. As the United States was settled, European conventions became limiting in the context of the new world. This led to natural disruptions and the creation of new values and vision.

And the New World Vision has played an important role in shaping our approach to business and marketing. American ingenuity and entrepreneurial spirit have shaped the disruptive ideas at the core of many success stories. But Disruption is not exclusive to America. It is a global idea with a simple construct: Convention/Disruption/Vision. While there are many examples of disruptions that transformed life in the United States, does this automatically translate into a uniquely American flavor of disruption in American business today? Yes.

EUROPEAN CONVENTION	DISRUPTION	NEW WORLD VISION
• LIBERTY + RELIGION	• NO COMMON ROOTS	• PERSONAL LIBERTY
• CONFORMITY	• SEPARATION OF CHURCH	• INDIVIDUAL FREEDOM
• MONARCHY/BARONIAL	AND STATE	• DEMOCRACY
• COMMON LAW	• UNLIMITED LAND	• POSSIBILITIES
• APPRENTICESHIP	• SHORT SUPPLY	FOR EVERYONE
	OF LABOR	• CONSTITUTIONAL LAW
	• MULTIETHNICITY	• ENTREPRENEURIAL
	• DISTANCE FROM	• MOBILITY
	EUROPE	• PRAGMATISM

American ingenuity is by definition Disruption. Henry Ford's vision of democratizing automobile transportation when he transformed the working class into consumers by paying them three times the norm was extremely disruptive. By applying mass-production techniques to home building, Levitt and Sons took the American Dream of land ownership and a home and made it attainable for the average family. And by believing in endless possibilities at a time when there were no new earthly frontiers to explore, the American aerospace program was able to put a man on the moon by disrupting the conventional technological barriers.

America's entrepreneurial spirit is embodied in the start-up operation, especially when the start-up concept is metaphorically related to the American Revolution. This explains why the usual roster of American disruptive case studies includes the likes of Southwest Airlines, Apple Computer, and Federal Express. It is no coincidence that each of these stories begins with the infancy of these companies' existence.

They were all born as start-up brands that succeeded in disrupting established categories. Each of these companies challenged the bureaucratic, aristocratic category leaders by democratizing their categories and providing more imaginative and pragmatic solutions for their customers.

Southwest's decision to not try to be all things to all people enabled them to focus and execute their business in a way that other, larger carriers feared doing because they could not conceive of relinquishing underperforming segments. The incarnation of Apple's Macintosh literally opened the world of user-friendly computing to the mass market at a time when IBM was reluctant to acknowledge the emergence of a shifting marketplace. Federal

Express took aim at the inefficient and monopolistic U.S. Postal Service, creating healthy competition that resulted in a reaffirmation of the work ethic in the category.

These classically disruptive examples are born of powerfully American ideas, which seem to illustrate that Americans are less driven by convention and are perhaps more receptive to the Disruption methodology. But this is not quite the case.

The fact is that American conventions may seem anti-conventional. In reality, though, they are as rooted in driving our behavior as conventions that exist anywhere else in the world. The key difference is in understanding that some of America's cultural conventions are inherently disruptive because they encourage visceral and innovative thinking, and thus can explain our abundance of disruptive American marketing examples. These success stories were aided and abetted by American cultural conventions that facilitated their disruption.

So, if the American business environment embraces ingenuity and entrepreneurial ideas that reinforce American values, what does this mean for established U.S. businesses? As American companies grow and mature, their corporate cultures risk becoming actively resistant to disruptive ideas. How can we explain this transformation in the context of the American argument? By examining the evolution of American ideological shifts.

The United States evolved from a challenger to a champion country and, with this transition, a secondary set of American cultural conventions evolved that discourage disruption.

This allowed U.S. culture and government to be lulled into complacency as the United States became a champion country. This was evident before World War I, in the 1950s and early 1960s, and again in the 1990s. However, each of these idyllic periods ended when the U.S. way of life was disrupted. Each time, the U.S. reverted to its challenger roots and values and acted as a champion/challenger country, responding with disruptive behavior.

Champion/challenger behavior

Just like the country itself, successful U.S. brands run the risk of becoming stagnant champions. And this risk is more prevalent in the U.S. since, by their sheer size, successful American companies grow from challenger brands into global champion brands more often than successful companies in smaller countries. The result is that the United States defines category conventions more often than other countries do. Consequently, if mature

U.S. companies are to survive, they must continually strive for success within the ebb and flow of champion/challenger behavior, or run the risk of once again becoming pure challenger brands in the future.

General Electric and IBM embraced champion/challenger thinking as they reinvented themselves under reinvigorated leadership. By the early 1980s, General Electric had little entrepreneurial spirit left and instead was a bureaucratic conglomerate without focus or vision. In 1981, Jack Welch took the helm and led with renewed entrepreneurial prowess and disruptive ideas. Similarly, the strong entrepreneurial spirit of Louis Gerstner's vision drove IBM's disruptive reinvention from being a hardware manufacturer to becoming an information solutions company.

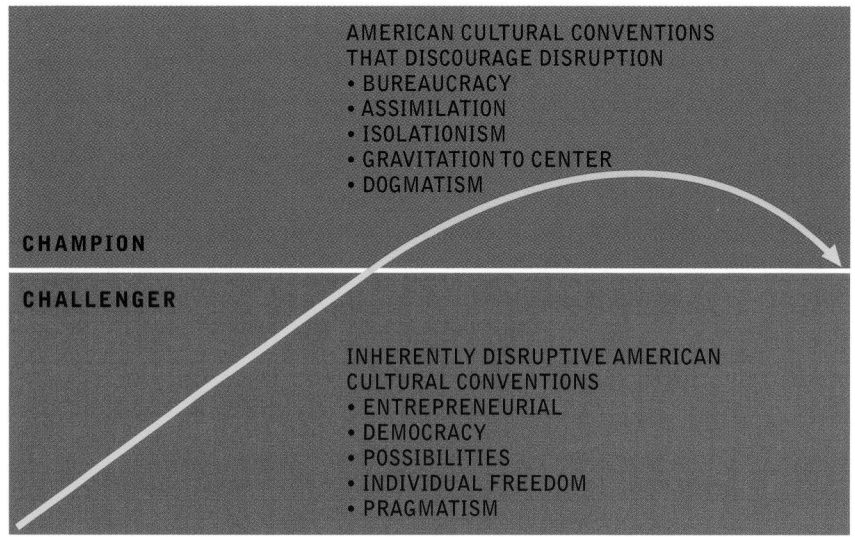

AMERICAN CULTURAL CONVENTIONS
THAT DISCOURAGE DISRUPTION
• BUREAUCRACY
• ASSIMILATION
• ISOLATIONISM
• GRAVITATION TO CENTER
• DOGMATISM

CHAMPION

CHALLENGER

INHERENTLY DISRUPTIVE AMERICAN
CULTURAL CONVENTIONS
• ENTREPRENEURIAL
• DEMOCRACY
• POSSIBILITIES
• INDIVIDUAL FREEDOM
• PRAGMATISM

Communicating Disruption

As U.S. champion brands strive toward champion/challenger status, advertising can be a powerful tool in signaling change and drawing upon the U.S. cultural conventions that facilitate disruption.

Jeans market leader Levi Strauss lost relevance and market share in the late 1990s by failing to react to the new category players and changing demographics. They turned themselves around by retooling their product lineup to address new segments, and by choosing to communicate the disruptive American convention of individual freedom and democracy through their "make them your own" advertising campaign. The spots featured a shopper's personal moment of grooving to her favorite song in front of the dressing room mirror. This approach was in stark contrast to the slickly produced Gap campaign running at the time, which seemed to encourage conformity and homo-geneity by staging identically dressed dancers moving flawlessly in unison. After stumbling in the mid-1990s, Apple Computer once again embraced its challenger heritage by bringing back its founder, Steve Jobs, and developing a new generation of computers that challenged convention and emphasized individual expression and possibilities. And Apple's comeback was signaled through the "Think different" advertising campaign showcasing amazing individuals, such as CNN's founder, Ted Turner, who had, in one way or an-other, disrupted life as we know it. Incredibly, Apple reclaimed its place in the market before any new products were actually introduced.

During the early 1990s, Visa was threatened by American Express's growth, which was spurred by its highly successful "Membership has its privileges" campaign, reflecting conventional category values of status and exclusivity. Visa was able to disrupt these perceived values by drawing on American challenger conventions of democratization and personal freedom as expressed in the "It's everywhere you want to be" campaign, which turned exclusivity into a weakness.

And non-U.S.-based global brands doing business in the U.S. have also cap-italized on American challenger conventions to effect a turnaround. Nissan's recent business turnaround was communicated by the "Driven" campaign that featured their chief American designer, Jerry Hirshberg, who discussed his disruptively pragmatic approach to design and engineering. This adver-tising was particularly groundbreaking in that it celebrated the Americanization of Nissan in the U.S., something that a Japanese company had never previously done.

Each of these examples illustrates brands in various states of evolution from champion to challenger to potentially neither. How can U.S. champion brands anticipate threats and use Disruption to remain in a leadership posi-tion, despite challenging marketplace shifts? How can they be appropriately disruptive, rather than defensively disrupted and thus continuously maintain the role of champion/challenger?

Acknowledging the Need for Disruption

By recognizing and acting upon the following seven disruption triggers, U.S. champion brands can navigate the ever changing landscape of American business. When confronted with these challenges, champion brands should look to be guided by the ideals of the ingenuity and entrepreneurial thinking upon which their company was originally founded, and the challenger con-ventions that can help foster successful disruption.

1. If You Are No Longer Setting the Category Values

This is a good indication that you have crossed the line and are now embracing conventions that inhibit disruption. This was certainly the situation that the U.S. automotive industry found itself facing in the late 1970s and early 1980s, when the Japanese changed the conversation from style and flash to substance and value. One wonders what the U.S. automotive market would look like today if Ford had gone back to its roots immediately and taken a disruptive risk instead of retrenching to an isolationist, dogmatic stance. Had Ford been quicker to reclaim category values — as it finally did in 1986, when it emphasized ergonomics and design with the Taurus sedan — perhaps the Japanese would not have been able to capture more than a quarter of the U.S. light vehicle market.

2. When You Are Relying More Heavily on Deals and Promotions

This could mean your brand has assimilated toward centrist category values, rendering attempts at differentiation internally unpalatable. As a result, today we are seeing an acceleration of commoditization in many not yet mature categories, such as wireless communications and Internet service providers, where deal has replaced differentiation. This type of environment can create opportunities for challenger brands that embrace disruptive conventions. EarthLink has successfully disrupted the ISP category by differentiating itself from America Online's "members only" version of the Internet. EarthLink proclaimed themselves the "#1 Provider of the Real Internet," which carries an implicit First Amendment message. EarthLink made the distinction between those consumers who were trapped in AOL's walled garden and those users who want an enriched, all-encompassing Internet experience, all the while protected by EarthLink's steadfast commitment to the issue of Internet privacy.

3. When You Feel Invincible

You have probably isolated yourself. Failure to recognize changing marketplace dynamics along with potential new competitors will make you vulnerable. Facing these challenges head-on will be vital in securing your position within the marketplace. Polaroid's recent bankruptcy protection filing might have been avoided if Polaroid had returned to their foundation of ingenuity and innovation and reinvented themselves in accordance with the prevailing trend of digital photography. As the sole provider of instant images for decades, Polaroid had every right to claim leadership in the digital revolution. But their inexperience in dealing with credible competitors may have left them blind to the marketplace appeal of the vision that lay beyond the convention that a camera required film.

4. When the Competitive Set Changes

It is a signal that conventions have probably changed as well. For the U.S. soft drink industry, the swift acceptance of bottled water as an alternative to carbonated soft drinks signaled the consumer desire for healthier alternatives to sweet and heavy soda drinks. Category archrivals Coca-Cola and Pepsi were caught off guard by European brands Perrier and Evian as they began to entrench themselves in this exploding segment of the U.S. market. Pepsi, who often behaves as a champion/challenger against the iconic Coke, drew upon this challenger heritage and beat Coke to market with its Aquafina brand. Coke eventually launched the Dasani brand four years later, which has yet to catch up to Pepsi's initial success.

5. When Your Customer Base Begins to Look Different

This could indicate that your marketing message is in danger of losing relevance. The U.S. wireless category has its roots in telecommunications, where the most lucrative customers are mature and belong to the upper middle class. Wireless marketing therefore tends to target the same user in both its central message and its mainstream media. But adoption of wireless service has skyrocketed among young, urban, ethnic users. Cingular Wireless's success with their "Express Yourself" campaign can be directly attributed not only to their celebration of diversity and personal freedom, but also to their astute, disruptive decision to market to previously undervalued consumer segments.

6. When Your Customer Base Fails to Look Different

This could signal failure to capitalize on demographic or societal trends. When entrepreneur Ray Kroc started the U.S. quick-service restaurant (QSR) business, his success in establishing McDonald's was aided by the growing mobility of the U.S. population and recognition of baby boomer buying clout. Overall industry growth in the 1970s and 1980s was fueled by the seemingly endless supply of 18- to 34-year-olds, the core QSR user. Since the early 1990s, one of the few brands to achieve significant same-store sales growth is entrepreneurial Wendy's, who has recognized the lucrative opportunity beyond the 18-to-34-year-old demographic. By using its mature founder, Dave Thomas, in advertising to appeal to an older demographic, Wendy's has been able to achieve gains in both frequency and size of average check.

7. When You Cannot Articulate a Clear Vision for Your Business

This situation manifests itself in many ways, both internally and externally, and can, consequently, not only damage your business performance, but lead to a malaise that starts from the inside and works its way out. This often results in confusion and alienation among employees that enable centrist and counterintuitive behavior in the absence of any clear direction. Brands without a vision have probably already ignored at least one of the previous seven disruption triggers as they drift in the marketplace. With luck, there will still be time for them to embrace challenger values and find their vision through disruption.

Disruption is a powerful tool. It can reignite the ingenious and entrepreneurial soul that undoubtedly lives in the DNA of all American brands. Just as it took immense courage for the American founding fathers to break with convention, it will take thoughtful fortitude for established U.S. organizations to venture beyond the status quo.

2. DISRUPTIVE ORGANIZA- TIONS

When first thinking about disruptive companies, some famous names spring to mind: Virgin, 3M, Apple, Nike, and so on. Typically, these companies are acclaimed for their visionary product ideas, great technological leaps, or innovative advertising. But such advances are often the result of core disruptive qualities that lie at the heart of the company: either in the fabric of the business strategy or in the management culture.

These disruptive organizations bring a genuinely new perspective to the way business is conducted, which is often disturbing for competitors. The industry map changes irrevocably and competitors struggle in the newly created framework.

Whether the disruption lies at the core of the company or occurs after the birth of the organization, these disruptive companies generally hold the same beliefs and goals over the long-term, giving both internal and external participants a sense of trust, confidence, pride, and continuity.

What we see in all of these disruptive companies is that they are in love with being different, but not necessarily in love with change.

Whole libraries have been written about change. About as many volumes will soon be written about "change fatigue" and how to deal with it. Change in large organizations is often inwardly focused and is driven by boardroom talks and management processes. Invariably, there is a belief in a trickle-down effect from top management to the whole organization, which in reality stumbles over human, psychological, administrative, or practical hurdles. Personal resistance to change is always underestimated, and traditional change processes often affect one discipline instead of running through the whole organization. The application remains ancillary to many of the worries or interests of internal constituents, which means intended changes often fail to reach critical mass.

But change and Disruption are, in our eyes, two very distinct phenomena.

Disruptive organizations are focused on changing how things work, not primarily on changing themselves. Their disruptive approach can come from anywhere, but usually arises from observation of the outside world, not from self-referenced analysis.

Key Characteristics of Disruptive Organizations

First, we usually see a childlike talent for expressing the vision of the organization simply and what it means specifically for everyone involved, at all levels (not just for executives). We also find this in the vision of putting a man on the moon and returning him safely to earth, laid out in the 1960s by John F. Kennedy, a promise that satisfies both the left and the right side of the brain. Often, we find a unique *sens de la formule*, a visual image or a metaphor. Behind its naïve expression, this childlike vision is far from innocent. It often gives an implicit but brutal redefinition of the other players — and what they are not. Disruptive companies use their childlike vision to reposition the rest of the world.

Second, Disruptive organizations thrive on doing, not lecturing. And they do it close to the ground, in action, not simply at the level of vision. All the companies we studied have a combination of passion and pragmatism and a strong emphasis on providing tangible evidence of the company's disruptive approach, offering all constituents proof that something radical is going on. This proof is not provided by the management, but by the frontliners, the sales staff, the reps: the most visible people.

Finally, because disrupters look at things from the outside in, these organizations share a radical view of their place in the bigger world that redefines the nature of their interaction with partners, suppliers, and users.

Boundaries are therefore more blurred in disruptive organizations. For example, users become producers, and companies find themselves part of a network where some of the traditional business fences vanish. The turf they are protecting is in their minds, it is in the idea.

1. Childlike Vision

Lush, the Cosmetic Grocer

When Mark Constantine started Lush, the purveyor of fresh, handmade cosmetics, he visualized himself not as a supplier of youth fantasies and over-packaged luxury goods, as many cosmetic brands probably see themselves, but as a grocer, a self-appointed cosmetic grocer, with a company culture and values more often associated with the food world than with the world of cosmetics. This overall vision of himself and the business he was in was highly disruptive, and guided the total development of the company and the Lush brand. Grocers have a personal relationship with their customers. They sell only fresh, natural products by the pound.

This disruptive strategy pervades the attitude and the tone of voice that radiates from the company: no nonsense (a grocer talks about the weather and asks how the kids are doing rather than holding philosophical debates or selling jargon) and a sense of humor — elements dramatically absent from the conventional cosmetic world.

By employing the grocer metaphor and references from this other world, Mark Constantine does not just bring a new marketing idea and positioning to his brand, he creates an inspiring yet very explicit message for his staff and communicates his strategy and vision in just one word. Now, this is fresh.

Southwest, the Singing Airline

Southwest fought a legal battle for more than three years against established carriers to get the airline off the ground. Herb Kelleher's vision for Southwest Airlines was rooted in a radically new idea of what an airline should deliver at an emotional level: fun, a laid-back style, and simple kindness — a set of values that had so far been judged incompatible with the serious business of running a reliable and safe airline business.

Behind the overall *joie de vivre* that exudes from the Southwest flying experience, there is also a different approach to customer care and service, which challenges the usual servant/served model so common in this business. The Southwest transactional model is more on equal terms, adult to adult (or sometimes even child to child) — a model that is gathering momentum in the service business today.

In the Southwest model, front and back office can serve very distinct but complementary purposes. The back office guarantees a well-run operation and reveals solid management, while the front office — consisting of flight attendants singing safety instructions and serving midflight jokes in place of lunch trays — provides a unique flight experience, which has since inspired many no-frills airlines around the world.

Southwest proved that you can have an emotional and lighthearted rallying cry and still be a serious player in a serious business.

2. Frontliners Provide the Evidence
Greenpeace's Actors

Greenpeace activists surely represent a radical redefinition of what staffs are about and the message they should be sending to the public. Of course, the noncommercial and activist stance of the organization is largely responsible for the passionate and engaged nature of the staff, but it goes beyond that, and is the result of a carefully articulated mission and culture.

Greenpeace activists have taken the word *act* to its extremes and brought its theatrical meaning into the non-governmental world. Part of the Greenpeace vision is to create images, not thoughts, and this vision is expressed almost exclusively in the doing — in the acting and the performance.

Greenpeace activists have responsibilities as actors. Their task is to create a sense of drama around the situations they bring into the limelight, often contributing to the dramatic plot themselves. As brand experience becomes the latest buzzword in the field of brand management, one might want to rethink how staffs could act for their business more directly, instead of simply letting the brand do all the stage work.

Nike under the Skin

Nike has many frontliners performing the dance of the brand. The Ekin are a unique breed of sales reps who go to sports stores, educating sales staff in the products' most sophisticated technical features and infusing staffers with their passion for sports. The Ekin are renowned (even within Nike) for their obsessive and extreme love of a particular sport, which is their life blood. And, it is allegedly within that very closed group of Nike staff that we can find the highest proportion of Nike Swoosh tattoos.

This hard-core passion must be combined with a rebellious and irreverent spirit, a combination that also guides the selection of Nike's most valued performers, the athletes. Nike has an implicit contract with the athletes with whom they contract: They are expected to perform as individuals, not just as athletes.

When looking for the true spirit of Nike, look no further than John McEnroe, Andre Agassi, and Eric Cantona. They have genuinely performed for the brand, not by following behavior guidelines and smiling at the camera, but by expressing their rebellious spirit in sports. Most of them are associated with vivid, visually dramatic acts and moments that stick in the mind of any sports lover and crystallize for anyone else working at Nike what the company is really about. Nike athletes play a powerful integrative role for the company; they embody the brand.

Nike also focuses on carrying this spirit through to its business partners — especially its advertising agency, Wieden & Kennedy, which has the mission of bringing it to life for a number of target audiences. When I first interviewed to work for the European office of Wieden & Kennedy in Amsterdam as a strategic planner, the only question the creative director asked me was, "Have you ever been arrested?" I won't tell you what my answer was, but I did get the job....

Salespeople as Hosts

A similar empowering approach was used in the United States by Nordstrom, who recruited staff not on the basis of their sales expertise but on their personal ability to take on responsibilities and run a business within the business. Nordstrom broke many of the conventions ruling the world of department stores, such as that of territory-based jobs, whereby you sell socks or you sell ties, but not both. The overall theme crafted by Nordstrom was that the store should be operated more like a home, in which staff would be hosts. As a host in your own house, you welcome guests (not clients), make them feel comfortable, and try to find out whether they need anything. This metaphor of the host at home conveys the high expectations that Nordstrom had of its sales staff, both tangible and emotional. It also ensures that the company has a guaranteed critical mass of personnel, a prerequisite for the success of such a disruptive program.

Salespeople as Financial Analysts

The Spanish clothing brand Zara disrupted many industry rules, such as the practice of outsourcing all production to third parties. But what made the disruptive strategy of Zara so interesting is the way it totally redefined and elevated the role of its staff.

Zara views its salespeople not as passive shopkeepers, but as financial analysts. Empowered with the task of gathering and feeding essential sales and transaction data to the headquarters near La Coruña at the speed of light, the shop staff at Zara stores all around the world make the idea of real-time inventory and retailing a reality. The combination of this real-time information-sharing and the disruptive approach of producing 60 percent of the goods in-house means that Zara can work with almost no inventory and still have new designs in the stores twice a week, as opposed to the six weeks it traditionally takes most competitors to introduce new merchandise.

What is so clever at Zara is that there is a clear and direct connection between this disruptive staff profile and the business objectives, whereby results are shared. In such a context, the risk of staff resistance to this new job profile with increased responsibilities is minimized. As they are giving more information, they are also getting more information.

3. Radical Interaction with Partners

The User Produces, and Vice Versa

Having understood that the new customer will soon be asking for a new type of interface from the organizations they deal with, some businesses have already disrupted the conventions of the customer relationship.

With any database marketing activity comes the concern that the organization will know stuff about customers that they do not want known and cannot fully control. Dell took the concept of coproduction and applied it to its customer relationship marketing. Any Dell customer has full access to the total history of his or her interaction with Dell, the time and contact name of the last call to the help desk, the status of a brochure request, and so on. This new form of contract between the organization and its customers is disruptive news for most of the business world, which still operates by a logic wherein they handle the customer and not the other way around. For many businesses, the prospect of customers playing an active part in handling the relationship is frightening. Why should customers meddle with a company's processes and products? Why not?

Linux, Open for Business

There are some similarities between Dell's approach to customer management and the philosophy behind the success of Linux, an organization of open system software programmers, totaling 35,000 worldwide, which has managed to generate servers that claim 35 percent of that market.

In the 1980s, as the PC became a mass-market product, users demanded simple user interfaces and the highest possible degree of compatibility. Only a minority of very sophisticated users noticed a deterioration in the quality of off-the-shelf code, particularly as they perceived it in Microsoft products. Linux emerged in the early 1990s, fueled by a distaste not just for Microsoft products but also for its business practices, and quickly attracted a large group of developers to write new code. Linux pioneered the open source concept, which is fundamentally about collaboration not just between developers, but also between developers and users, reflecting the blurring of boundaries between producers and users.

Before Linux, during the period when Microsoft dominated the market, the working business model relied solely on exploiting customers' lack of technological expertise. Linux established a new vision, which includes a disruptive business model that challenges the convention that the backbone of the software market is the logic of the copyright. Today, this new paradigm of "copyleft," as some developers put it, challenges fundamental conventions in the relationship of markets, firms, and governments.

In the last few years, disruption has shaken up the world of software out-sourcing, pioneered by the Indian software industry.

Until recently, most companies such as IBM would rely on local suppliers to handle their call centers — supposedly the ideal way to control and manage sensitive customer contact and private customer data. Today, it is very likely that my medical record with the local hospital is actually being kept some-where in Delhi. American Express conducts all its card business back-office operations out of Delhi. Companies such as Infosys or Wipro have estab-lished themselves as high-performing suppliers of outsourced software, thereby refining the traditional interface between the organization and its information partners. With a small front office in Silicon Valley, the real work is done by an army of programmers based in Bangalore, Madras, or Hyderabad. These partnerships represent a new cultural turn in business, maybe one of the most powerful business interfaces between the north and the south.

Manchester United: Who's on Our Team?

The most famous football club in the world provides another compelling example of modern coproduction. A survey published by UFA Sports in 2001 found that 26 percent of European football fans thought that Manchester United was the best club in the world, two-and-a-half times as many as those who chose Barcelona. ManU has almost 14 million fans across Europe, and in Britain it has nearly two-and-a-half times as many fans as Chelsea, the Premier League team with the next-largest fan base. Manchester United announced a joint marketing deal with the New York Yankees, revealing its aggressive stance in global sports culture.

From a relationship point of view, it seems bizarre nowadays that until ManU, no one (at least no one in Europe) saw the possibility of redefining a football club as a brand and its fans as the engine of a powerful media and financial system. Of course, not everyone could pull this off.

Mark Oliver, from Oliver and Ohlbaum, a media and sports consultancy, says that Manchester United was a "brand waiting to be discovered." Prior to the 1990s, Manchester United had accumulated 20 years of relative failure in the form of ongoing challenges and dramas. Nonetheless, the club had gen-erated an unusual level of support, partly as a result of the plane disaster in 1958 that killed eight of the club's players. The disaster shocked the world.

This heartbreaking event contributed to seeding the legend of ManU, as well as the extraordinary talent of the club's players in the 1960s.

The myth began to develop. ManU was more than just an ordinary football club, but it needed someone to listen to the voice of the fans and reveal the team's magic.

At the heart of the ManU story was the realization that fans are many things: They are consumers; they are apologists; they act as a medium. A passionate fan is worth 10 times as much as a moderate fan. Fans create their own system and dynamics around the idea of the team; the fans are the team. Behind this is the disruptive thought that people derive their values more from each other than from material goods.

Manchester United's market capitalization of nearly $1 billion is attributed to the many thousands of season ticketholders — the fans who attend every match, who regularly buy shirts and merchandise, and who subscribe to the club's newspaper. Behind the aggressive commercial agenda is one important point to remember: Respect the fans, because the fans are part of the team. The fans make the brand.

The Way to Approach Things

As the western world drifts slowly but surely from techno-optimism to greater techno-skepticism, we believe that the human factor will prevail in most disruptive organizations. How we approach things — that is, the psychological and social implications more than the technological issues — will stimulate the next wave of disruptive thinking and practices.

As a result, a genuinely disruptive organization usually has an impact outside of the traditional realm of business. It is a social and cultural agent that has shaped and continues to help define a new paradigm, which will often have an impact on popular culture.

This is one of the reasons that disruptive companies often communicate a clear and powerful message. Advertising, in particular, has the power to show quickly and indelibly the true character of an organization. Everybody from top management to support staff can see their company's ad on TV and say, "See, this is it. This is the real face of my company."

3. DISRUPTING MARKETING CONVENTIONS

Disruption is based on the premise that fresh ideas can be generated through the systematic challenging of conventional beliefs and patterns of behavior. As a business practice, Disruption pays off when these fresh ideas force audiences to positively reassess a company's offering. This chapter is concerned with how Disruption can help us, as practitioners of the discipline of marketing, reassess the way that we work and identify some of the conventional beliefs and practices current in the marketing and advertising industry that we can fruitfully disrupt.

Today's business writing has taken as its central preoccupation the importance of creativity to successful businesses. In order to achieve profitable results in the "idea economy," companies must increasingly rely on the creativity of their employees in order to gain a competitive edge. One might think, therefore, that it would be second nature for marketers to seek out disruptive ideas and strategies. But this would not seem to be the case. Even as marketing teams are charged with achieving breakthrough results in increasingly demanding market conditions, they all too often seek to do so by following conventional marketing practices.

If one definition of insanity is repeating the same mistakes and expecting different results, then its marketing corollary is repeating these conventional practices and expecting breakthrough results. Of course, conventional practices are based on conventional beliefs, which often go unexamined in our day-to-day work. The economist J.M. Keynes once remarked that those who claim to practice economics without working with any particular theory are simply in the unconscious grip of some earlier theory. Marketers who are plying their trade every day may claim that they have no time to consider the fundamental principles of marketing; but this merely means that they are trapped, unthinkingly, within the existing framework of conventional thought.

In this chapter, we look at a different convention of marketing thought in each section and suggest how it might be disrupted to positive effect. We do not pretend to be the first to debunk some of these conventions. We also make no claim to exhaustiveness — there are surely many more conventions waiting to be disrupted. We merely hope to start a habit of thought that others will pick up on.

Everything Starts with the Consumer

The notion that the customer is always right is probably as old as marketing itself. The need to put the customer first is still one of the mantras of today's businesses. Belief in the importance of placing consumer interests at the center of business strategy gained momentum during the long economic boom of the postwar years, as the big packaged goods companies, such as Procter & Gamble and Kellogg's, built their empires. These companies were among the first to disrupt the contemporary convention that the idea of a business was to create a product and then find someone to sell it to. Their disruptive insight was that this logic should be turned on its head: Why not first find out what consumers want, and then give it to them?

Thus, the consumer's needs and desires were placed foremost among considerations when deciding what products to take to market. This placing of the consumer at the heart of business strategy was accelerated by new thinking in the 1960s about benefit-based marketing, most powerfully crystallized by the marketing theorist Theodore Levitt, who pointed out that consumers do not want four-inch nails; they want four-inch holes. A recent article caught the current flavor of consumer-centric thinking. It proposed that we had moved from the era of unique selling propositions (USPs) to that of *my* selling propositions (MSPs): "People will need a level of passion and commitment to a brand to bother being an active partner — hero status ideally" (Julian Martin, Admap, May 2000).

Today, then, customers are not only right, they are heroes. This is conventional wisdom, and it is inherently limiting. To think about why, we might recall Henry Ford's remark, "If I had asked the public what they wanted, they would have asked for a faster horse." Today's equivalent might be, "If I had asked the public how they wanted their coffee, I doubt that they would have requested a double short caramel skim cappuccino."

The disruptive notion here is simply that the *idea* is the hero, not the customer.

Heroic business ideas rarely come from letting the customer make all the decisions. Most people cannot tell you what they want but, in trying to do so, they base their decisions on logic, familiarity, and past experience. As insistent as we can be in marketing on generating new insights, it is often self-defeating to go into research and see whether consumers buy our ideas. Operating in this way confuses consumer input with marketing output. Of course, there can be little argument that businesses need to treat their customers with respect and gain their input. But the real challenge is for the company to generate original ideas, so that it can be seen as a hero in the customer's eyes rather than the other way around. Today's most exciting companies generate ideas that they believe in with conviction, and that they believe people will follow in the marketplace (often regardless of the decision of a focus group).

In other words, leadership brands attain that status by leading their customers. Jeff Bezos says, "Where some companies go wrong is they only listen. Even if they do a good job of listening, it is not enough because you have to do things your customers would never think to ask. That is where invention comes in." Similarly, the Coca-Cola company has the stated aspiration of continually "surprising and delighting" customers. You cannot surprise people with something they asked for in the first place. And it is hard to truly delight people by giving them what they expect.

Leadership brands are customer-*informed*, but they are idea-led. At best, they move ahead of the customer, based on their own guiding ideas of the future, and the customer follows. Apple, Sony, and Starbucks are all companies whose success is based on their ability to generate surprising and original ideas that transform a customer's perception of what their product is (be it laptop computers, gaming consoles, or coffee).

In the idea economy the disruptive mantra that may serve us best is not "everything starts with the consumer" but, rather, "everything starts with the idea." If we are to create greater shares of the future for our businesses, we have to find ways of generating great ideas.

Branding Is Added Value

The conventional view of branding is that it is an exercise in adding value to a product offering. A brand is seen as a set of values, impressions, or associations that can enhance the meaning and relevance of a product or service over time. The intangible nature of this added value means that it is often regarded as something of a luxury by CEOs and CFOs. Very few companies think about branding as an investment. It is accounted for as a cost, and is often regarded as a cost that should be among the first to be cut when the company is not meeting its targets.

We would agree that it is more and more difficult to justify a brand as a set of values or emotional benefits that get transmitted in lofty and expensive brand communications. But thinking of brands in this way in the first place comes from the conventional, overly linear nature of the branding process.

As companies set their business objectives, they typically start at the corporate level and follow up by setting sales and marketing objectives and, in turn, communication objectives. Branding gets dealt with most noticeably at the communication stage. It is the last leg of the objective-setting relay race. The brand is added value: something we bolt on at the end in order to give our product or service more of a competitive edge in the marketplace. Again, we would suggest that this conventional wisdom is wrong.

THEN

BUSINESS PLAN

▼

MARKETING PLAN

▼

COMMUNICATION STRATEGY

▼

CREATIVE IDEA

▼

MEDIA PLAN

Branding, by its very nature, is not optional. If you do not position yourself in people's minds, they will do it for you. If we accept David Ogilvy's definition of a brand as "the consumer's idea of your product," it becomes clear that a business cannot control whether it has a brand. It can only hope to control or manipulate what the brand stands for in consumers' minds. Companies, whether they know it or not, cannot decide whether to add on a brand to a product.

Given that any in-market product already has some kind of brand, and given that this is not just an add-on feature, what is the best way to think about branding? We suggest that a brand should be thought of less as a set of values or associations that create differentiation for a product and more as a living business idea that lies at the center of everything a company does.

A brand is a living business idea

The brand is a CEO, not an agency or a consultant. It is defined through behavior, not by residual impressions. When thought of like this, the brand lies at the heart of a business. It is the cohesive force of an organization, the idea that gives the company its *raison d'être* and sense of purpose.

The notion that a brand is a living business idea does not mean the idea should be businesslike in the conventional sense — it does not have to wear a suit and tie. Businesses begin and end with people, so the ideas that they run on should be human ones. Apple is a great example. Apple revolves around the idea that it does not make computers, it makes "tools for creative minds." This idea underlies Apple's advertising campaign. It also determines what types of hardware it makes (stimulating tools that encourage you to keep a life log with music, sound, and image), the way it communicates with internal and external audiences, and the way it takes its products to market (radical new retail experiences). The iMac emerged from this thinking. It could not have come from a company that saw its task as simply to produce another beige box that would sell at the right margin.

Without an inventive and inspiring business idea at the heart of a company, that company will find it harder to achieve breakthrough results. With such a guiding idea, businesses can act more like organisms than mechanisms. The brand becomes behavior — a way of life, a way of thinking — for its employees and its customers. Think of Virgin's Robin Hood mission to take on the big guys and win on the public's terms, or the spirit of play around which Nike is reinventing itself. Employees at companies with living business ideas at the heart of them feel empowered to think of more creative ways to deliver real value to their customers, because they have a clear intellectual and emotional understanding of what that company stands for and where it wants to go.

Ultimately, branding and business building cannot be separated.

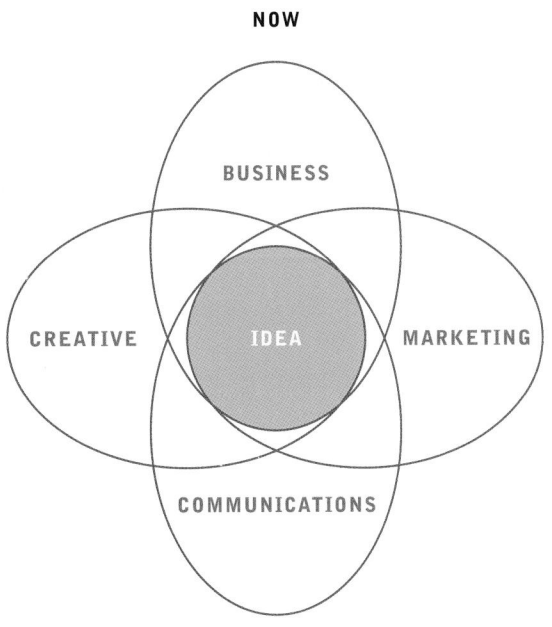

It is time to disrupt the conventional belief that branding is the domain of marketing or communication. It is the domain of business itself.

The Future of Marketing Is One to One

A conventional belief that has taken hold in recent years is that the future of marketing is about one-to-one, individualized communication. As relationship marketing grows and the Internet offers new routes to reach individuals in individual ways, broadcast media and the very idea of broadcasting have come to be seen as anachronistic. Such media are, it is said, impersonal and inaccurate. They create enormous waste, and fail dismally at the task of giving consumers what they want, when they want it. Broadcast media are the dinosaurs of the information age.

Recently, marketing writers such as Regis McKenna have offered arguments about the true nature of brands and branding that effectively suggest that if branding means anything in the future, it will be as an extension of information technology. McKenna discusses what makes a strong brand and concludes that "branding, in terms of brand creation and image, is dead... Strong brands endure because of their distribution infrastructure." This kind of argument — that brands are simply prisoners of their distribution channels — usually goes on to suggest that marketing communications as we know them will be replaced by the entirely rational operation of Web-based decision makers that act as proxy for the emotionally disinterested consumer. This dovetails with the argument that the marketing of the future will be targeted to an audience of one.

The disruptive view here is to reaffirm the importance of broadcast as the best way to create excitement and distinction for brands both

within *and beyond* their target audiences.

Simply put, brands need fame, and broadcast media are still the best way to achieve fame.

Many of the successes we have with clients are predicated on brands reaching icon status in the public domain. Brands that enter the bloodstream of popular culture take on a life of their own and therefore become more resilient to economic or competitive threat. Absolut, Apple, Energizer, Sony Playstation, Wonderbra, and FCUK, the British clothes brand, are all examples of brands that broadcast media have exploded into the public domain, where they are talked about, adored, dissed, appropriated, and parodied.

They have become public property. This is, as the owners of these brands have testified, of enormous economic benefit. These brands have a scale and reach far beyond that which most brands achieve on similar marketing spends. While we pay attention to the net present value of an investment, we must not underestimate the power of net presence value.

The original 1984 spot for Apple is a powerful example of this. It was the first time the Super Bowl was effectively used to launch a brand instantly into the public consciousness. Of course, that was a disruptive idea at the time, but it would not be so now. Fifteen years later, dot-coms spent ill-conceived millions on the Super Bowl in an unsuccessful attempt to replicate that success. The objective — to achieve an instant critical mass of public awareness — was not a bad one. But the method used to accomplish it was based on conventional thinking. Perhaps these brands could have staged PR stunts, run promotions, or created content-based events on a scale that would have achieved the mass awareness they were looking for.

Icon brands are in the fame business, and, as Jeremy Bullmore has pointed out, there is something in the nature of real fame that means it needs to be indiscriminate. For instance, of the millions of people who know about Britney Spears, only a fraction will ever buy one of her records or a ticket to one of her concerts. Yet her brand value is incalculable when all of the other people who know who she is and have opinions about her are considered. It transforms the relationship that her fans have with her into more than just a preference. It becomes a statement, a part of who they are. To take an example from closer to home, Sony PlayStation in the United Kingdom has thrived on the fact that its devotees enjoy the idea that the rest of the world does not understand and may even be reviled by the brand and its "weird" advertising. Whether it is fame or notoriety, the key point here is that brands can gain hugely from being known outside their target audiences as well as within them — and broadcast is the best way to effect this.

Broadcast media also continue to provide valuable context for consumers to assess your offer, before engaging with the brand at a more individual level. The massive growth of E*TRADE across the 1999-2000 period in America (a brand that successfully harnessed the Super Bowl to continue its rapid build of momentum) was fueled by tremendous broad-

**AIMING OUTSIDE
OF YOUR CATEGORY**

cast media spending. This brand understood the age-old need to create a mass presence before making individual house calls. Broadcast media set the stage for successful one-to-one approaches as the brand matured and the marketing environment became more competitive.

Broadcasting is not limited to businesses with exorbitant advertising budgets; the Virgin PR machine, Absolut-sponsored events, and the live presence of FCUK through T-shirts, all demonstrate the value of broadcasting the company message through different means. But broadcast-led brands are becoming the disruptive ones in today's environment, where one-to-one marketing often takes precedence. Certainly the one-to-one approach has its place, but it is unwise to underestimate the value of the fame that broadcast can create for brands.

Marketing Is about Market Share

As product proliferation and parity increasingly become the norm, marketing activity seems to be focusing on gaining ground on the business's immediate competition. The fight for incremental share increases is becoming ever more fierce. But the focus is on gaining share of a market that has its parameters defined according to manufacturer-led beliefs and habits of thought. The disruption here is a simple one: the act of asking "What market are we really in?" Or to put it another way, "What are we really selling?"

In today's environment of consumer hyperchoice, companies compete for mindshare more than market share. Brands have to compete within the context of the lives of consumers, who may view their choice in an entirely different context from that defined as the competitive set by the business concerned. Think of the opportunity cost of a significant purchase like a sports watch. People might weigh the cost of buying such a watch against a down payment on a sports car, or a yearly gym membership, or anything that has to do with their self-image or self-definition. The market in which a sports watch brand competes might therefore be more fruitful if described as self-image rather than sports watches.

Approaching it from this angle immediately suggests ways of overturning conventions of communication, of transforming the language in which watch brands have traditionally communicated. Is it necessary to show the watch in its advertising? Is it necessary to show the person wearing it? Or is it possible to present the brand in an original way by placing it in the context of the consumer's potential range of self-image choices? Perhaps the watch should not only be sold in watch shops, but placed next to other self-image-type products such as clothing, fragrance, or even cars.

Of course, thinking like this can also lead to a profitable disrupting of the conventions of pricing in your market as conventionally defined. If you define your own market, you have a chance to control your pricing. We can be certain that everybody knew seven years ago that nobody would pay $3.79 for a cup of coffee. But back then, nobody knew what a double short caramel skim cappuccino was. Once you understand that the conventional definition of a category is just that — a convention — then you are free to set your own rules.

Successful Marketing Depends on Consistency

The trend toward consistent, carefully worked-out, long-term business strategies grew out of the widespread economic and political consensus of the postwar world. Just as governments became convinced that the only way to cope with the violent downturns and upswings of the business cycle was through carefully planned public investment programs, so corporations began to believe that their long-term futures could be ensured if they made the right plans. Business strategy, the more idealistic of the business community believed, could be made into a branch of science. The deep recessions of the 1980s and early 1990s, and the rise of the information economy, changed all that. Governments became all too aware of their impotence in the face of the global forces of capital, and companies discovered how hard it is to make long-term plans in the warp-speed markets of late capitalism. Jack Welch, CEO of General Electric, caught the new mood when he declared, "Our strategy? We run like hell and then we change direction."

Of course, strategy is not dead. Successful companies such as GE and Microsoft still pursue long-term goals and have broad ideas about how to get there. But they recognize that these plans, such as they are, must be provisional, subject to constant revision and, where necessary, transformation. In a world where, as Andy Grove of Intel puts it, "only the paranoid survive," nobody can rely unthinkingly on the same unchanging beliefs and models of thought. Yet this is precisely what happens in the marketing community. Despite the fact that our industry should be at the forefront of change and adaptability, we often find ourselves working with models and ways of thinking that valorize consistency above all other virtues, to the detriment of a brand's ability to thrive on change.

Normative data from decades ago still acts as the yardstick for many communication models, despite the divergent ways in which communication has been proved to work today. Research models that were designed to test advertising made and received in a completely different consumer environment are still used, in part because of the "consistent" data that this allows us to view. Never mind that the data from this test is based on wholly false assumptions about the way people consume advertising today — it allows us to make some very interesting correlations with data produced in 1958. The overvaluation of consistency is also evident in the approach that agencies and marketing departments take to creating brand communications. Brand communications are held accountable to a painstakingly worked-out model called a brand essence or brand DNA. The more complicated and elaborate this model is, the better. Once we have fixed the "truth" of this brand, it shall never be allowed to change — and neither shall its advertising. Agencies frequently impress upon their clients the value of a long-term, consistent campaign, with a single creative idea. The longer-term it is and the more consistent it is, the easier it is for the agency to sit back, collect the money, and knock out another one when the media plan requires it.

Some guiding truth

Now, to a certain extent, we are playing devil's advocate here. We would not suggest that it is not a good idea to try to define some guiding truth about your brand. But this truth should create a future for your brand, rather than define its present by nailing its past, as is all too often the case. Neither should a brand truth model attempt to set an exhaustive template for the brand's communications. Agencies and marketers too often play the role of brand-essence fundamentalists, checking each new communication in painstaking detail to ensure that it stays true to the sacred text of the Brand Essence. The fact that agencies often assign to themselves the role of brand guardians is another symptom of an attitude to brands that is defensive rather than creative. In our view, brand truth models should be simple, future-positive rather than just future-proof, and flexibly interpreted — springboards to creativity rather than checks against brand heresy.

Furthermore, the brand's truth should be defined as something more than just a rational description of the product or service. If your brand's truth is defined as a higher-order idea, such as "tools for creative minds," then it is better able to accommodate and inspire new ways to serve customers, and thus new revenue streams. This is the strength of the notion that brands are living business ideas.

Neither should we underestimate the value of branding ideas that remain the same over a long period of time. But the point is that we must be vigilant, to the point of Grove-like paranoia, about their continuing relevance to consumers. We must constantly be thinking of new ways to revitalize and reinvent long-term campaigns. Absolut is a good example of a consistent long-term branding campaign that has exploded out of its home on the back pages of magazines and into the new media opportunities of Internet, sponsorship, and content creation, ensuring that it stays at the leading edge of cultural trends.

The bottom line may be that one must be consistent in belief but dynamic in action. All too often, though, the overemphasis on consistency of belief is allowed to stymie the dynamism of a brand. Emerson said that "consistency is the hobgoblin of little minds."

There is little doubt in our minds that conventional thinking is built into the very structures of many client organizations and agencies. Advertising agencies have struggled to come to terms with the new worlds of interactive and immersive media, in part because they were saddled with conventions of thought about the best way to reach customers that had not been questioned in 50 years. Marketing departments often find themselves in territorial battles with the rest of their organization, and construct cast-iron models and rules for brand communications as a means of regulating and justifying their budgets.

"We are all marketers now"

One disruptive conclusion to challenging these marketing conventions would be to argue for the abolition of marketing departments. Their very existence as separate departments within organizations reinforces the convention that marketing is an added-value discipline that should be bolted on at the end of a company's supply chain. Peter Drucker once remarked that "we are all marketers now." Many businesses are coming to recognize that every part of their organization must be focused on the delivery of its ultimate product or service. The best way to do this is for everyone in the company to work with a clear understanding of the values and attitudes of their company, and to feel empowered enough to put those values into action in new and profitable ways. This is why it is so important that we begin thinking about brands as living business ideas. The ultimate organizational implication of this way of thinking is that the marketing discipline should be broken up and redistributed throughout the organization in more creative and disruptive ways, involving all of its people. Your company's brand is too important to be left to the marketing department, or, indeed, the advertising agency.

In this chapter, we have tried to outline some of the key conventions of thought among the marketing community that we think are most ripe for disruption. These conventions are partly responsible for the fact that so much of today's marketing and advertising is formulaic and lacking in imagination.

You may not agree with some of our conclusions, but we hope that we will inspire you to search for more conventions to disrupt. The powerful thing about such a method of thinking is that if you disrupt a convention, you are forced into thinking of an alternative solution. If branding is not about added value, then how else might we justify its existence? We have already given our answer — you may have another one. You may even question the validity of a conventional belief, only to conclude that it is true. The important thing for all of us is not to allow our behavior to be governed by outmoded conventions of thought that we have not even bothered to question.

"Successful companies base themselves around fixed core values, but at the same time, adapt to a world that is in constant motion. The key is to understand the difference between the sacred and the unsacred, between what should never be changed and what can be changed."

GARY HAMEL

DISRUPTION

AT WORK

You have just been exposed to some stimulating thoughts. By now you may have some questions that you did not have before. How do you go about applying Disruption?

This second part enters into the heart of the subject, and explains in detail how we practice and apply Disruption. We call it "Disruption at Work." By the end of this part, you will realize that Disruption can be applied by anyone, given the right stimulus.

Neil Dawson, our agency's head of planning in London and the most recent arrival among the authors of this book, was immediately confronted with putting Disruption into practice. He gives us his initial reactions in Chapter 4, "First Impressions."

Chapter 5, "State of the Art," is obviously a key chapter. It describes in detail how Disruption is practiced in South Africa. Why not London, New York, or Paris, you may ask? The answer is that our agencies in Johannesburg and Capetown live and breathe Disruption more than anywhere else in our network. You may not know much about South Africa, but this is where Disruption has been fine-tuned.

Our South African agency has created an emblematic culture. **John Hunt**, the founder of our agency there, with Reg Lascaris, heads what can be seen as one of the best agencies in the world. It was elected Agency of the Century in South Africa in 2000. John has written Chapter 5 in collaboration with **Marie Jamieson**, the head of planning in South Africa, and it will demonstrate how a company embraces Disruption from top to bottom.

No other creative director knows more about Disruption than John. He is an incredible evangelist. His work combines fresh creativity with many sound strategic insights. As you will see later on, he has achieved great Disruption results, in terms of both business disruptions, such as with Standard Bank, and communication disruptions, such as with Nando's.

In Chapter 6, John and Marie provide a step-by-step description of how Disruption workshops are run in their country. These workshops have become a universal model throughout our network. The good news is that they have made the process anything but dry. Using inspiring tools and visual aids, the process is lively and fun to be part of. It helps our clients shape new visions for their companies, and the agency to reflect these visions in great advertising. As John himself says, "Great campaigns are the benefit of the process. They are a natural extension." He adds, "Our objective is to be seen as smart thinkers that happened to do great ads. Not by accident."

Our clients participate in Disruption workshops, but often much of the Disruption work is done internally. We need tools to help us think out of the box. Chapter 7 is therefore devoted to describing the tools used for Disruption. Acting as a common grammar, these tools serve as a stimulus to inspire thinking within the agency. They correspond to each step on the path that leads the brand from today to tomorrow. **Fiona Clancy**, Worldwide Strategic Planner, who has put her intelligence and enthusiasm into Disruption since its early days, describes these tools. She explains how to use them and why they offer a better chance to create new market spaces.

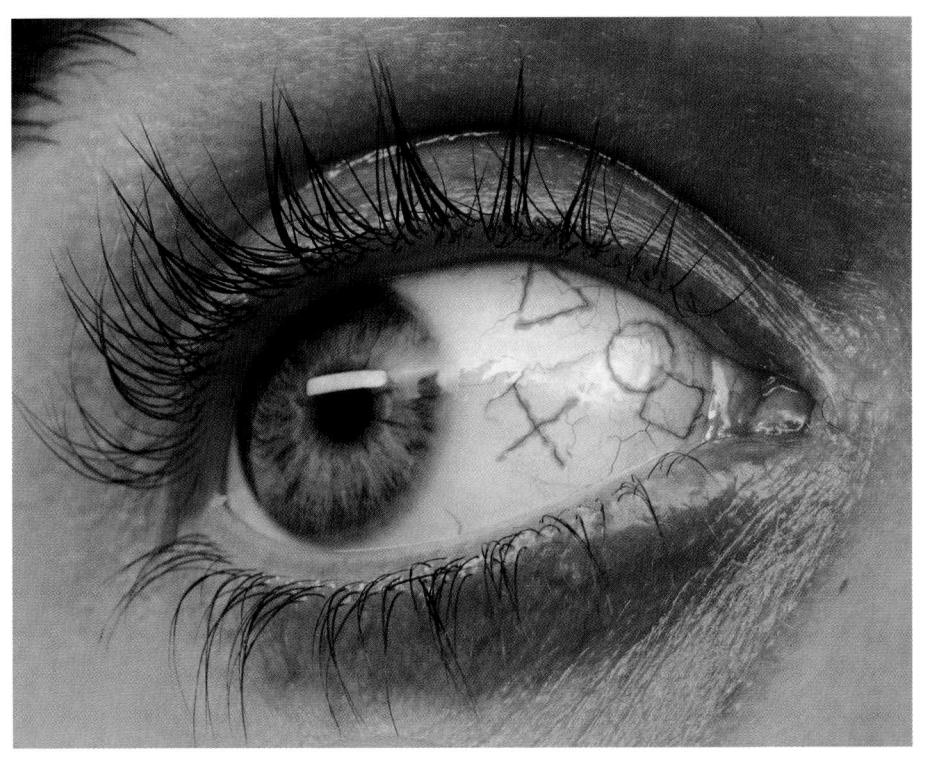

4. FIRST
IMPRESSIONS

"Strategists may have a lot to say about the context and content of strategy, but they have, in recent years, had precious little to say about the conduct of strategy — that is the task of strategy-making. No one seems to know anything about how to create an original strategy. Managers may know how to embed quality disciplines, re-engineer processes and how to reduce cycle times, but don't know how to create new, innovative, wealth-creating strategies."
Gary Hamel, "The Search for Strategy," *Sloan Management Review,* 1998

Hamel's observation is relevant to anybody who works in the marketing and advertising business. A cursory read of the major handbooks leaves you with the troublesome impression that strategic development is often a conventional, linear process rather than a creative skill. The business-market-brand-consumer context followed by the identification of the role for advertising and the creative brief are the all-too-familiar reference points for the agency strategist. (Indeed, how many agency pitch presentations still follow this so-called logic?) While they are certainly important foundations of thinking, agencies need to approach them from new and fresh perspectives. And yet rarely do we deviate from these familiar paths. If the thinking follows the same rigid approach whatever the problem, is it any surprise that so much of marketing and advertising output is wallpaper?

The fundamental importance of Disruption is that it demands a fresh look at the development of ideas. This allows us to break free of conventional wisdom and familiar, often uninspiring, approaches.

My first encounter with Disruption came at another agency in 1997 when my chief executive at the time gave me a copy of a book, entitled *Disruption*. Whether this was a subtle hint about my thinking abilities or simply something that he thought I would enjoy, I decided to read on. Two things have remained in my planner's tool kit since then:

• The register of advertising expressions, which I have often used in strategic debate. As an analytical tool, it encourages client and agency alike to consider all the possibilities of a brand approach and can create a common understanding. (This tool can also highlight the advertising conventions in a marketplace very well if you use it for analysis. See chapter 7.)

• The three types of conventions identified in the book and the wise advice that business breakthrough is not necessarily the result of direct opposition but often is achieved by laterally attacking conventions or not taking them at face value.

Both of these I have found far more useful than the usual "Let's think outside the box" or "How can we differentiate?" types of question that so often frame strategy development.

So, my very first impressions were sufficiently positive for me to borrow two tools! In the course of more recent exposure, I have had the opportunity to give Disruption more thought. While Disruption cannot be a panacea for all strategic and creative ills, it does encourage consideration of the key challenges for agencies and planners. Here, then, are my second "first impressions."

How Can Agencies Maintain Their Role as Strategic Advisors to Clients?

Much of the recent concern in the advertising industry has been that agencies are no longer seen as the key strategic partners for clients. The industry's perceived obsession with creative execution and a limited commitment to integrated communications have encouraged clients to look elsewhere for advice. The ad agency's traditional, self-appointed position as guardian of the brand has been challenged from a wide and sometimes unexpected variety of organizations.

At the same time, there has been a growth in the influence of consultants, be they of the management, brand, or research variety. This is due partly to their independence from the creative product. The underlying longer-term fear is that agencies will be relegated to a purely executional function, while the added-value thinking is done (and paid for!) elsewhere.

Disruption has the potential to address this because it is committed to the generation of what clients are looking for in an increasingly fragmented media landscape: ideas that transcend advertising and can run through the heart of their brands. And the way Disruption does this is crucial.

By blurring the lines between strategy and execution...

...and bringing fresh perspectives to bear, it breaks down the traditional, linear model of agency process from strategy to brief to execution.

In so doing, it prevents the often artificial separation of strategy and execution to which we are vulnerable. Disruption exploits the crucial advantage agencies have over any consultant: our responsibility for both strategic input and creative output and our cultural mix of strategic and creative minds. One of the founders of British advertising planning, Stanley Pollitt, described the relationship between account manager, planner, and creative as one of "controlled friction," and this mix is what continues to leave agencies uniquely placed to generate outstanding creativity. Using Disruption, we can assume a preeminent position as the generator and guardian of the big brand idea, and then take responsibility for advertising execution, using our specific skills.

ACCOUNT MANAGEMENT   PLANNING

CONTROLLED FRICTION

CREATIVE

As Robert Jones, in *The Big Idea*, puts it, "A big idea is the soul of the organization. It's not a form of words; it is the organization's essence." From Tesco's "Every little helps," to British Telecom's "It's good to talk," agencies have proved their role and value to clients. Because it is dedicated to such ideas, Disruption can ensure that we play a larger role in our clients' business.

A System That Is a Way of Thinking

"When the Old God leaves the world, what happens to all that unexpended faith?" Don DeLillo, *Mao II*

The "Old God" of marketing has been exposed. Think of the unique selling proposition, the use of demographics to define targets, and the deployment of gap/need analysis. Even terms such as positioning seem curiously static for today's brand environment. The original principles of marketing seem irrelevant to the challenges for today's brands. Marketing is under increasing pressure to deliver and be seen as accountable. It is thus no accident that we have seen a recent return to the mechanistic advertising research methodologies and black-box techniques. Add to this a widespread tendency to formularize brand vision and brand architecture (pyramids, wheels, onions, etc.), and it seems that the "unexpended faith" is being diverted into systems, regardless of any proof of their effectiveness. The risk is that the system becomes the end in itself.

In this context, my reaction to a proposed system of any kind is, "Do we really need another one?" And, yet, Disruption is not a system in the manner of those already described. In each stage of the Convention/Disruption/Vision process you are encouraged to look at things differently. The focus on the brand vision ensures that this is not simply a system that is limited to creative execution. Instead, it encourages a role for advertising that will inject new life into the brand as it strives to achieve its vision.

And Disruption is not a system with boxes to fill in...

...or rules to follow, which is what so often limits thinking. The strategy debate can be reduced to a semantic one, as the "system" demands that you write a brand vision or a promise in a specific fashion. I once worked with a major food client who required that every proposition be defined as "the critical and unique benefit which will motivate people to choose our brand over any other." Unsurprisingly this system generated neither original strategies nor inspirational creative work. The system made sure of that. The Disruption process, by contrast, is open-ended and expansive. It demands both analytical and creative input. The tools are there to stimulate and encourage thought, rather than being an end in themselves. The fact that, in our network, we are invited to develop our own tools to augment those on offer is a confirmation of its flexibility.

Malcolm McLaren once famously described the Sex Pistols as "an attitude, not a band." In the same way, Disruption is an approach or a way of thinking rather than a system.

Creativity Cannot Be an Optional Extra

"The modern economies will be constrained not by lack of resources but only by lack of creativity and ideas." Charles Handy

"The search for value has led companies to seek efficiency thru' downsizing, rationalizing and right-sizing approaches that eventually result in a diminishing level of return. But what will fuel growth in the future? Growth will come thru' mastering the skills of creativity and making them actionable." John Kao, Harvard Business School

It is now widely recognized that creativity is at the heart of many successful businesses, from Apple to Virgin. Business success is an output of creativity, rather than creativity being a tool of business. There is an independent U.K. fashion brand called YMC (You Must Create). This is a very clear statement of their brand attitude. Disruption seems to say the same thing.

The strength of Disruption is that, by adopting the Convention/ Disruption/Vision approach, it is likely that radical, new, or redefined visions for brands will emerge. This, in turn, will require more interesting and original creative solutions that express those visions.

The importance of this should not be underestimated in the world of advertising, where most agencies themselves draw a clear divide between the creative (i.e., award-winning) jewels and the hardworking, effective accounts. If we consistently apply Disruption to a client's business, we are embracing creativity of thought *and* execution. By encouraging a change in our approach to business problems, we are more likely to change the way we think about the solutions.

How Can We Break Free from the Constraints of Traditional Client-Agency Relationships?

One of the key criticisms of traditional agency processes and structures is that they exclude the client at key stages of strategic and creative development. The Advertising Agency Register in London cites "involvement" and "collaboration" as key factors for clients short-listing agencies as equally important, alongside the more predictable areas such as creative reputation and the personalities of senior management.

From my initial impressions, Disruption is, by definition, a collaborative and participative process between advertising agency, client, and other key communications partners. It is not simply a debate about whether advertising is on strategy.

It offers a level of involvement that most agency processes cannot usually achieve.

This is particularly important given that Disruption invites clients to commit to groundbreaking ideas and alternative visions for their brands. These demand bravery, intelligence, and judgment. You can deliver such ideas only when you work as a team. Collaboration of this nature between clients and their communication partners should be both more enjoyable and more productive.

So, as well as being a way of thinking, Disruption is a process that can disrupt the client-agency relationship itself.

Do We Have License to Retrofit?

"... The rationale of creative work after it has been developed will become much more important than the initial creative brief."
Stanley Pollitt, 1969

This prediction seems to often be either forgotten or ignored. It refers to the way Pollitt thought planning would develop. There is a certain purist planning perspective that holds that the creative brief should inform and inspire the creative work in a neat, precise, and sequential fashion. Postrationalization and reviewing the brief in the light of the creative work is viewed with skepticism, as if it were in some way underhanded. Neither volume of the APG's (Account Planning Group) planning textbook, *How to Plan Advertising*, even refers to this area. And yet, this is precisely how some of the greatest creative campaigns are developed and evolved with the help of planners. Briefs are not sacrosanct, and creative work is often considered in light of the spirit of the brief rather than the letter. Planners are the midwives of creative work as much as they are the inspiration.

Disruption legitimizes and encourages this behavior. The Convention/ Disruption/Vision format can be written and rewritten at any stage in the process. Provided you can identify the idea, you can then revisit the format and see how it might work. You can be fairly sure that "the future's bright, the future's Orange" went some way to informing and defining their brand idea of optimism. Similarly, the creative expression of FCUK has developed the spirit of what is now described as "the antifashion fashion brand."

So, Disruption encourages planners to do what comes naturally.

Thus, here are my first and second impressions of Disruption:

• It offers a different approach to the conventional and, hence, by definition, flawed approach to the conduct of strategy.

• It is open-ended enough to avoid the limitations of the mechanistic methodologies and processes, which are increasingly prevalent in marketing and advertising.

• It protects the position of the agency by exploiting its core strength as being responsible for both strategy input and creative output in the development of big ideas.

• It is likely to lead to more original and effective creative work.

• It breaks down the barriers that frustrate and limit the scope of client involvement and replaces them with partnership.

• It legitimizes and encourages a fluid role for planning — one nearer the free reality of the process of creative development, rather than the linear theory.

It is obvious that there can be no formula for original creative thinking. Indeed, it would be ironic if there were a system for alternative thinking. The appeal of Disruption is that, as an approach, it increases the chances of being *more* innovative and *more* creative *more* of the time.

aids. the new struggle.

Segregation isn't a thing of the past in South Africa. Everyday people with HIV/AIDS are treated like second – class citizens. Fight the discrimination. Support Wola Nani on World AIDS Day December 1st. For more information call (021) 237 385.

5. STATE OF THE ART

When it comes to practicing Disruption on a daily basis, our partners throughout the network say they are inspired by our agency in South Africa. Is it because of the way the agency is run? Or is it due to the country in which this agency operates? We believe that the answer is both.

South Africa is a land of contrasts — beautiful mountains and arid plains; unspoiled beaches and picturesque wine country; urban shacks and undulating bushveld, where lion, elephant, and rhino roam. It is also a land of contradictions — Western sophistication and tribal lore; cell phones and drumbeats.

This is the Rainbow Nation. The land Nelson Mandela calls home and the beloved country to all its children. It is the most exciting place in the world and the world in one country.

In 1991, our agency became one of the architects of the peace campaign that brought together South Africans from all walks of life, and helped pave the way for constitutional negotiations and democratic elections. Our agency received bomb threats from extremists for its trouble.

That agency milestone was followed by another when Nelson Mandela asked us to represent his party, the African National Congress (ANC), in the country's first-ever democratic elections. We received more bomb threats, our phones were tapped, and we lost a few clients who did not want to be associated with "the ANC's agency." As compensation, we got closer to South

Africa's miracle transformation than most.

By living and working in South Africa, we have probably had a crash course in Disruption — like it or not. The status quo never holds in this country. Yesterday's conventions evaporate in the morning mist. It keeps you light on your feet and, to survive, never mind succeed, you have to have a disruptive attitude. And this attitude has to be high-octane and all-pervasive.

Disruption in Our DNA

Perhaps the reason for winning against the odds is that Disruption has always been in our corporate DNA. Looking back, we were putting Disruption to work even before there was a name for it. In our early years, there was no Disruption methodology for us to go on. In South Africa, we depended on disruptive instincts. We were a Johnny-come-lately agency and attracted many clients who were mavericks taking on entrenched interests. The way to get noticed was to challenge the status quo and disrupt the balance of power. So, that is what we did.

Despite the iconoclasm, the purpose was always clear. This was not being different for the sake of being different. Everything was based on a strategic imperative, although, in truth, we often crossed our fingers and hoped like hell it would work. There was risk, but it had been calculated. Dynamic, highly successful brands benefited hugely from intrusive campaigns hatched in our early years. The ads may have had a surprising quality and taken the category into unexpected terrain, but they had strategic gravitas, too. They exploited a competitive weakness or capitalized on "unused" knowledge of the sector in question.

We were first introduced to the formal, structured version of Disruption in 1998. We liked it straight off. Jean-Marie Dru and his book explained us to ourselves. Our contrarian behavior had a name. There was a whole philosophy to it. Even a methodology.

We felt vindicated.

This methodology demonstrated that challenging convention was much more than a sign of schoolboy impudence. It made strategic marketing sense. This is showcased by the strategic gains made by numerous clients: Standard Bank of South Africa, Savanna, South African Airways, Standard Corporate & Merchant Bank, the AIDS awareness campaign, Nando's (today a global chain of chicken restaurants), all showcased in the following pages.

Disruption was used to give extra impact and pertinence to these campaigns and many more. Simultaneously, the methodology has been employed by clients to address strategic business issues. We have found that clarity of strategic purpose often springs from a disruptive approach to a business or industry. Iconoclasm enables senior executives and ordinary staff to take a step back and gain a new perspective.

Disruption can be applied in so many ways. You can apply it horizontally or vertically. You can apply it at an organizational level or a brand level. You can drill up or drill down. You can look at Disruption from a business point of view or a marketing point of view. From a communication perspective or simply from an advertising perspective. You can disrupt via full-scale versions of the methodology or fast-track versions. You can apply it formally with clients at workshops. You can apply it informally back at the agency. In a group or even on your own.

For us, Disruption has no rules. It has no clear beginning and no end. All we know is that, whenever we have applied it, it seems to give a clear direction. And, looking back, it always seems to deliver definite results. Disruption's optimum value is unleashed when you take it, embrace it, absorb it into your culture. Make it part of your DNA.

By doing so, you switch on the power that comes from constantly changing the rules of the game.

Six examples of Disruption in South Africa
Standard Bank

It is unusual for a major corporate client to go to its ad agency and say, "We need to change; help us do it." That was the start of a major transformation at Standard Bank of South Africa. A key factor contributing to their readiness for change was a hostile takeover bid. However, theirs was not a knee-jerk response to a threat, but a commitment to a new way of banking that would roll out even after the takeover battle had been won.

The Disruption process resulted in a shifting-gears strategy that pointed the organization in a new direction. Not only was complexity to be replaced by simplicity, but silo thinking would give way to unified goals; passing the buck would be superseded by a willingness to take ownership of problems; autocracy would go, and people empowerment would come in. The snarl often associated with big institutions would be replaced by a smile.

The drive from the top was powerful. And, it needed to be, because a fundamental shift was necessary if reverence for complexity was to be supplanted by a culture that prized simplicity. This happened at a time when complexity seemed to be on a global roll. After all, in new knowledge economies, it is conventional to see a correlation between complexity and value. Many specialists wrap themselves in the mantle of complexity because of this assumption of added value. Information technology innovators do it. So do some financial experts.

The Disruption was an especially daring leap for Standard Bank, because they had a reputation as a high-tech financial services player. They helped pioneer electronic banking in South Africa. Their systems compare with the best anywhere. Some could argue that they had an interest in reminding customers just how complex modern banking could be, since this would reinforce their reputation as one of the rocket scientists of financial services. Instead, the bank put a kink in the conventional wisdom.

The human truth is that people do not want complications. They want simplicity they can trust — that makes their lives easier, that saves them time. The disruptive insight is that true masters of complexity make things seem easy, not difficult. The apparent effortlessness of simplified service delivery masks exceptional technical skill and absolute dedication.

This led to the vision: "Simpler. Better. Faster." This is both a summary of

SIMPLE®. BETTE®. FASTE®.

corporate values and the payoff line in the bank's post-Disruption advertising. It is at once a promise to clients and a clarion call to staff. From this vision, the agency presented a customer credo that would help guide everything the bank did, both internally and externally:

Here's a bank I would like to bank with . . .
The world has its finger on the fast-forward button,
so I need all the help I can get.
But I would like them to understand it is people who make connections,
not modems.
I would also like them to understand their real job is to make
a complicated thing simple, not the other way around.
And whether I am smart or not, not much is gained by treating
me like an idiot.
And lastly; I don't expect my bank to be perfect,
but I do expect it to never stop trying to be that way.
Because when I give you my money,
I give you my trust.
Standard Bank. Simpler. Better. Faster.

This vision and this credo have guided the bank in everything it does and says. All advertising showcases the consumer benefits of "Simpler. Better. Faster." The bank's recruitment forms ask, "Are you the sort of person who can make us simpler, better, faster?" Performance appraisals ask employees how they have helped to make banking simpler, better, faster.

The belief system can be reflected anywhere. It even plays out on bank ATMs. Previously, when you used a Standard Bank ATM, a little cartoon character appeared and slowly walked from left to right carrying some papers while your request was carried out. Today, that little guy races across the screen.

It is not only the customers who notice the difference. Independent industry and media observers are picking up on it, too. For instance, the Best Emerging Market Bank Survey run by Global Finance magazine hailed Standard Bank as the best in South Africa. In addition, it was named one of the best on the continent of Africa and in the Middle East. In the S.A. top brands survey for 2001, Standard Bank was ranked eighth within the 10 most admired companies in South Africa. It achieved the highest score among all financial institutions for relationship (trust and confidence).

Convention Banks are generally slow, cautious, and bogged down in their own processes.

Disruption True masters of complexity simplify people's lives.

Vision Simpler. Better. Faster.

Savanna

Another client who allowed us to be disruptive from the outset was alcoholic beverages marketer SFW and their Savanna cider brand. At the time (the late 1990s), the alcoholic fruit beverages sector was one of the fastest-growing liquor markets in South Africa. Four established brands commanded more than 80 percent of the market. Although two SFW brands dominated, competitors were starting to threaten. Against this backdrop, SFW approached the agency with a view to disrupting the status quo through a new launch. SFW gave us free rein, with one stipulation: that the launch strengthen SFW's overall market position. This was no small challenge, as extensive trial had already occurred within the sector and strong perceptions had taken root.

The key convention was that cider was a woman's drink. Ciders tended to be mild and sweet. At best, men saw cider as an initial thirst quencher. They then moved on to another drink. For a new launch to succeed, all these paradigms had to be disrupted. The vision was that of an international trendsetter. The disruptive idea was to take a product born and bred in South Africa and give it all the attributes and positive associations of a premium international brand.

Everything about the brand, from the name to the distinctly different bottle, contributed to the international image. The international platform legitimized a significant price premium (25 percent above the market average). It also led us naturally to a distinctive, stronger, drier cider that shattered the "sweet and feminine" conventions. All communication emphasized dryness. TV and print ads featured dry humor, with headlines such as "If love is blind, why do surgeons make so much money?" and "I was trying to daydream, but my mind kept wandering" and "Lie on a bed of roses and put your tulips around one of these." The payoff line proclaimed, "Savanna. It's dry but you can drink it!"

This disruptive strategy's success is illustrated by comparisons with the lackluster performance of a competitive launch that occurred three weeks before Savanna's introduction. This launch embraced all the market conventions and took a mainstream approach. Despite huge distribution muscle, introductory pricing 10 percent below the market average, and the support of a budget 10 times higher than Savanna's, this newcomer was still left trailing, in market share terms.

Savanna, in contrast, exceeded initial sales projections, fulfilled the strategic objective (overall reinforcement of SFW's position), and created pride among South African trendsetters across age ranges, income groups, and genders. Savanna makes a perfect toast to Disruption.

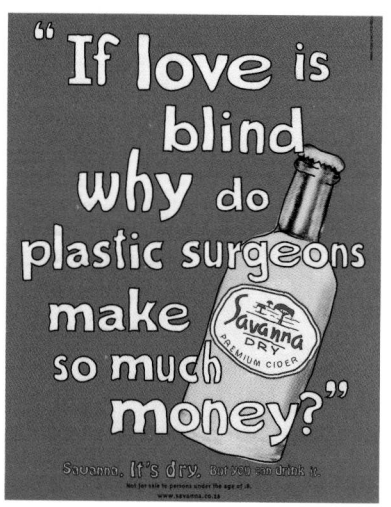

Convention Cider is a woman's drink (sweet and weak).

Disruption Express the dryness of the taste through dry humor.

Vision An international trendsetter.

South African Airways

Airlines always seem to sell themselves on product features and service. Their pitch is based on the distance between one row of seats and the next or the width of the smiles on the faces of the cabin crew. The focus is internal. This convention is compounded by a taboo among global players. You never beat the patriotic drum. It might play well back home, but you could offend international traffic.

You disrupt all of the above by deliberately playing on pride.

In the apartheid era, some international passengers refused to fly the old SAA on principle. Since then, the new SAA has come to embody the hopes of a new democracy. And guess what? Non-South Africans are not offended by SAA ads that reflect newfound pride and self-belief. They share the hope that this new democracy will succeed and become a beacon and blueprint for other African countries.

The vision here is one of African pride and hope, taking off with a resurgent SAA. The disruption was to create an SAA brand anthem that was also an ode to South Africa — ultimately setting up the proposition, "Fly the South African Dream."

The anthem proclaimed:

Because we dance when we're happy
Because we dance when we're sad
Because now we live side by side like we've been doing it for years
Because "ja well no fine" makes sense to us
Because we say "sharp!"
Because our past is as bad as the future is good
Because you are never too old to graduate
Because the streets are our malls
And the trees our temples
Because we sing two anthems
And speak eleven tongues
Yet we fly one flag

This is a much bigger pitch than claims built on whether there is 31 inches or 30 inches of leg room. It takes SAA on a flight from pariah status to self-respect. It encourages South Africans and their well-wishers to acknowledge SAA as their airline.

Of course, it is a bonus when you can call in the world's favorite president and give him a starring role in advertising that puts a smile on newly discovered national pride. Nelson Mandela, the Grand Old Man himself, pictured relaxed, rejuvenated, and ready to rock 'n' roll, helped Fly the South African Dream.

Convention Airlines generally use features and services
to sell themselves.

Disruption Create an anthem that celebrates our diversity
and idiosyncrasies and encourages South Africans to take their
airline into their hearts.

Vision Proud carrier of the South African dream.

Standard Corporate & Merchant Bank

You know you are dealing with a different breed of banker when the only time they can see you is between 5:00 and 11:00 at night. So, that is when we arranged our Disruption workshop with the team from SCMB. These deal-driven executives drive some pretty exotic vehicles. They arrive in sports cars, not the standard upmarket yet understated sedans you would associate with the banking sector.

The SCMB team members do not conform to anyone's mental picture of bland bank employees. In fact, they do not seem to conform very much at all. These guys are a corporate elite. They work crazy hours, have nonconformist lifestyles, and provide the creative spark that generates some highly imaginative deal structures. In any integrated financial services group, market banking operations are high profile. Their successes have impact on the bottom line, on investor and public perceptions, and on staff morale throughout the organization.

Yet merchant bank advertising ignores the merchant banker. It is invariably a hymn of praise to the deal and the stature of the merchant bank's client. It can be an exercise in client name-dropping. These product-focused "brag ads" never spotlight the thinking behind the deal. The deal makers themselves are anonymous contributors. The disruption in this case was simply to lift the veil, publicly showcase the deal makers, and discard the brag ads.

Therefore, our advertising executions demonstrated that great ideas do not keep office hours. They can occur at any time — if you deal with a merchant bank with the requisite level of creativity and dedication. The scenarios show a lot of attitude. They are in your face, while reflecting a contemporary 24x7x365 lifestyle.

One commercial opens on a very elegant woman in a very expensive apartment as she strides angrily out of the bedroom and shoves an armful of men's designer shoes into the washing machine. She cuts the sleeves off all the suits in the wardrobe; she places a large slice of salami in the CD player and a huge frozen prawn inside a black leather chair cover. She then writes a message in lipstick on a huge mirror hanging on the wall: "You B..." However, her scribbles quickly turn to calculations, flow-charts, and jottings, as the title comes

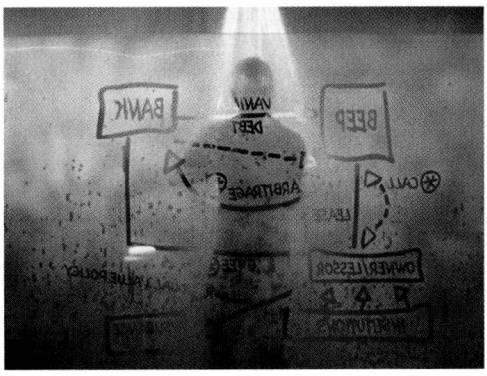

up and explains, "Great ideas don't keep office hours. SCMB."

Another execution opens on the interior of a steamy bathroom. The shower door is closed and fogged up. We see the outline of a man inside. We hear him singing at the top of his lungs, and from his movements we can see he is really into his song. The singing stops. We see him stand still for a moment and then his movements change. From the outside of the shower we see letters and numbers being scribbled into the condensation on the glass. Again the title comes up: "Great ideas don't keep office hours. SCMB."

Interestingly, SCMB staff confess to moments of intense self-recognition when viewing their own commercials. Within six months, market awareness and perceptions were the best ever, while SCMB's merchant banking peers rated it first in six categories in a prestigious Pricewaterhouse Cooper survey (corporate banking, international trading, money markets, Internet banking, retail lending and deposits, and capital market bonds and derivatives).

Convention You choose an investment bank on the strength of its reputation and solidity of its performance.

Disruption Use the attitude of the staff as a reason to believe the performance.

Vision Inspired performance round the clock.

aids. the new struggle.

Prejudice isn't dead in the new South Africa. Ask one of the 5 million people in this country with HIV/AIDS. Fight the discr

PUBLIC TOILETS
NON-AIDS ONLY
OPENBARE
KLEEDKAMERS
ALLEENLIK NIE-VIGS

port Wola Nani on World AIDS Day December 1st. For more information call (021) 237 385.

TBWA HUNT LASCARIS CAPE 708078/1

AIDS Campaign

South Africa's HIV/AIDS status as the country with the world's highest prevalence rates raises huge issues. In Africa, AIDS is both a national tragedy and a family and community affair. Care has to be family- and community-based, as no African government can afford to create a sufficiently comprehensive public health infrastructure to handle ever growing caseloads. In this environment, de-stigmatizing AIDS is critical. Greater tolerance is a prerequisite for greater support and engagement on both family and community levels. This background shaped South Africa's first regional AIDS awareness campaign (in Western Province). In order to warn of the dangers of discrimination and intolerance, the campaign branded AIDS the new apartheid. This was both a shock tactic and a call to South Africans to stand together to fight it. The apartheid parallel identified the issue as the new struggle, the new battle against discrimination, where AIDS victims were literally exiled from their home villages.

To ram home the AIDS-apartheid linkage, the campaign borrowed the look of racist signage from the period from 1948 to 1994. In those days, South African park benches, toilets, buses, and amenities were marked Slegs Blankes or Blankes Alleen (Afrikaans for "whites only"). Second- and third-class amenities were posted Nie-Blankes Alleen, showing they were for nonwhites only. The typeface and signage design favored by the apartheid government were used by the AIDS campaigners. But the groups being separated this time were AIDS sufferers and nonsufferers. Signs went up on buses, beaches — every spot where the old apartheid authorities had announced their system of racial privileges. Viewers were taken aback. Less than five years after the dismantling of apartheid, the signs rocked many people back on their heels. The campaign became a major topic of conversation. For many families, this was the first time the A word had been used in anything more than furtive discussions. Conventionally, you do not get people on your side by evoking their worst nightmares. Yet this was precisely the technique that was adopted. The disruptive imagery was so strong, it could not be ignored. This satisfied a key ambition of the campaigners — to jolt audiences out of AIDS denial. The campaign provoked controversy, but the core objective could not have been more forcefully achieved.

Convention AIDS is a plague that should be isolated.

Disruption Use the memory of apartheid to force people to
confront their current attitudes and behavior toward AIDS sufferers.

Vision The new struggle (an enduring social issue that we must
confront together in order to fight).

Nando's

Nando's is a client that has been disruptive right from the start of their relationship with us. Specializing in hot, spicy chicken, today they are an international chain of restaurants. *The Economist* hails Nando's as one of its
New Millennium brands. Even in the old millennium, they ruffled feathers.
Fast-food advertising conventions dictate that you sell the deal by vacuum-
packing appetite appeal and family imagery. A cute Labrador retriever on
the storyboard is another plus. Nando's decided not to go there. Their competitors were outspending them six to one on that particular corner. Nando's
staked out their own turf instead.

Their vision called for irreverence. Spiciness is a product feature *and* part
of its brand personality. The disruption was to use irreverent social com-
mentary to show Nando's closeness to customers, not saccharine-rich pic-
torial clichés of square-jawed fast-food dads, moms with perfect teeth, and
engaging kids with happy, smiling faces.

Nando's became famous for cheek as well as chicken.

When raging veld-fires blacken pastureland near freeways, Nando's sticks
signboards in the scorched earth, claiming these spots as Nando's Peri-Peri
Picnic Sites. (Peri-peri is a chili-based sauce. It is notoriously hot at
Nando's.) Nando's sends up everybody. When TV viewers had to cope with
a succession of hard-sell, price-driven retail ads from national supermarket
groups, Nando's struck a chord with the public by producing a parody that

counted even the cash register receipt as a product benefit. The brand claimed a first for sex scenes on South African TV when it revealed the secret of its fresh chickens, with the feathers flying in an amorous barnyard love-fest. Nothing is taboo.

Instead of using lovable family dogs, Nando's used a guide dog for the blind. This dog was so in love with Nando's, it made a detour and led its owner straight into a lamppost. When the powers-that-be ordered the commercial's removal, Nando's recut the ad, inserting all the cute family and lovable doggy clichés. While controversy raged, the chain's share price went up 20 percent and research confirmed that this was one of the most noticed and best-liked Nando's ads of the year.

Nando's irreverence has moved onto a whole new level with the latest campaign. It takes a no-holds-barred look at the reality of life in South Africa today. TV satirizes the incessant bank robberies, falling standards in our ambulance services, and consumer cynicism about the national lottery. The central character of the series is a mixed race comedian — another disruption. Conventional wisdom dictates that South Africa's mixed-race community speaks neither for blacks nor for whites. The ads demonstrate that a mixed-race comedian can speak for us all. His tongue-in-cheek confrontation of our social taboos flies in the face of political correctness, yet it resonates deeply across the broad spectrum of South African society.

At the start of the 1990s, irreverence was an unknown property in this category, yet, in a decade, irreverence has helped the Nando's brand become a national institution. Today, only Nando's can highlight — even criticize — things that are not right in our country and community, and they get away with it. As the brand has evolved from opportunistic challenger to irreverent spokesperson about life in South Africa, more and more South Africans unite behind the brand.

Nando's is still outspent by competitors, but they delight in giving the opposition a basting. Nando's advertising regularly wins awards for effectiveness, as irreverence perks up sales among South Africans who conformed for too long. At the same time, the chain has successfully grown from a single store in Johannesburg's south side, into a R1 billion a year global operation.

Convention Fast food generally uses appetite appeal
and family imagery to sell itself.

Disruption Promote desirability through spicy attitude
and irreverent spirit.

Vision Use a spicy icon (not just a spicy chicken recipe).

Let us leave case histories aside for the time being and return to the subject of Disruption on a more general level.

Disrupting Ourselves

We cannot suggest that our clients and other companies embrace meaningful change while we remain static. We not only disrupt clients, we disrupt ourselves. Applying the same methodology, we define conventions within our own industry and challenge them. We are ready to create new visions of the future on our own behalf and act on them. In this way, Disruption has become a winning, day-by-day philosophy within the agency.

Ideas factory

This has led us to develop a new agency model and a new agency vernacular to describe some of the new processes that spring from serial self-Disruption. We have become a creative solution finder for clients. Solutions are not always focused on communication. They are not always led by advertising considerations. We refuse to define ourselves as *simply an advertising agency*. We are an ideas factory, an ideas company. This act of re-definition leads us in some surprising directions.

Getting out the Silo

If ideas are your primary product, you better start developing systems that enable you to generate a bigger, better flow of them. One way to do this is to break down walls and barriers. Get out of the silos — the little boxes marked "client service," "creative," "media," and so on. Pool ideas. Work together. This has led us to adopt the concept of fusion as a smarter, freer, more inclusive way of doing things. It is not integration by another name. It goes way beyond that. There is much more to fusion than assembling a range of communication skills under one roof. We walk the talk. In our fused state we bring together all the disciplines for a single, fused brief. In the same room at the same time, we assemble practitioners from above-the-line advertising, below-the-line advertising, public relations, promotions, digital relationship marketing, and sponsorships.

It is a forum for all the talents. They share in the challenge and the opportunity. The intention is to thrash out the Big Idea. At this stage the ideas are media-neutral. In our state of fusion, there are no preconceptions and no preconditions. This permits a 360-degree scan of the horizon. Most important, every idea is equal.

Getting Ideas to Ricochet

Once an idea has been hatched, the challenge is to get it to *ricochet* across communication formats and media types, creating synergies and additional impact with every successive hit.

There is no guarantee the idea will be an advertising idea. It might be a smarter way of doing business or building relationships with consumers. Often it *is* an advertising idea or an internal corporate communication idea. But the brainwave could just as well be a concept that works best as a PR campaign or as a direct marketing ploy. It could be a promotional concept or a new way of encouraging product trial.

When an idea really starts to ricochet, the synergies overlay one another in rapid succession. The idea may work superbly well on TV, then ricochet over to the Internet. The interactive nature of the Net may create a voting platform or lead to a competition that is then taken up by radio. Alternatively, an industrial theater idea may ricochet into cinema or become a PR stunt that is picked up by the news media.

The aim every time an idea bounces from one format to another is to create a quality connection with consumers, maximizing their attention and involvement.

Workshops

A Disruption workshop — or a series of them — provides just such a link to the interconnected developments that impact business today. A workshop can focus on a specific advertising challenge or any marketing, business or strategic issue that has a client company worried or excited. New workshop formats and procedures have been developed as a consequence of this vision of a Disruption workshop as an engine of change, which the agency and client jump-start together.

Diversity and democracy characterize the new South Africa. This means Disruption in the Rainbow Nation is multicultural, not predominantly pale and male. Representation is drawn from every level of a client's organization. The decision makers are present, but so are office juniors. Freedom of expression is guaranteed.

Every idea has value, no matter what the source.

The logic of the Disruption methodology provides inner discipline, but great emphasis is placed on fun and theatricality to encourage spontaneity and creative leaps into the business future. We have discovered a link between fancy dress and flights of fancy. Pirate outfits and Mickey Mouse ears may make an appearance. They keep pomposity and bureaucratic thinking at bay while encouraging individuals (and organizations) to try on new personae.

But, after role-play and creative freewheeling, comes a concerted effort to turn kick-butt concepts into practical propositions that will drive forward an organization or a marketing campaign. Focused workshop exercises ensure that ideas are harnessed and put into context. By the end of the workshop, key deliverables have to be evident. (And are.) They are democratically spot-lighted by voting processes that identify the best ways of addressing specific challenges that currently face the organization.

Every suggestion or initiative engendered by a workshop is doable because every concept has been scrutinized by people from every level of the organization. Every planned development has the potential to fire up a client's staff and obtain their buy-in because all ideas spring from within. They are not imposed by outsiders.

A Disruption workshop generates enthusiasm as well as new ideas.

Huge forward momentum becomes evident. Attitudes change. A joint sense of purpose develops between internal departments and individuals within the client company as well as between the agency and client. You have identified new opportunities. You cannot wait to come to grips with them. Together.

We have carried out dozens of Disruption Days in South Africa, and hundreds throughout the network, from New York to Hong Kong, from Guatemala to Indonesia. Something always comes out of these workshops, whether it is a new vision for the brand, new product ideas, or new ways to define the brand portfolio.

The most recent workshops took place in Mexico for Pepsi and in Paris for Beiersdorf's Labello and Axa Insurance. Workshops are currently being prepared in Frankfurt for Henkel and in London for Cadbury.

Creating Better Clients

Complete openness to new ideas and total flexibility are needed if business is to optimize the opportunities created by a fast-changing world. It is a challenging platform to work from. As an agency and ideas company, you are seeking a larger share of the future for your clients and their brands. This wider mission demands a lot of our people — and of our clients.

Today, we refuse to take on new clients until they have been through a Disruption workshop with us. It helps us get close to them and frees us to do better work. It may lose us a new client occasionally, but we have to take the risk. Sacrifice comes with the territory. We cannot ask for courageous leaps from clients if we do not have the courage of our convictions.

The good news is that Disruption is rarely a client killer. Quite the reverse. We find that Disruption allows us to create better clients. This discovery was accidental but, then, so was the discovery of penicillin. If the aim of marketing is to create a loyal customer, the aim of an advertising agency must surely be to create a loyal client. The better the agency, the better the client you should create. We know an agency is supposed to create great ads, but track the process to its roots and you see that great communication is never possible without great clients. The client is the cause. The ad is the effect. Create enough great clients and great advertising will look after itself.

But how do you create a great client?

In a post-Disruption environment we find we no longer sit on one side of the desk while our client sits on the other. We are all on the same side, sharing ideas. I guess what we are trying to say is that the Disruption process and the post-Disruption level of understanding take the ego out of the idea. When an idea emerges, it is not your idea or their idea. It is *our* idea. It belongs to us all.

New attitudes come to the fore along with new ideas. We have post-Disruption clients who look at a proposal and ask, "What's disruptive about that?" They do not want the supposed safety of yesterday's solutions. They want a breakthrough. This has to be an agency dream come true — clients who set the creative pace. They enjoy new ideas. They are not fearful of them. As a general rule, we find clients who have been disrupted are eager to innovate. They are receptive, not defensive. Interaction between the agency and the client's executives improves markedly. Adversarial position taking becomes a rarity.

These days, we disrupt both clients and non-clients. Our clients recommend the process to industry peers and the next thing we know we are working on a new Disruption project for an outside organization. These outside organizations have been as diverse as a chain of movie theaters and a large firm of attorneys.

Disruption Inside an Agency

Disruption is a powerful tool. You start out reinventing your clients and end up reinventing yourself. To give one example of internal Disruption, we have started to reexamine long-standing approaches to idea generation within creative teams. Of course, teams still consist of an art director, a copywriter, and a creative director. But, in the quest for ideas, why not bring in an architect, a theater director, or an engineer to broaden the base of experience? We have had creative teams who bounce ideas off a stand-up comedian. We think out of the box by moving out of the box and interacting with outsiders. It has become standard practice for us to disrupt a problem as soon as it occurs. For instance, we found we were having a problem with lengthy meetings. Our disruptive solution was to create chairless meeting rooms. It is amazing how time efficient you can be standing up! Experimentation is hardly likely to end there. Structures and conventions are challenged from all sides once the Disruption genie is out the bottle.

Disruptions Improve Communication

Our fast-food client, Nando's, does not wait for us to go to them for a meeting or a briefing. They have set up their own alternative boardroom on our premises because they want to be part of what goes on at the agency. They want to break down the "us" and "them" mind-set. They want shorter lines of communication. Their disruptive solution? Put their boardroom into our offices.

Be proactive

For our part, we find ourselves more frequently submitting ideas to clients without waiting for a brief. Ideas start ricocheting and we start acting on them. We believe fast is better than slow. If business proceeds at the speed of thought, then quick thinkers must enjoy competitive advantage. But only if they refuse to wait for slow processes. Why wait for clients to brief you on a project if you have shared a Disruption experience with them and some great ideas have already been generated? Why not be proactive and develop concepts or an entire execution for the client? We have now set up a creative team that works solely on proactive idea generation on this model.

We have the capacity to move before waiting to be told. These fast-tracked concepts are not thrown straight back at us with an instruction to "go through proper channels" or "give us an order number." Disrupted clients are delighted we have done something on risk. If they like it, they will commission it *after* the work has been done. It is upside down, but it works. Disruptive clients are great to work with. There is more fun in the process, less formality. You still work effectively and with a sense of strategic direction. But you cease to be a supplier. You are welcomed as a partner. Because both parties want very similar things. You are engaged in a joint quest for solutions. You set the bar higher.

Good Is the Enemy of Great

If change is to be embraced, not feared, why not change something fundamental like your own agency credo? We started out as a strident, confident,
young agency that proclaimed, "Life's too short to be mediocre." We
believed in dreaming big. (Still do.) We made no secret of our ambition to
be the first world-class agency out of Africa. Is it possible to freshen the
vision, making it more inclusive at the same time?

Our creative stuff bought into the early versions of our credo big-time. But
if every contribution is to be encouraged and cherished, we surely need a
simple credo that can transform every input. We want our creatives to be
motivated to a higher level, but account management, media, everyone, must
feel that way, too.

The Disruption Agency

As we are rapidly becoming known as the Disruption Agency, any new credo
has to fit snugly with the disruptive quest for better performance and
smarter solutions. We have borrowed an old Bill Bernbach line — "good is
the enemy of great" — because it works for us and points us all in the right
direction. It sums up the agency philosophy. It can be applied whether you
are sorting the mail or answering the phones. It is inspirational quality control no matter what you do. Good is often the polite word for mediocre. It is
another way of saying, "This is acceptable." It confirms the status quo. We
want to represent the opposite of this.

A Better Life for All

In our experience, agents of change do not wear Superman outfits and get
undressed in telephone booths. They are ordinary people who are capable of
extraordinary things. The greatest agent of change we ever came across was
in his mid-70s when he strolled into our office. He was gray round the temples, soft-spoken, and incredibly humble. His name was Nelson Mandela. The
man was unfailingly polite, almost diffident. His vision of the future was "a
better life for all."

Nelson Mandela was (and is) an instinctive disrupter. He is not constrained
by convention and not frightened of rocking the boat. Disruptions set in
motion by South Africa's first democratically elected president have
changed the country forever.

(For more on Disruptive South Africa, refer to Exhibit A, page 296.)

6. WORKSHOPS

Disruption workshops are an important way to enact the method.

We must thank Tiger Brands, an early adopter of Disruption, for working with us and helping to hone the procedures. Tiger is the largest manufacturer of FMCG (fast-moving consumer goods) brands in South Africa. They allowed us to run Disruption workshops on all key brands, plus an overall workshop on the group as a whole. Working together with Tiger helped us develop the process and introduce refinements to the workshop format. But the basic tasks of a workshop have always remained the same. They are:

• To assess the conventions that govern the market or business status quo

• To set a new vision for the brand (or the organization)

• To develop disruptive ideas that will take the brand beyond category conventions in a manner calculated to deliver specific advantages to the organization and take it closer to its vision

A workshop may last one or two days. Most generally, it will last a full day. The framework and overall objectives have remained unchanged. However, as we gained experience, we learned valuable lessons. We applied those lessons as we went along and brought new elements to the Disruption process. The workshops have unleashed a flood of disruptive ideas that are revitalizing companies and redefining market categories. Ideas can be radical — like the launch of new killer brands that at first glance appear certain to destroy old favorites that have contributed to a client's bottom line for decades, but achieve new growth instead. On other occasions, forgotten brands have been turned into the flagships of the product range. Entire budgets have been turned upside down to reallocate internal resources and change the marketing mentality of both the manufacturer and its franchise operations.

Workshops have revolutionized recruitment policies at client companies, creating employers who hire for attitude, not just aptitude. New recruits have become agents of a cultural revolution — because the organization wants it that way.

Workshops regularly demonstrate that sacred cows make the best hamburgers. One challenged a company's definition of itself to such an extent that it provoked a cultural revolution. As we have seen, the Standard Bank of South Africa repudiated complexity and the supposed value of sophistication. Instead, it embraced simplicity and applied it at all levels and to all processes. This act of reinvention is achieving significant gains in efficiency and morale.

Another workshop induced a client to reassess all internal structures to ensure they became customer-friendly. This reversed established norms that sometimes put convenience for the company ahead of convenience for the customer. On many occasions, disruptions are radical without being so far reaching, such as the adoption of new packaging materials, concepts, and colors. In at least one instance, a packaging disruption has spawned a new social trend among the under-30s: the habit of drinking straight from the bottle rather than having the alcoholic beverage poured into a glass. It was not enough to drink this premium brand. One had to be seen drinking it from its distinctive bottle.

Workshops not only foster change, they are subject to change. By the end of 2001, at least 10 key learning concepts had been logged and applied to the original process, bringing a new look to workshop formats. Here is the list so far:

- Input is key to output
- Creative research can uncover so much
- Keep up the pressure
- The power of fun
- Tool up for inspiration
- The overall mix is crucial
- Decision makers are critical
- Naïveté is okay
- Rotate the mix
- Have a sense of direction when you close

Input Is Key to Output

An early lesson for us was that input ahead of time has massive influence on the quality of output at the workshop itself. Typically, it will take the agency a month to prepare for a workshop. Days of interviews with executives, staff members, industry figures, or consumers might be needed before we have a picture of the issues at stake. An "organizational health check" may also be indicated to gain insight into culture and morale. Background reading includes annual reports, industry reports, and relevant research.

But, at the end of the day, it is the client's workshop as much as ours. The agency brings a host of insights to the table, but on the day of the workshop, it is critical to keep the input session interactive. Client representatives must be encouraged, and feel free, to expand, debate, and challenge points so that we are all fully immersed in the issues.

Our groundwork, plus interactive immersion, enable us all to describe the conventions that apply in the area we plan to disrupt.

Disruption is not anarchy. It is a strategically directed shake-up.

Creative Research Can Uncover So Much

We also learned that readily available research and standard interviews may be insufficient for real insight into a problem. Creative research techniques may be called for. We sometimes undertake mystery shopping, taking a hidden camera into client outlets and those of competitors. Seeing is believing. Screening the results of these forays can be cathartic for a client's workshop team. When senior executives see what actually happens at store level or among the staff of franchisees, eyes bulge and jaws drop.

This is no exaggeration. Film taken by our mystery shopper was shock therapy to one CEO. The shopper was in the market for a top-of-the-line product carrying a premium price. Presumably, VIP treatment for any customer was warranted. But the sales consultant did not rise to greet this high-net-worth individual, though he was aware of the nature of the sales inquiry. He sat at his desk, with his feet up, while he completed a lengthy (and personal) conversation on his mobile phone. When the consultant began to pick his teeth on camera, senior executives among our guests came close to apoplexy. It was downhill from there. No, the obviously bored consultant could not give the customer a full-color brochure of the product. He had only one himself (though thousands had been distributed to outlets). The consultant could make a black-and-white copy. That was the best he could do.

A few minutes' video footage like this can be more powerful than a year of conventional research. Agency insights cannot be dismissed. This is at once a reality check and a slap in the face. The issues have to be addressed.

We had some consolation for this particular brand. Our mystery shopper also checked the outlets of a major competitor — again going top-of-the-line. The salesperson for Brand X denied all knowledge of the product. Allegedly, it was no longer available — though it was in plain view.

The focus of our candid camera often shifts from our clients and their retail support to consumers. We run pantry checks and wardrobe checks, taking photos of contents to provide insight into usage, buying patterns, and what consumers consider essential. We carry out accompanied shopping trips to observe and film actual behavior. It can be more illuminating than ticking off answers on a questionnaire. In one case, in-store interviews on the value of two-ply versus one-ply toilet paper showed consumer sentiment solidly in favor of the premium product. One housewife claimed she bought only two-ply. Yet our camera showed only one-ply in her cart. This type of mismatch is not at all uncommon.

Cameras may be taken into a parking lot and drivers asked to take photos of the favorite part of their vehicle, the part they connect with most. We may even hand out disposable cameras and ask consumers to take them home and photograph what they see as the most important features of a product, the features with the most meaning or appeal.

Where we suspect there might be a problem putting feelings into words, why not ask consumers to capture them in pictures? And why limit yourself to standard methodology when disruptive research often unearths so much more?

Keep Up the Pressure

As we said earlier, most workshops are run over a single day. There is a lot of ground to cover and usually only 10 hours to work with. This means the participants work intensely. Deadlines have to be set. Workshop teams have to perform at pace. This does not mean the output is slapdash or ill-considered. We find we can keep up the tempo and keep up the standard.

Participants cut to the chase and cut out the waffling. They are decisive. They are often daring as well, perhaps because there is no time for second thoughts. Lack of time need not be a constraint. It can accelerate you toward simple, straightforward ideas that are supremely doable. Key decision makers and senior staff can rarely afford two days away from their desks, but they can make one day available. At first, we thought crazy time compression was a problem. It is not. It focuses the mind wonderfully when you have got no time to waste. Bill Gates said that these days business proceeds at the speed of thought. That is pretty much the pace of one of our workshops.

The Power of Fun

We have found that, the more fun workshop participants have, the more likely they are to make quantum leaps in their thinking. Logical processes can become laborious. Lighten up a little and you leap a lot further. We are looking for spontaneity, especially in the early stages of the workshop, when we tend to be in blue-skies mode.

Fun and theatricality are not a digression. They do not trivialize Disruption. They lead to quality ideas. They are usually the magic potion that keeps us going through a very taxing schedule, jam-packed from beginning to end with tight deadlines and mental pressure. We have found that 20 people sitting around a table with smiles on their faces produce more than 20 people with frowns on their foreheads.

Tool Up for Inspiration

You cannot expect ideas simply to flow. Inspiration has to be prompted and directed. You need tools for this job. So, we created a toolbox of devices to help spark new and disruptive thinking. These tools enable you to apply a range of projective techniques to shift you out of your current paradigm. They vary, but generally include the following:

- Our "Wear a Different Hat" exercise
  (encouraging you to think differently by taking on a new personality)
- Specific quickie exercises
  (short and sweet ways to cut to the quick of organizational
  and brand issues)
- Our Headlines exercise
  (a method of projecting workshop participants one year into the future
  to encourage a leap of the imagination into winning scenarios)

Simple tools like these can inspire great solutions.

Overall Mix Is Crucial

Getting the right people to the workshop is key. You need a representative sample without going overboard. The process can become unmanageable if too many participants turn up. We have run workshops with just 10 people. We have also worked with 50 participants at a time. But 20 to 25 participants is probably ideal.

In our view, Disruption demands diversity. We do not invite just the personnel from the department most affected by the problem. This is a multidisciplinary approach. We like to see a broad range of executives, but we do not want an all-executive lineup. We want office juniors as well as divisional heads. We want technicians as well as marketers, typists as well as financial directors. The agency tries to match the client contingent one to one. But, when a client wants to send a large team, the ratio might come down to one agency staff member for every two to three members of the client's staff. We ensure the agency team is at least as diverse as the client's contingent. Usually we are a lot more eclectic and unstructured — unless it is the client's second or third Disruption workshop, when they may try to outdiversify us. We also play wild cards. We might let our lawyer loose once in a while. We have invited a couple of housewives to join us. We once brought in a child psychologist. The key is to invite both those who are close to a particular client or industry and those who are not close at all.

Decision Makers Are Critical

Whoever else you invite, make sure you get the key decision makers there. This is essential. Do not take no for an answer. Entrenched practices often come under scrutiny. Radical change may be suggested on the day of the workshop. If key decision makers have not been part of the workshop process and have not experienced the Disruption dynamic, they cannot possibly share in the enthusiasm for a new beginning.

It can take months of conventional business presentations to convince these decision makers of the desirability of change — by which stage problems might have become more acute or opportunities might have slipped. In addition, a key decision maker may be the main resister of change and the person most in need of Disruption! You cannot go to work on these people if they are not at the workshop.

Naïveté Is Okay

Junior staff members and those unconnected with the key department or industry can make a telling contribution. Often the most basic question, the challenge that shifts paradigms, comes from a junior staff member or someone with little or no knowledge of the business. Naïve and uncensored questioning is the driving force behind the Disruption process. Albert Einstein remarked that the thing that made him different was his ability to ask the most childlike questions.

Rotate the Mix

We have also learned that rotating the mix of workshop participants stirs things up nicely. Participants are split into four teams, with representatives from both the client company and the agency spread across each team. The team structure creates a competitive element. Each wants to come up with the best insight, the most thought-provoking visions, and the most radical disruptions.

But, we have found that it pays to constantly change the personnel on the teams. Different individuals spark when in contact with fresh recruits. As the interpersonal dynamics change, so do the perspectives.

That is the positive reason for personality rotation. There is also a negative reason. We have found that dominating personalities can impede the free flow of ideas from other participants. If the personalities are rotated among several groups, the negative vibes can be contained, while the dominator begins to see that he or she might be part of the problem rather than part of the solution.

A Sense of Direction at the Close

The workshop process takes you from general, unconstrained, blue-sky mode at the outset to increasingly specific action points as the day goes on. We have found that a mechanism is needed to give a sense of climax and closure to the process. Simultaneously, you need to shine a spotlight on the ideas that have the capacity to take the client's organization forward.

As South Africans, we are a new democracy and we like the idea of voting, of putting our X next to the candidate we think can get the job done. So, our climax is provided by a voting session at which participants endorse the "candidate ideas" they like the best. At the end of the day, each participant is given 10 colored stickers. As their final contribution, they vote for the ideas they like best. They can put all 10 stickers next to one item on the wall, vote for 10 different suggestions with one sticker each, or allocate any number of stickers they like to a particular concept. Voting spotlights the best ideas and illuminates the way ahead. You have closure. You also have a sense of clarity.

A Workshop Warning

We have found that a Disruption workshop is hugely powerful, explosive even. Human chemistry is unpredictable at the best of times. Be aware that ideas are not the only things that are thrown around. Sparks can fly! You are working with a varied mix of people and different personality types. In addition, the workshop may be the first forum in which the entire senior management tier has sat down together and openly thrashed out the key issues that impact their destiny.

At open workshops involving such a broad cross section of the organization, there is no way to cover up or control the agenda. The big issues have a way of surfacing. There is no place to hide. As the issues are raised, they are dealt with. On some occasions, deeply felt emotions come to the surface. Sometimes, the debate becomes so heated that senior executives can almost become violent. We take the heat out of the situation and thank them for their candor. The air has been cleared and we can move on.

Invariably, by the end of the session, the way ahead is apparent and general agreement is achieved on what the priorities are and what needs to be done. New and stronger bonds within the organization are evident. So is a possible solution. Or a whole host of solutions. But, remember, solutions do not come easy. Some tension and drama may be involved.

The Workshop Process

Our workshops follow a standard format:
1. Warm-up.
2. Convention hunting.
3. Visioneering. (Items 2 and 3 create a brief for the workshop —
   what needs to be disrupted and ideally what the goals should be.)
4. Disrupting.
   (These ideas are prompted and channeled in three different ways.)
   a. Wear a different hat.
   b. Specific, quickie exercises.
   c. Making headlines.
5. Voting and close.

1. Warm-up

We start our Disruption workshops with brainteasers or puzzles, which demonstrate that the seemingly impossible can rapidly become possible. There is a different subtext or message to each exercise.

One might illustrate the power of listening. If you listen carefully, you realize what is required and rapidly come up with the answer. Another indicates that there is not just one, single answer to a dilemma. Several approaches may work. Thinking in terms of only one correct answer keeps you blinkered when other possibilities are out there. Another test is designed to illustrate the advantage of looking at a problem from more than one angle.

The tasks in this warm-up session are fun, and break the ice between the client and agency teams. As well as brainteasers, we also use word challenges and modified parlor games, which we have unashamedly stolen from a myriad of sources. Here is a small sample of some of the tests. (Answers are at the end of this chapter.)

EXERCISES

What is the next letter in the sequence?

Read the above. What is odd about it?

BSAINXLEATNTEARS

From the line of letters above, cross out six letters, so that the remaining letters, without altering their sequence, will spell a familiar English word.

Other, more interactive, teasers include pushing a straw through a potato (it takes confidence, sudden force, and the correct angle of approach). Or balancing two forks on a matchstick (proper counterbalance is the solution). Or balancing eight nails on the tip of a single nail (first create a trellis of nails and then find the correct point of balance).

They all sound impossible, but are actually quite easy to do. By the time everyone has stood up and spontaneously grouped into competitive clusters to attempt the impossible, our workshop is on its way.

Coming Up with Answers

In the early days, we once made the mistake of not giving solutions until the next day when the teams were stumped by a particular word challenge. One executive then went home and wrote a computer program to hunt for the answer. Next day, he came back with thousands of permutations, but no solution. All he had to do was step back and listen to what we were actually asking him to do, not what he thought we wanted. He had the answer in 20 seconds.

The puzzles take participants into blue-skies mode. The idea is to open horizons and open minds. The subtext of the warm-up session is that just about anything is possible and discovering new solutions is fun.

2. Convention Hunting

Each team has to consider the conventions that characterize four key areas or planets:

- Corporate matters
- Marketing
- Communication
- Consumer issues

Preparatory work, research, and interviews provide some direction here. But you always miss something at the preparatory stage. The chemistry from the teams ensures that you fill the gaps. New perspectives are provided on each planet in turn.

A corporate convention might involve a company's culture, branding policies, staffing structures, or perhaps mission, vision, and values.

A marketing convention would typically cover issues arising from the four P's of marketing (Product, Price, Promotion, Place). Perhaps the client has always sought price advantage and never a price premium, or a brand's packaging format and design have followed a rigid pattern for years.

Communication conventions may involve media choice or executional clichés when crafting a message.

Consumer conventions normally focus on consumer perceptions, habits, attitudes, and prejudices (e.g., the notion that frozen food is not as fresh as vegetables from a greengrocer's or that prepacked baby food is not as good for junior as that made by Mom).

Whatever the conventions, they are logged as each of the four teams reports back. This initial list is then consolidated and rationalized into one collected set of key conventions across all four planets. We keep a keen eye out for connections or key drivers. There is often a root cause — a convention that influences all others and defines the worldview of the organization. In our experience, the dominant driver that connects to and affects the rest is usually found on the corporate planet. This discovery has had massive influence on our use of Disruption. It tells us that the marketplace cannot be separated from the business place, that business issues are key and have to be addressed if a strong platform for marketplace success is to be set up.

3. Visioneering

For this segment of the workshop, we put participants into teams and challenge them to develop the most relevant and inspiring vision.

Visioneering is particularly challenging, because many managers claim that they already have a vision. And they do. But we find that these visions are often clouded by corporate-speak. Executives often confuse an objective such as leadership or being the lowest-cost producer with an overarching vision of what their brand or organization might become. One does not replace the other; they can live side by side.

Essentially, what we are looking for in our visioneering session is more consumer language, the *how* that will enable a connection with the consumer. This vision must guide us in everything we do and influence how the organization acts internally and externally.

Teams are encouraged to use simple, everyday language when setting out a vision. We kick-start the process by quoting examples of the power of simple, inclusive visions. For instance, Apple's long-term business vision is "digital lifetime." Or, what about their 2001 communications vision "tools for creative minds"? Or, Richard Branson's vision on his entry into financial services: "I am gonna change the way people think about money." Then there is IBM's "solutions for a small planet" (the statement that redefined the way IBM thinks about itself and others think about IBM).

Because the conventions have already been established in the first working session, the visions that emerge in this segment are invariably disruptive visions. We are already on the road to change, spurred on by the conventions we have identified as being inherent in the marketplace.

Clarity Before Disruption

Once all teams have presented their vision, everyone is given one colored voting sticker. All participants then vote for what they believe to be the best vision. By the time we have finished the visioneering session, we all have a pretty clear idea of the challenge facing us for the rest of the day. By this stage, we have a consolidated set of conventions to disrupt, and we have general consensus on the vision we should be aiming toward. All that remains is to generate the ideas to get us there, the ideas that will break the mold and give the organization a unique and competitive position in the marketplace.

4. Disrupting

4a. Wear a different hat

Our first Disrupting session is generally the Wear a Different Hat exercise. Here we are back in blue-skies mode. There are no constraints. You can suggest putting a shop on the moon, if you feel like it. Reality is suspended. We are looking for new thinking. What better way to "think different" than to think like somebody else, to wear someone else's hat? These hats are representative of powerful personalities or company cultures that have proven themselves in the business world. We use the hats to deliberately create a little theater, to get people out of their workaday personae and transport them to a totally new way of thinking.

The hats are kept in colorful boxes. Additional contents usually include a T-shirt, maybe some other props, and always some information sheets to help get participants into character or culture. So, one box and set of outfits might turn you into a new Richard Branson, the archdisrupter known for his refusal to rest on his laurels and his compulsion to constantly challenge the norm. Alternatively, we might decide to dig into the Disney box and enter

a childlike world that is all about theater, people, and family values. The Disney regalia includes Mickey Mouse T-shirts, masks, and ears, plus information such as annual reports and distinctive Disney ideas. At Disney, you might be onstage or offstage, but you are critical to the outcome of the entire performance. It is a smiling, colorful environment. It takes you into a world of fantasy. The mind-set you evoke in Disney mode can lead organizations in surprising new directions.

We might delve into our Nordstrom box and examine their uniquely empowering corporate culture. This is the organization where the number one rule is to use good judgment in all situations. The number two rule is that there are no other rules. This level of freedom (and responsibility) sorts out the "Nordies" from staff members who might never fit in at the company. The non-Nordies feel more comfortable in situations governed by a procedure manual.

Then again, we could turn you into a wannabe for Sony, a company famed for its commitment to constant NPD (new product development) and never-ending innovation. Or perhaps you prefer to be the next Steve Jobs? If so, you take on the Apple mantle of new technology solutions.

There is even a pirate box when some corporate swashbuckling seems to be indicated. Put a couple of executives into pirate gear, complete with pistols, eye patches, and cutlasses, and see them take on new personalities. The results are remarkable. Their organization has behaved like the regular, spit-and-polish navy for years. Now is their chance to be more colorful, to contemplate the business equivalent of pillage and plunder. It is more fun being a pirate than being in the boring old navy. Let them experience the freedom for a while. The piratical executives begin to appreciate how restrictive and limiting the old environment could be.

There are lots of different hats on hand but, on the day of the workshop, we will choose four, one per team. Whatever personality or culture you end up with, it will invariably take you out of your own box and force you to think in a completely different way. There is something awe-inspiring in the transformation that occurs before our very eyes.

4b. Specific Quickie Exercises

After fantasy, we start moving back to reality. We are now looking for rational, how-to responses that will help the organization make practical progress. So, we focus on specifics. Depending on time availability, we give the teams a series of tasks that hone in on particular problem areas. These exercises will be customized to organizational needs. It is not a random selection. One focused task is the One Thing exercise. Workshop participants are asked, "What is the one thing holding us back?" Participants then have 15 minutes to decide what that one thing is and how to disrupt it to make it their greatest strength. One Thing feedback might focus on corporate culture, reward structure, inefficient systems or technology, or lack of consumer awareness. You never know where the spotlight will fall. All you do know is that a key challenge will be identified and a turbopowered 15 minutes will then be spent generating ideas to make this an area of strength rather than a weakness.

In another exercise, we may give a team 15 minutes to identify the most important driving force in their market, and then demand that they generate ideas that will enable them to take ownership of it. Other variations might focus on specific moments of truth, media choices, or corporate challenges facing the organization.

These quickie exercises are developed specifically for each workshop and are usually suggested by our up-front interviews with staff, executives, the trade, and consumers. It is remarkable how many workable ideas can be generated through 15 minutes of focused brain power.

4c. Making Headlines

In the Headlines session, the company concerned has supposedly made front-page news. The workshop participants have to tell us what they did to make the front page and how they did it. They are given various newspapers. Each front page carries a dramatic headline indicating some sort of corporate transformation.

Typically, the headlines will spotlight a mixture of specific actions and general shifts achieved by the organization. These headlines approach the organization from various perspectives. The company might be a service organization, generally reliant on staff, franchisees, or dealers who are perhaps not the strongest link in their chain. In a case like this, we might include headlines such as "Staff take XYZ company to unprecedented heights" or "Dealers lift XYZ to all-time high."

If we are focusing on one major brand or division within a company, we might include a headline such as "Death of XYZ division — yet company stronger than ever" or "Death of XYZ brand yet sales surge." If the company operates in a price-sensitive environment, our headline might proclaim "Price has never been so high — nor have sales!" or "Price at all-time low but bottom line more buoyant than ever!"

In all cases, the aim is to help executives to think beyond the norm, to ask, "What if?"

We are trying to solicit disruptive ideas that will propel the organization into the future described by the headline but, by now, we are also looking for ideas that are realistically feasible. Therefore, all newspapers are dated exactly one year from the date of the workshop. We stress the need for a directly actionable slant. We want only practical, workable ideas that are rooted in reality. This ensures that by the end of the workshop we have a host of potentially feasible solutions that complement the blue-sky flights of fancy from the earlier sessions.

5. Voting and Close

The final vote is the culmination of the workshop. There is a buzz about the place as votes are cast. As we mentioned earlier, all participants are enfranchised with their 10 colored stickers. Each participant fixes stickers to ideas written on the charts that have been hung from the workshop walls. In the process, he or she identifies the action points and priorities for the organization.

Some go big and pick one Big Idea. Others drag out the process and agonize as they allocate their stickers one at a time. By the end of the process, heavy clusters of voting stickers will be evident. These are the winning ideas. Nobody can miss them. These action points are doable because the people who have to carry them out are all at the workshop, or else their colleagues are.

All votes are equal. The voting outcome is never padded in favor of the bosses. This encourages individuals to champion ideas and express a view, which, in turn, helps unblock stodgy thinking from crusty individuals within the organization.

The voting creates a clear sense of direction. The way ahead has been signposted. The voting also gives individuals a sense of achievement. The workshop process has led to a definite conclusion. Participants are tired, but have the consolation that they have contributed to something meaningful.

During the workshop, notes are kept on all insights and comments from workshop participants. All key learning concepts are logged. These are also included in the final report. This document from the agency's strategic planning department restates the original problem and describes past practice and long-standing conventions. It then outlines the disruptions that will break the mold and carry the organization forward.

How Disruption Works with Clients

Disruption has a great effect on our relationship with our clients. It creates a very strong spirit, whatever the level of seniority. It opens up the mind to new scenarios, and it shows to what extent ideas can come from anywhere. It allows us to break with conventions on the spot.

It Breaks You Out of the Rut

In more than one case, Disruption has led to a veritable road-to-Damascus experience for some senior executives. They may start out as Disruption skeptics (which is fine). This may lead to almost zero input from the teams to which they are assigned. Or, worse still, lots of input is received, but it is all negative. They denigrate other people's ideas or use formulas like "we've tried that before" or "that just won't work" to torpedo suggestions.

Three-quarters of the way through the workshop, however, it becomes clear that the other teams always seem to be coming up with new ideas and possible solutions. They are also having more fun. These teams often include individuals who had nothing to say earlier on when they were part of a skeptic's group. No one can miss the contrast between the energy level in a skeptic's team (low to zero) and the effervescence of the others.

Seniority, a strong personality, and prejudice against the process can inhibit proper involvement and idea generation. In our experience, however, individuals stuck in this mode are intelligent enough to recognize this, and competitive enough to realize that peers and subordinates are starting to look like heroes of Disruption while they are stuck on the sidelines.

At this moment, a complete transformation occurs. These individuals then go on to generate the most powerful ideas of all. They have been transformed by the Disruption experience. But it is usually things — conventions and constraints — that have to be worked on, not people. A breakthrough here can involve a single issue or an entire corporate culture.

Inspiration from a Higher Source

A simple example of a Disruption breakthrough occurred when low morale and/or the absence of camaraderie were identified as a key corporate convention preventing one of our clients from becoming great internally. The ritual of quarterly reports to superiors was denting morale among junior and middle managers. These inevitably became destructive, fault-finding sessions because few managers encourage subordinates to grow by courting danger and making mistakes. It is so much easier to log the flaws and kick butt.

By going into the Disney box, one executive happened on the concept of the three o'clock Disney parade. A parade is a way of showing what you can do in a very public way, but it does not involve public humiliation. It is fun. It is theater. You look forward to it. Workshop participants later voted the parade concept as potentially the most disruptive challenge to the quarterly gripe sessions. Subsequently, the client company decided to keep the quarterly reviews, but introduced fun elements and aspects that celebrate success. The emphasis has been switched. The company now parades the achievers and praises the positives. Morale is up. So is team spirit. Improved retention of junior managers is in prospect. So is management continuity and more meaningful mentorship. One of the things holding them back has been transformed into one of the things propelling them forward.

It Removes the Blinkers

The most dramatic headlines in our Headlines segment sometimes cite the death of a brand, but the ideas generated from such a headline have led to the real-life launch of more than one new brand. The idea of a new brand launch may never have been previously entertained because the new brands would directly compete with the brand being disrupted. But, once conceptualized and brought to market, the power of portfolio synergies has enabled the brand owner to claim a much higher overall market share.

Change to the "brandscape" was once gradual, some would say glacial. But there has been a meltdown in recent years. Old, established brands become casualties at a faster rate. Conversely, new brand heroes achieve a faster rate of takeoff. Brands ensure continuing relevance by embedding themselves in contemporary lifestyles. But lifestyle change can be rapid today, as consumers vote in cash for the brands they like and trust, and withhold this financial endorsement from those that fall from grace. This switch in loyalties can occur at a bewildering pace. Disruption workshops have a knack for crystallizing these issues and prompting an imaginative response from marketers who realize that gradualism is ceasing to be an option.

In another case, a headline warning of the death of a division caused one company to seriously review the organization with a view to rooting out inefficiencies. As a result, they are on track toward a divisional amalgamation that will generate operating efficiencies while delivering higher, long-term levels of customer satisfaction.

The Idea Is More Important than the Source

In the disrupting section of a typical workshop, the process begins to take on a life of its own, with solutions coming from the most surprising sources. We had one instance where a divisional big cheese and industry-wide expert (age about 50) said something like, "We cannot do that! It'll cost a fortune and hold us back for weeks." Up popped a junior propeller-head from IT. "Yes, we can. I can write new code for that in half an hour and it won't cost us a cent." Guess what? The junior was right, but would not have dared to express an opinion until he was gripped by a little disruption fever. In fact, without the Disruption process, he might never have had the opportunity to make the suggestion directly to senior management.

In another instance, a non-distribution person suggested that his organization outsources its distribution functions. The suggestion was aired in the presence of an executive who was extremely proud of the in-house fleet of delivery vehicles. It caused a furor at the workshop. However, the outsourcing idea was subsequently implemented, saving the company a fortune in direct and indirect outlays.

In yet another instance, someone from the agency suggested that a company's remuneration policy be turned upside down. The existing pay policy was weighted toward set salary scales determined solely by seniority and length of service. It was proposed that pay rates should, rather, be driven by commission and incentives. This was based on an insight from internal interviews, which had indicated that most staff were not hungry enough, and that the current salary policy entrenched corporate conservatism.

There was an immediate outcry from those who supported the conventional remuneration policy. The naysayers predicted disaster. It was not possible to carry out such a radical change, they said. It might be possible to move gradually toward this model, but it would take years. Before the agency team had a chance to submit the post-workshop report endorsing the suggestion, the client had already started implementation! They achieved buy-in from staff, who realized a shake-up was essential. The sales curve responded almost immediately.

Disruption's Creative Clout

Sometimes it is the "old, gray men" who surprise you. For example, one financial director was invited to a workshop out of courtesy. There was little expectation that he might actually make a creative contribution. He was an accountant, for Pete's sake. Surprise, surprise: He turned out to be a closet radical!

Similarly, we often find that closet radicals can be hiding away in the research and development department. All too often, people expect the thinking of these individuals to be boxed in. In fact, they have minds bursting with ideas. To tap the creative flow, you simply need the right tool kit.

Another Workshop Warning

Once a workshop has established its own dynamic, the courage of workshop participants comes to the fore. They grasp nettles they shied away from previously. The process highlights problems and opportunities with increasing clarity as the workshop continues. But it is not always the client's team that has to swallow a bitter pill and prepare for changes that might be unpalatable. It can happen to the agency as well.

We do not write escape clauses into the process. Advertising is not sacrosanct. Nothing is. Once the teams begin coming up with ideas about conventions and how to disrupt them, the action points start to crystallize. The facilitators from the agency can neither stop nor divert the process.

One Disruption workshop led to the inescapable conclusion that it would be best to stop advertising. The agency could not duck the issue. The recommendation was therefore made that advertising come to a halt until other key issues had been addressed. The brand concerned gained long-term credibility by improving various aspects of the product and not launching a new advertising campaign until significant organizational and operational matters had been fixed. The agency and Disruption gained credibility, too. Our recommendation that advertising be suspended cost us money, but it was the right thing to do. The implicit promise of a Disruption workshop is that the best idea wins. A good idea deserves to be implemented, even if it hurts.

Disruption Satisfaction

There is nothing more satisfying than watching the transformation that occurs between the start of a workshop and its closing stages. A senior executive walks into the room wearing pinstripes and carrying a briefcase. Natural reserve prevents him from saying much at the outset. You stick him in a pair of Nando's "Honey-I am-Home" boxer shorts and a "funky" cap and he takes on a whole new personality, while providing you with a series of in-your-face ideas that challenge everything about the old corporate culture. An executive who never saw himself as an ideas man realizes he has it in him to be a creative powerhouse. Anecdotal evidence is that this has transformed careers as well as organizations.

Proof of the Workshop "Pudding"

The value of a Disruption workshop in achieving personal revitalization is relatively easy to recognize. But what about a workshop's value to an organization? Value here appears even more impressive if you apply the most basic test of any new product: Does it engender repeat business and broader product trial? The answer is an emphatic yes.

If you measure Disruption workshops against the usual criteria applied to new products, you find yourself asking a range of commonsense questions. Is the product easy to use and fit for its purpose? Is there demonstrable payback or practical value every time you use it? Is the product durable? Can you use it again and again, deriving benefit every time you unpack it and switch it on? A Disruption workshop scores high against a checklist like this.

Many clients have become serial disrupters, making use of workshops at regular intervals. They change the workshop parameters each time, crack a problem or explore an opportunity, move into implementation mode, and come back for more. The cumulative effect of repeated workshops is to splice Disruption into the genetic code of the corporation. There can be no greater product endorsement than this.

Our workshops are in a constant state of development. Each iteration is an opportunity to learn more; to refine workshop techniques and processes, to apply new concepts. Enhancement is constant. We at the agency do not know where workshop development will end. To be honest, we do not want it to stop. Even when things work out exceptionally well and there is a real buzz at the end of a workshop, we know we can do better.

According to Hollywood folklore, Sam Goldwyn's idea of a good story line was one that began with an earthquake and worked its way to a climax. If that is the yardstick, then our workshops have begun to shake things up nicely, but the real fireworks are yet to come.

Answers to Our Brainteasers
EXERCISES
• The answer is S. Instead of OTTFFS, think of the numeric sequence 123456. You complete this sequence by adding 7.

Now go back to OTTFFS and add a final S (for 7).

• The odd thing is that the word THE is printed twice.

It is also odd how few people notice.

The eye scans quickly instead of *reading*.

• Take this exercise literally. Go over the line and cross out S I X L E T T E R S, and you will be left with the word banana.

Brainteaser Courtesy of Roger von Oech at Creative Thinking, Menlo, CA.

Whether their history is industrial or colonial,
there are so many great temples to travel —
with their noble architectures, echoing sound chambers,
and the buzz of people going off to far-flung destinations.
You look up at the destination boards
and see just how far you can go by stepping onto the train
at the platform. The coffee in the station café seems infused
with greetings and farewells you are watching.
The excitement of a thousand possibilities is in the air.

7. TOOLS

"The art of creativity is the ability to see relationships between things where none exist." Thomas Michael Disch

How much harder to set aside relationships that already exist and start fresh. Remember those visual games in which you were supposed to be able to see a picture in the pattern on a piece of paper? Squinting, with your eyes deliberately out of focus, the picture would suddenly and wondrously appear. Once you had seen it, though, it was all you could see. What did it look like before? Your earlier, naïve perspective is irretrievable.

Maybe that is why, in the communication business, pitches are so prevalent. Trapped in their own ways and habits of thinking, clients tend to turn to outsiders for fresh thinking. Equally, those in creative businesses love pitching — with everything to learn, and nothing to lose, they are starting from a blank sheet of paper. If both agency and client can get pitch thinking without having to go through the pitch process, then everybody gains. And that is what the discipline of Disruption is all about.

Disruption as a Discipline

It sounds Machiavellian — the concept of a discipline or craft skill designed to disrupt — until you realize that all we are trying to disrupt are conventions, the basic assumptions, the common wisdom that maintains the status quo and inhibits our imaginations. It has to be a discipline insofar as we want a rigorously questioning approach to tackling every problem, great or small, shared around the network.

But how do you make a discipline out of Disruption without destroying its very essence? And how can you institutionalize this discipline across a network of 9,000 people? The problem is that a formal process is both inappropriate and impractical. It would be anathema in a disruption culture — creating boxes for people trying to think outside them. Nothing destroys creativity and spontaneity more quickly than dogma.

A Discipline of Play

Disruption can be successful as a discipline only if it is playful. We are looking for fresh, imaginative thinking, even in the analysis stages of a problem. Play is surprisingly hard for adults, who have mostly forgotten how. In traditional advertising agencies it has been tolerated among the creative staff, but not condoned among others. Yet its value, both to the individual and to the company in terms of amplified creativity, makes it a modus operandi worth rediscovering.

Nobody expresses this better than the master toy maker, Mr. Kjeld Kirk Kristiansen, owner and CEO of Lego: "Children are our role models. They are curious, creative and imaginative. They embrace discovery and wonder. And they are natural learners. These are precious qualities that should be nurtured and stimulated throughout life.

People who are curious, creative and imaginative — who have a childlike urge to learn — are best equipped to thrive in a challenging world and be the builders of our common future."

So, we have made play a discipline and our discipline playful.

To stimulate such play, we have put together a vast box of tools, models, and processes, which range from rainmakers for big ideas to investigative and observational analysis techniques. This toolbox has much in common with a box of construction toys. While the tools are arranged in zones of strategic focus, all are designed to offer maximum opportunities for trial and error, constructing and deconstructing brand possibilities. The box is called Disruption Central.

Why Disruption Central?

Because, while play is essential as a guiding mood and set of values, the subject of Disruption and disruptive thinking is serious business. We are not in a make-believe world, but in the real one, trying to realize great futures for our clients. So, when designing a framework for our tools, we wanted a concept that brought with it a sense of adventure and purpose. And one that resided at the heart of the company. The grand, central train stations of the world seemed an appropriate metaphor; hence, we call our toolbox "Disruption Central."

In Disruption Central, there are currently more than 20 tools and exercises to choose from and adapt as the occasion requires. Why so many? Why not? There is more than one way to skin a cat. In fact, there are benefits to having so many options. While preserving a sense of freedom, as well as a sense of fun, the multiple choices encourage a natural assimilation of the Disruption mind-set. As you dip in and try out different things, the disruptive approach will seep in. It keeps you on your toes, constantly tackling problems from different angles.

The exercises are arranged in zones or sections that reflect their purpose. There are three central zones that capture the core of idea-generating thinking: the ● **Conventions Zone** which helps us take a thorough look at where the brand is today and identify conventions that govern the current marketplace; the ● **Disruption Zone**, which consists of exercises and processes designed to locate the ideas that will accelerate the brand's progress toward the Vision; and the ● **Vision Zone**, which is focused on imagining new futures for companies and brands.

Around these are two zones that affect the thinking at all stages of creativity and development: the ● **Context Zone**, in which we seek to determine the factors that influence consumers and the marketplace, or will do so in the future; and the ● **Connections Zone**, which inspires creative thinking about the way a brand makes connections with people.

Finally, we have an important checkpoint, the ● **Evaluation Zone.** Here, we have our own approaches to measuring the impact of the idea on a brand — procedures designed to anticipate and accommodate disruptive ideas and recognize impact beyond communication and brand likeability.

The Tools Themselves

How does a tool become a Disruption tool?

Most of them have been developed on the job by planners and others trying to figure out a problem. Each is identified by an icon that appears on the computer screen and that one can click on for a full description and examples of how to use it.

Disruption Tools

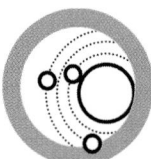

Convention Planets®
For a defined competitive set, this tool reveals the underlying assumptions that currently constrain the brand in the market place.

The Purchase Funnel®
A direct marketing tool which can shed light on the conventional marketing dynamics of a category.

The Idea Behind the Idea®
Based on the premise that several heads are better than one; that discussion between people with different perspectives is one of the most stimulating environments for idea generation.

The Brand Integrity Check®
A quick test to make sure that the ideas are credible, relevant and motivating to the consumer.

Corporate Prism®
A good way of plotting your findings from a culture-mining session, and seeing how the internal facets of the brand impact on the external.

Lighthouse®
What client does not want his brand to beam a light for people to navigate their lives by?! It helps people look up to the stars instead of looking down at the problem.

Consumer Connections Wheel®
A tool designed to audit any chosen target audience's naturally existing connections.

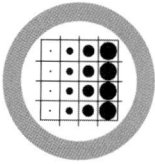

The Migration Matrix®
This maps the brand's aptitude to personalize and customize connections.

The Connections Approach®
Expresses the connections idea in a concise, deliverable statement which then informs the connections scenario.

Relationship Thermometer®
A simple diagnostic designed to gauge the depth of relationship with the brand.

Conversation Gauge®
A way of assessing a brand's standing through its presence in conversation.

The Brand Game®
A research technique designed to explore dimensions of the brand: consumer relationship, and the company that the brand keeps in the consumer's mind.

The What if Process®
The what if process makes a great starting point for the conversation. 'Stealing' ideas from other eras and other categories opens up possibilities.

Big Idea Wheel®
If you are not able to convene a big meeting to toss around ideas, the Big Idea Wheel is a helpful 'what if' model to spin ideas on. With this tool you can make big ideas bigger.

The Ladder®
A multipurpose tool with which to explore roles for different modes of communication.

The Vision Grid®
Helps articulate the behaviors that the vision should inspire in the company behind the brand.

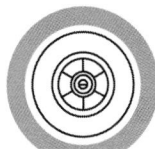

Brand Connections Wheel®
Provides the base framework for enumerating and analyzing connections between brand and audience.

Brand Connections Clock®
Assesses the importance of the timing of connections for an audience.

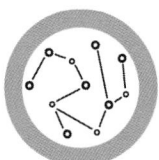

The Connections Scenario®
Provides a collaborative planning framework for moving through the advocacy chain while meeting the needs thrown up by the Clock.

The Persuasion Sequence®
A methodology for planning connections architecture, is used to test the logic of the connections scenario.

The 7 Killer Business Questions®
Designed to help ask clients the right questions right at the beginning.

The Weatherfront Check®
A macro perspective, this is about assessing the potential impact on the brand of what is happening in the world.

Evaluation Framework®
Principally a device for prioritizing the desired consumer response to a given campaign. Tracking is then set up against agreed criteria.

The Idea Impact Monitor®
This serves as a basis for exploring the broader impact that an idea can have on a brand's status within the marketplace, both directly and indirectly.

One of the most used and most useful tools is the star of the Conventions Zone, the Conventions Planets, which was derived by asking the very simple question, "Why?" Why do we see things the way we see them? Why does the marketplace operate as it does? How have the mobile handset manufacturers been caught in the commodity trap in such a young market? Why do people resent their banks?

We find that the answers to these questions are usually embedded in assumptions made by the key industry players, which affect marketing decisions and strategy and, in turn, dictate communication strategy. All these things — the way the key players behave, the way they market their products and services, and the way they communicate to their customers — have an impact on the way consumers feel and act. The Conventions Planets tool helps us plot out the links between assumptions and actions, determine the causal relationships, and identify the points at which the relationship with consumers breaks down. You can see where the status quo is open to challenge, or where there is a latent, untapped truth or opportunity to build on. In the case of Jameson Irish whiskey, we found both. We had to break a classic marketing convention — that if you have a genuine, discernible, and advantageous point of difference you should shout about it — to escape being buried as a niche player in the whiskey market ("the Irish," as an occasional change from a Scotch), before we could explore a positioning as a frontline liquor that would be right for the brand. Another review of the Planets for icon liquor brands led us to observe that all the icon liquors were competing for the same drinking occasion or mood — upbeat, clubbing, "up for it" — leaving an interesting space for an equally glamorous but more relaxed, conversational, "chilled-out" mood sharer, perfect for a mellow, rich whiskey best sipped neat or with water. Our recommendation for Jameson was a territorial strategy — corner the "sofa bars," the lazy, late-night jazz bars, the laidback Sunday conversations, the mellow beat. The brand's advertising became an invitation to this mood: "What's the rush?"

A territorial strategy? This jargon comes from another of our classic tools, the Ladder. We use this in a variety of ways (to identify and then disrupt communication conventions, to explore brand visions), but its principal virtue is the way it insists on strategic focus. There are six registers, or areas of focus, on the Ladder.

Top of Mind	Attribute	Benefit	Territory	Value	Role

For Jameson we were trying to establish a *territory* in a very literal sense, because place and time have such an influence on one's choice of drink. For FCUK, the British fashion brand, the communication focus has been on *value*, an antifashion point of view shared with the target audience, rather than on a territory that is the convention among fashion brands (dress in X brand and you belong to its universe).

Many brands tend to focus on *attributes* and *benefit*; what a brand has or does differently and the benefit to the consumer lead naturally to a selling proposition. The communication for the dish soap PRIL shows that the product is so effective that husbands and guests actually volunteer to do the dishes. It is a classic benefit illustrated humorously. All batteries tend to claim that they last longer, and in essence Energizer is no different. But the brand has built a fantastic *"top of mind"* device in the Bunny, which they are now using as a unique brand attribute in their "Bunny inside" umbrella campaign.

Big retailers tend to focus on attributes to attract customers — prices, services, opening hours, range, and so on. So, Mexico's department store Palacio de Hierro is highly disruptive in its approach. It has given itself a *role* as the women's champion in a macho and conservative society, with advertising that celebrates a distinctly and defiantly feminine attitude to life. "Top of mind" saliency is of great strategic importance to spontaneous purchase decisions, sometimes in surprising categories. While much of the travel industry works on the basis that holidays are long planned and premeditated, Thomas Cook works hard on triggering the impulse decision to get away, by confronting you with visual reminders of just how dreary life is in the United Kingdom, with the line "It's time to leave the country."

Context

The secret to great creativity in strategy is asking the right questions from the very beginning. We have an investigative approach to context. The Context Zone contains a variety of tools, which range from microscopic to macroscopic in focus. We take a fresh look at events on the surface and then search for underlying patterns and structures from which to assess their depth and importance.

From a business angle, we start with the Seven Killer Business Questions, which serve as reminders of the issues we need to understand if we are to tackle the problem in the right way. We have one set of questions that we try to answer ourselves in advance of meeting new clients, and a second set that we use as a basis for first-meeting conversations. One question that we enjoy discussing is, "What is the cost of maintaining the status quo? Can we estimate how much it will cost the business not to change?"

From a consumer angle, we have two tools that are designed to explore the relationship with the brand. The first is the Conversation Gauge, which evolved from the insight that brands exist largely in the public domain, even at a domestic level, and therefore they are the subject of conversations. While traditionally we have concentrated on what the brand is saying to consumers, and to some extent (via focus groups) on what consumers want to say back, we rarely consider what people are saying about a brand among themselves.

Such a study revealed a strategic flaw in McDonald's strategy for marketing to children. They reached a point where no amount of Happy Meal activity in mature countries in Europe seemed to increase the frequency of family visits, and they began to ask profound strategic questions. Exploring the problem through the filter of conversations exposed the key issue. Ironically, as a brand that prides itself on being a family restaurant, dedicated to promoting strong family relationships, McDonald's Happy Meal activity unwittingly had the reverse effect. Happy Meal activity did indeed encourage children to request a trip to McDonald's more often, but so frequently that parents began to resent the nagging.

As in physics, for every action, there is an equal and opposite reaction. The more children begged, the more parents said "No!" The obvious solution is to change the nature of the conversations.

The second tool is the Relationship Thermometer. This was inspired by an insight we had when working with a pharmaceutical client in Paris. Upsa, a division of Bristol-Myers Squibb, was expert in analgesics. They observed that while doctors focus on the symptoms that are causing an illness, they sometimes neglect to treat the pain that accompanies it, which may be even more debilitating. One of the reasons for this is that it is difficult to gauge how much it hurts because that is a highly subjective issue. So, they devised the simplest possible scale as a way of objectifying the conversation about a patient's level of pain. You might put on a brave face and say that it is not too bad, but if you are asked on a scale of 1 to 10 how painful it is, you might be at point 8 of your personal tolerance level. And that is what the doctor needs to know to treat you.

We have borrowed the same idea to help us gauge the depth of relationship that people feel with a brand. We give them a thermometer and ask them to tell us how warm or cool their feelings are, and why. We use the same principle to ask clients about their company's appetite for risk.

A more macroscopic view of the context is provided by the Weatherfront Check, an exercise adapted from a scenario-planning course that senior planners from around the world attended in February 2000. Taking each major weather front in turn, (i.e., social, technological, economic, environmental, and political), the task is to identify possible futures pertinent to the brand, and then make sure that strategies are in place to tackle them. The trick is to focus on treating as priorities both the issues that emerge as important and those that emerge as uncertain.

Disruptive Ideas

It has traditionally been left to the creative teams in agencies to come up with ideas. But here, it is everybody's responsibility to see if they can come up with an idea that moves the brand faster toward its vision. The tools in the Disruption Zone are mostly collaborative, designed for teamwork. We find that cross-disciplinary teams, which include clients, yield much more interesting ideas than single-discipline partnerships or solo acts. It often takes more than one person to spot an idea, and the chances are that it will be amplified in seconds by the rest of the team.

We look for ideas with particular characteristics:

Disruptive ideas: Inspiring, refreshing, daring ideas that defy market or category rules.

Media-infinite ideas: A strategy, concept, or idea that can be adapted, amplified, and communicated through many different forms.

Media-infinite ideas sound like a holy grail. How do you set out to have a media-infinite idea? Creative ideas are rarely born in a vacuum, unattached to a medium. You can develop a strategy or come up with a concept that is media-neutral, but an idea needs a form of expression. So, any kind of communication idea will have a medium of origin. Rather than deny these ideas because they are within a particular medium, we have a formal process for getting underneath the idea to arrive at the core concept. It involves asking a simple question: "What is the idea behind the idea?" Once we have defined this, we can rebrief on a media-infinite scale.

The same question is also useful if you come up with a cracking idea for a brand that you know is right, but you do not know why it is right, or how to brief for a second execution or next year's campaign. This could have been the case for Sweden's SBAB campaign, which orchestrated all the communication around an unrepeatable event; a football tournament. Working through the "idea behind the idea" exercise delivered a way to evolve into Year 2.

SBAB in Sweden offers housing loans via the Internet and had a 5 percent market share in 2000, while four big banks had more than 90 percent. The objective was to give SBAB a high profile as the small but energetic challenger. On the basis that you need to act like a challenger if you claim to be one, their big idea was to challenge the banks to a game of football (explained in detail in Chapter 9).

The real question, though, was what to do to keep up the momentum afterward? Once they realized that the idea behind the idea was about challenging the banks for real, they had a repeatable formula. They even came up with a rule of thumb: that is, an idea was only good enough if it was visibly painful for the other banks. In year 2, their campaign consisted of men wearing sandwich boards outside the other banks, comparing their rates for housing loans. When bank managers chased them away, it served to earn them positive news coverage at the banks' expense.

In lots of ways our Disruption tools are no more than a series of good questions. The classic disruptive question has to be "What if?" We have a set of 21 "What if?" questions, derived from examples of brilliant mold-breaking strategies, to get our creative juices flowing. We use these in meetings as limbering-up exercises to help us come up with the scenario that works best for the business at hand.

We get a lot of inspiration from other people's great ideas. It is so refreshing when you come across a company that has broken free of market conventions. Recently we put together an analytical model inspired by radical advertising work that did not follow the norms of either brand argument or product advantage. In fact, advertising was not the primary medium. Rather, the big idea resided in some action that the brand had taken. And the role of advertising was to publicize this action. In an attempt to identify and categorize what these actions could be, we have developed the Big Idea Wheel. We use it to try out ideas and see how big we can make them.

Of course, you have to come back to earth at some point. When you have generated wild and surprising strategies or ideas, it is important to make sure that the brand can live up to its promise, and that people out in the real world are going to care. We have adapted a classic model, more commonly used to derive ideas in other companies, to be our Brand Integrity Check. The three criteria that a proposition must pass are simply:

1. It has to be true to the product or brand,
2. It has to be motivating to consumers,
3. It has to be distinct from the competition.

Visions

Identifying a vision for a company or brand is about defining the future market space of which we want a larger share. When working on visions for our clients' business there is only one place to start: *chez le client*. Often there are visionaries not only on the boards of client companies or in the marketing departments, but on the shop floor or in the mail room. Customer-facing staff can have devastatingly simple and clear insights to share with us. It is very inspiring to meet such people, so we make it part of our formal procedures to undertake this culture mining. We have a skeleton questionnaire that provides a guideline for the conversations.

What is a vision? While it is an inspiring term, it is vague in meaning and so overused that it is in danger of losing its luster. We insist on being concrete when it comes to visions. For us, a vision is a projection of the company or brand into the future. A vision is more than an advertising proposition or a brand positioning, it is a total culture. It utilizes all elements of the mix. It speaks to all interested parties.

Some of the most useful exercises in the Vision Zone are dedicated to tying down a vision, making sure that it has substance, that it can genuinely act as a catalyst for the company, that it can expand into the targeted future market space. One of our senior planners in Paris developed the Vision Grid, which prompts you to work through the desired effect of your vision on four key aspects of the brand or company's relationships and direction.

Based on the simple axes of internal and external focus, crossed with brand or company emphasis, we assess the potential the vision offers to inspire the employees, the R&D department, the brand positioning in the marketplace, and shareholders or opinion leaders. If we find that a vision statement does not inspire or lend focus to the company in every quadrant, we go back to the drawing board.

Of course, since we are ambitious for the brands in our care, we expect our ideas to have a big impact on the marketplace. But exactly what impact are we looking for? Defining and articulating goals and objectives is key to any evaluation process. Misunderstandings are surprisingly common, particularly when implicit expectations remain unvoiced. To prevent any kind of error by omission, the London planning department has developed a broad-based evaluation model: the Idea Impact Monitor. In conjunction with clients, we review and define the impact we want an idea to have in six different domains: the corporate world, the marketing world, classic communication measures, the consumer world, the internal culture, and the wider cultural context. Setting clear targets and prioritizing form the basis of a highly constructive discussion with the client. (Beyond sales results, it is important for PlayStation or Absolut to make an impact in the wider cultural context, while internal culture is all-important to the SNCF, the French Railways). Assessing performance against the criteria set then makes for a second very lively, multidisciplinary session.

What do these tools and exercises have in common? You will not find the word Disruption in most of them. What you will find is a playful spirit, a restless energy, curiosity, naïveté, a change of perspective. The Disruption is in what we construct with these tools.

Disruption in Evolution

We currently use all these tools, and more, on a daily basis in our practice of Disruption. But who knows what we will use tomorrow? As people adapt them to specific market or client needs and develop new exercises, the contents of Disruption Central will mature and evolve. There will be the old favorites, the well-worn toys that never fail to spark the imagination, and there will be the bright new games, the new frameworks that keep us from settling too quickly into our own comfort zone. Nothing is more alarming to a company that prides itself on its ability to think disruptively than the thought of slipping into conventions ourselves.

One of our mottos is this:

Disruption is the art of asking better questions.

The discipline of Disruption lies in making sure that we are all curious enough and energetic enough to continue to ask them.

DISRUPTION

SCOPE

How might you apply Disruption to the various areas of marketing in your company to create more value? This third part takes us in detail through the many communication disciplines to which Disruption can be applied.

Chapter 8, "Disruption across Disciplines," looks at how any communication discipline can take the lead in marketing a company or brand. **Gavin Hilton** and **Alastair Maclean**, from our offices in London and Paris, provide numerous examples in direct marketing, PR, internal communications, design, and so on, and observe that Disruption is all the more effective when its intervention is least expected. **Richard Lewis**, who has been in charge of Absolut worldwide for more than ten years, then explains how disruptive PR has helped make Absolut what it is today.

Then we fly to Sweden, a country where advertising is not highly regarded, even by the people in our agency there. In Chapter 9, "Street-Level Disruptions," our friends in Sweden, **Johan Almquist, Anna Qvennerstedt, Claes Kjellström,** and **Albin Gustafsson**, show us examples in which media advertising is the consequence of something else, such as a disruptive event.

Louis Gavin is a very talented designer — maybe the most well-known designer in South Africa — and a partner in another of our South African agencies. In "Tactile Disruptions" (Chapter 10), he discusses concrete disruptions that you can touch and feel.

We move next from the tangible world to the virtual world of the Internet. Is there a need for Disruption on-line? When everything has been newly created, does the concept of an established convention exist? **Heather Albrecht**, who left our company some time ago to start a digital consultancy in Australia, offers some insights in Chapter 11, "Disruption On-line." She demonstrates that in each phase of the marketing continuum — from building awareness to acquiring loyal customers — there is always an opportunity to disrupt. Heather's knowledge of case histories is so vast that we have decided to showcase them on-line in their native medium. Then **Neil Lawrence** and **Paul Worboys**, the heads of our agency in Sydney, offer us the fruits of their interactive experience with Sony PlayStation.

Disruption does not typically connote something positive. It is often associated with an interruption and at times may be controversial. The paradox is that Disruption, as we use it, is constructive. How can we talk about Disruption in the era of permission marketing? **Laurie Coots**, our chief marketing officer worldwide, explains, in "Disruption, Interruption, Permission" (Chapter 12), that Disruption is in no way synonymous with interruption, but, rather, is a sustainable phenomenon that can lead to effective permission marketing ideas.

How can media placement help companies and brands make a more meaningful connection with consumers? **Monica Karo**, our worldwide media director, explains in "Disruptive Media Planning" (Chapter 13) that media planning is all the more disruptive when it is linked to the creative process. Monica personifies the creative side of media strategists. She is an idea person for whom media planning is an art.

This journey around the world then brings us to the United Kingdom, where **Trevor Beattie**, the charismatic chairman of our London agency, has totally disrupted the conventions of political advertising. He was Tony Blair's advisor for the 2001 election campaign. Together with **Rob Alexander**, Trevor gives us a rundown in Chapter 14, "Disruption in Political Advertising," of how they went about it. From the United Kingdom we move to Asia. Since the days of

Marshall McLuhan and the introduction of the global village, the world has become increasingly smaller. Such was the catchphrase of the 1990s. Yet we frequently talk about how complex the world is and, consequently, it seems to me that the world is becoming bigger rather than smaller. Some 80 percent of the world's GDP is produced by 20 percent of the population. What about the other 80 percent, and what about the markets of the future? What about disruption in countries where there is nothing to disrupt?

In "Disruption in Emerging Markets" (Chapter 15), **Gavin Heron** and **Sandip Mahapatra** take a stab at an answer.

To conclude Part III, we wing our way back to the affluent world. Chapter 16, "The Luxury of Disruption," answers the question, "How do you apply Disruption to premium brands?" Luxury goods have their own logic. They do not rely on research to determine their future. You do not approach Giorgio Armani and say, "Let's do some focus groups." **Adam Stagliano**, our specialist in brand architecture, explains how Disruption can be used to revisit a brand in depth. He suggests that more mass-market products need to behave like premium brands.

Part III does not obey the logic of the first two parts. Each chapter gives its own version of Disruption, independently of the chapter that precedes and follows it. In other words, you can start this part where you like and read it in the order that you like. If you have a passion for on-line, then skip directly to Chapters 11 and 12. If you are particularly interested in politics, go to Chapter 14. If you are more interested in the cultural differences between countries, go to Chapter 15. If you prefer thinking about concrete and tangible disruptions, then open Chapter 9 on "Street-Level Disruptions" or Chapter 10 on "Tactile Disruptions." Finally, for a high-level perspective on giving value to brands, go directly to the last chapter on "The Luxury of Disruption" (16). It is very inspiring.

8. DISRUPTION ACROSS DISCIPLINES

When you first picked up this book, did you flip through its pages, possibly from the back? Did you pause to look at interesting diagrams or illustrations? Did you stop at the page overleaf and immediately begin to read this paragraph for an explanation as to why the page is black with white type instead of the usual white with black type?

If so, then a number of things have happened. Someone thought about your likely habitual behavior and how to break it. And if this chapter had to compete commercially for your attention with the others in this book, then it may well have succeeded.

The idea is not new. When Laurence Sterne published *The Life and Opinions of Tristram Shandy* way back in 1759, his novel was littered with blank pages, black pages, upside-down pages, and a rambling narrative that played with the genre in which he was working in order to surprise and delight his readers.

The time and place you least expect it

In the communication business, we have overlooked Sterne. Too often we forget the power of doing the unexpected in an unexpected place. We cling to conventions about how we manage communication. By placing different disciplines in different boxes, we have taught consumers to expect packaging, direct marketing, PR, and advertising to follow the same rules.

The purpose of this chapter is to demonstrate that when we change those rules, when a Disruption idea is built at the time and place you least expect it, it is even more powerful.

To illustrate this, we have selected a few cases from seven network clients — Scoot, France Telecom, Leroy Merlin, the French Railways, Dubble, Virgin One, and Absolut — and we will briefly outline some of the processes that we use to make Disruption happen more often.

Be What the Others Are Not

We all know that we live in an environment where competition can come from anywhere. All companies are on a quest to find a sustainable competitive advantage. Put simply, companies seek to place a brand beyond comparison by being what the others are not.

Take **Scoot's** launch in the Netherlands as an example. The first thing you use when you have Internet service is a search engine. For non-connoisseurs, the difference between search engines appears minimal. How could Scoot be anything more than a glorified search engine?

We have all experienced frustration with search engines: They search, but with the information overload they give you, it is up to you to find what you are looking for.

By calling itself the first-ever "find engine," Scoot created a whole new category, which promised to eliminate the hassle of search engines. It is an idea that can take the Scoot brand into any number of diversifications.

Was it an advertising idea or a marketing idea? Who cares? It gave people what they were longing for. By the end of 2000, 1 million people called the service every month, and the Internet site currently receives 3 million hits a month. The "find engine" idea redefines Scoot for consumers because it is immediately and intuitively understandable.

Design can be a powerful tool for redefining a category because it works on the same intuitive level as the "find engine" concept. A first impression can make a brand feel both different and right. **Mobicarte** was the third prepaid mobile phone service in the French market. In the realm of new technology, this means you are nowhere. Employing Disruption in the design of the package has helped Mobicarte capture the number-one position with a completely comparable offer.

The market for prepaid mobile service is mainly teenagers — it allows them the freedom to control their consumption according to their fluctuating incomes. The package design took this independence one step further: While the competitors' offers were presented in boxes with instructions, similar to those of subscription phones, Mobicarte was launched in an iconoclastic cylindrical tube. The package design leads the rest of the communication on Mobicarte. It embodies a brand personality and, along with it, the promise of independence. In the mass of complex and ephemeral offers, Mobicarte is the only brand to emerge clearly.

Disruptive ideas can be the smartest way of entering a new market, because they allow brands to set their own criteria, but they can also help leading brands. Being an established leader can be a mixed blessing. You represent the category, but you also represent the conventions of the category. So what do you do when your market is shifting?

Be Where the Others Are Not

There are few purely masculine environments left in the Western world. From golf clubs to trade unions to the sacred arena of the football field, women have invaded traditionally male territory. One place continues to hold out: the do-it-yourself store. **Leroy Merlin** in France was a haven for DIY hobbyists, that hardy breed of individuals who compare calibrations and screws on a Saturday morning, safe in the assumption that they will not be pestered by their wives. But the company was ignoring a niche market of 50 percent of the population! This group was increasingly interested in DIY activities, but they called it "decoration," and, oddly enough, they were more concerned with the end results than with the therapeutic benefits.

Reframing women's perceptions of Leroy Merlin was a difficult challenge. The brand needed to switch its focus from selling the tools and raw materials to owning the end benefit of creating and personalizing the home.

This brand ambition was expressed in an unconventional way, through a series of mini-documentaries called *Du côté de chez vous* (close to home), in which eccentric people described their homes and how they personalized them. There have been some remarkable cases — a rotating home, a converted water tower,

a house in the shape of a painted red cube in the middle of a field. The testimonials are charming because even if the houses are totally off-the-wall, the people talked about decorating them as would you or I. Three hundred such films have been made since 1997. They have become a rendezvous point on the main TV channels during Saturday prime time. These films share an objective: to show that Leroy Merlin is there to help create your dream home.

To make these dreams into real projects, Leroy Merlin launched the first paid consumer magazine in France, entitled *Maisons en Vie*. It bridged the gap between upmarket glossies such as *Elle Déco* and *Maisons du Sud* and specialist DIY magazines. The magazine displays a dreamlike end result and then gives advice about how mere mortals can achieve it. With initiatives such as these, Leroy Merlin is the only store firmly entrenched in the category's biggest growth area — decoration.

This shift committed Leroy Merlin to changing its stores and the behavior of the sales staff. The promise expressed through the films and the magazines needs to be kept on the shop floor. It is an evolving process, but the company has a clear vision of where it wants to go.

Change the Actors, Not Just the Script

What do you do if you want to transform a public service into a service brand when 80 percent of your employees never have any contact with customers and the trade unions forbid the word *customer* in internal communication?

Such situations are more common than you think, and the usual response is a campaign on two fronts: soft-sell a customer service ethic while simultaneously soft-selling the brand on TV. Remember when British Rail told us "we're getting there"? Customers knew it was getting nowhere, and the railway people wanted to get where they wanted, on their own terms.

In 1995, the **French railways**, SNCF, were in perhaps a worse state, following the longest strike in industrial history. In the subsequent 18 months, we decided to stop brand advertising altogether. We recommended confronting the railway employees with their customers in order to inject real and enduring change into the company. The same people who were obstacles to change are gradually becoming active agents of change.

The first step was to launch a customer questionnaire in the national and regional press asking customers how the company could improve its service. Approximately 200,000 questionnaires were filled in, and the results were presented to railway staff from station to station throughout the country, as well as being published in the press. Afterward, the real work began. A national improvement plan was drafted, and staff from each of the 500 stations developed their own improvement programs, including such innovations as installing benches on train platforms and providing information on delays as well as communication training for clerks. It was only when these 500 plans, one for each station, began to be implemented that the SNCF started advertising again. The role of the advertising was then to inform the public of concrete, tangible commitments to service that the railway was making.

This has created a truly dynamic spirit for the company. In addition to years of uninterrupted growth in the number of passengers, 16,000 railway workers actually volunteered to personally question customers with a second questionnaire. These were the same men who refused to even utter the word "customer" a few years earlier.

For the French railways, this makes good sense. Who better to communicate customer needs than the customers themselves? Corporate communication needed to take the lead in making it happen, by avoiding the conventional approach of advertising before there was something concrete and credible to say.

In other circumstances, advertising can play a role in touching off a revolution within a company. A corporate advertising campaign redefined **France Telecom**'s mission from phone company to communication company, with the claim, "welcome to life.com." In this case, advertising took the lead. In order to make this credible, the workforce had to be made aware of the implications. Fifteen thousand France Telecom employees participated in a series of three-day events that we designed to help them understand France Telecom's vision of the future — a vision that they then communicated to their business-to-business customers as well as to the general public.

Many established public and private enterprises share this need for change, the need to redefine their role in customers' lives and in the economy as a whole. This change needs to be lived at all levels of the company. Changing the actors in this case means understanding that the employees are not just another audience. They need to be made catalysts of change.

Build Brand Communities

A motivated and effective workforce can set up a virtuous circle in which satisfied customers attract new customers. The first direct banking service in the United Kingdom was launched in 1990, with the appropriate name: **First Direct**. A great offer, but so ahead of its time that many people were unwilling to take the plunge.

The broadening of First Direct's base was built by the word-of-mouth advocacy of satisfied clients. The bank considers that the single best marketing investment is the quality of their phone service, rather than conventional communication and new product development. Today, First Direct is a real challenge to High Street banks. It is the fastest-growing bank and enjoys a level of loyalty and a capacity for cross-selling that is unprecedented in the sector.

Beyond being effective vehicles for spreading the brand message, customers can even become sales agents. The Dubble chocolate bar is the product of a joint venture between the celebrity charity Comic Relief in the United Kingdom and a cooperative of 35,000 Ghanaian cocoa farmers. Dubble is an ethical trade product. Imagine pleasure and conscience reconciled in one chocolate bar. Success, however, was limited by the fact that the company had only two salespeople.

The EMAP magazine group agreed to enclose the candy bars on the front cover of widely distributed boys' and girls' magazines at launch: *Smash Hits* for girls, and *Match* for boys. Children were encouraged to become ''Dubble Agents'' by means of the Dubble web site, and to ask for the bar at their local shops. By smart thinking about how to extend their brand, Comic Relief has provided ongoing funding through fair trade, and Dubble is forecasted to get into the top-10 most sold candy bars in the United Kingdom — and all for a tiny, tiny budget.

By making customers actors, we can create profitable brand communities. A brand community begins to exist when consumers start to talk about your brand, to share experiences and anecdotes in a positive way, over which you — as a marketer — have no control. To cultivate these communities, we have to think of stimulating the conversation beyond the message.

Find New Sources of Value

Existing customers and employees can thus be a source of great value, which we cannot exploit fully if we only think of them as targets in a conventional sense. The story, however, does not end there. Company employees can provide other sources of untapped value. A celebrated example is British Airways, which reengineered its complaints department with the idea that it adds value not just by isolating and solving problems, but also by sending information to the marketing department to help explore ways of improving service in the future.

Scoot is an innovative company, so it is hardly surprising that it represents another case of Disruption. In the United Kingdom, it has made its internal processes into an external source of value for customers. As a business directory, it also acts as a matchmaking service between consumers and businesses in their area. Customers call or log on with their requests and Scoot matches the relevant suppliers to the customers' addresses.

Scoot changed the rules of its market when it realized the potential power of building supply-and-demand models for each of its main category listings in every area. By analyzing the demand — say, for florists in a particular postal code — Scoot could tell whether there was over- or undersupply. When undersupply occurred, it was possible for targeted direct communications and the sales force to focus on specific businesses in that area, with the confidence that they would benefit through advertising using the service. This helped Scoot grow the subscriber base from 15,000 in the spring of 2000 to 60,000 at the end of the year.

With the bank **Virgin One**, a system has been created to turn nonconverted inquiries into a marketing resource. Virgin disrupted the face of U.K. banking when it launched its Virgin One bank account, an offset mortgage facility that calculates the interest on your borrowing daily, but only once it has subtracted any positive balances in your checking and savings accounts.

The financial savings of the product are self-evident, but at the same time consumers were reluctant to put all their eggs in one basket with account consolidation. Mortgage lock-ins or other practical requirements mean that the incubation period can be fairly long.

Although Virgin One was experiencing a growth in sales, it also had a growing file of unconverted inquirers. In addition, the major banks were developing similar products of their own and putting a lot of media weight behind them. Virgin could have ignored consumers (commercially foolish). They could have treated them all the same way (counter to the brand philosophy). They could have called them all and asked them why they had not yet signed up for the product (extremely expensive). Instead, they simply invited their customers to tell the company where to go, using a mailing that allows the customer to specify a reason for not yet having purchased — from "It's not the right time for me" to "Go away." Each reason is presented on a tear-off postcard with a bar code containing relevant prospect details. The recipient simply has to pop the card into a mailbox.

This prompted unprecedented levels of response and enables the agency to treat these responders in the appropriate way. Rather than clearing them off the database, we send them trigger communications when we know that the lock-in period on their current mortgage product is about to expire. With this activity alone, we estimate that a potential additional £4.5bn of borrowing for the bank has been created.

Finding Inspiration

These cases are all very different, but they have one thing in common: They were built from disruptive business and brand ideas. We need to make our antennae sensitive enough to pick up and recognize such ideas from any source.

Case in point: When **Ola**, the consumer brand for France Telecom mobile, was relaunched on October 31, 1997, at the end of a client meeting someone cracked a pitiful joke, "I suppose that makes it Ola-ween."

At this time, Halloween was known to only 5 percent of the French population. The launch strategy that came from this feeble joke not only kick-started France Telecom's entry into the consumer portable market but also integrated Halloween into the national calendar. It is now right up there with Valentine's Day and Mother's Day.

On the first Ola-ween, 9,000 pumpkins appeared in the gardens in front of the Eiffel Tower, making it the world's largest pumpkin field. It attracted both national and international media — 30 minutes of airtime on the main TV channels and one hour on radio, and it even made it to the front page of the *Herald Tribune* and the *New York Times*, as well as the national press. From this event we then promoted Ola-ween-themed offers in advertising among retailers.

The event-driven idea gave France Telecom the advance on the competitors; it appealed to a whole new audience of phone users. Today, Halloween is known by more than 80 percent of the French population and has fast become an institution.

Competitive value is defined by the quality of the ideas we find. The quality of the execution is a given. So our organization is necessarily devoted to managing ideas — from pooling as many ideas as possible to refining the single big idea that can inspire creativity in all the communication disciplines. In our direct marketing network, we have two tools to help us:

The **Mindpool** technique simply invites participants from throughout the network to contribute spontaneous ideas that respond to a headline challenge. It is amazing the insights that you can find when you open up the thinking process.

As an example, we were given the project of promoting a range of antibacterial cleaning products. Through Mindpool, we unearthed the insight that people tend to worry about hygiene more when they have children. We recommended that the client take each of the separate products out of the household cleaning shelves and make them a specialist range for homes with kids by placing them in the baby care aisle. The subsequent creative solution was at once simple and disruptive — the bottle designs for each of the products featured a "pregnant" bump on the front.

For long-term strategic development we have devised another process called **Freeform**. Freeform sessions last at least one full day and involve key team members from both client and agency, including sales and customer interface people, as well as marketing and communication staff, working toward a single task.

What is important is that the Freeform group can change the agenda at any time, as long as the output is relevant to the initial task objectives. This freedom helps disrupt the traditional journey through a prescribed agenda since the group can jettison anything they find unhelpful and include anything they find stimulating.

Freeform works to a deadline called the challenge session, where an outsider is presented the findings and has the job of challenging the groups to reappraise their thinking and help perfect the final recommendation.

The role of these two approaches is to make the thinking process nonlinear and involve people who do not recognize constraints and the normal way of doing things.

We have created some tools to help us, but the single most important thing is to keep our eyes on the goal, to set challenges beyond the authority of one particular communication discipline.

1. Be what the others are not.
2. Be where the others are not.
3. Change the actors, not just the script.
4. Build brand communities.
5. Find new sources of value.

Succeeding in these challenges means redefining the integration of communication disciplines. When it first became fashionable to talk about integration, we believed that we should be integrating messages above, below, and through the line simultaneously. As a result of this, the advertising looked like the direct marketing, which looked like the point-of-sale material, which looked like the web site at any given point in time. Remember the vocabulary? We proposed seamless solutions.

The cases that we have discussed show that any single discipline can and should take the lead: A packaging idea has made Mobicarte a completely different brand proposition; an internal communication effort has helped make the French railways commercially competitive; and by starting from a problem with distribution, Dubble has created a community of Dubble Agents. Absolut, as you will see on the following page, has built the brand as much through unexpected sponsoring and support of artistic initiatives as it has through advertising.

By building Disruption where it is least expected, we can engage the consumer in a meaningful dialogue, which in turn can help us create brand communities that enrich and become ever more profitable for our clients.

ABSOLUT DISRUPTION

Absolut has always assumed that consumers are smart, have good taste, are sophisticated (but not snobby), and have a great sense of humor. Just like Absolut.

These people are also social: They leave their homes and go to movies, clubs, restaurants, shows, museums, galleries, concerts, sporting events, and so on. They probably do this with friends and lovers, spouses and sisters, exes and nexts.

Before Absolut commissioned Andy Warhol to paint his version of an Absolut bottle, which subsequently became the campaign's most famous ad, it was acknowledged that (1) the brand already had an "arty" feel due to the bottle design, (2) many of the consumers had an interest in the arts, and (3) artists had an interest in the brand that went beyond consuming the product. Prior to "Absolut Warhol," it is safe to say that artists were employed in advertisements but not glorified by them. They were background players simply because brands and corporations did not see their selling power.

Alternatively, corporations like IBM or United Technologies would finance exhibitions at area museums to demonstrate their good taste or their commitment to the community. Typically, the artists had already been dead for at least 200 years, so they probably no longer benefited from the exposure. But Absolut saw a different equation:

People think artists are cool.

Artists think Absolut is cool.

Therefore, people (could) think Absolut is cool.

Warhol introduced the artist community to the brand. In short order, Keith Haring, Kenny Scharf, Ed Ruscha, and dozens of other artists, both established and rising, became friends of Absolut. And every painting, sculpture, drawing, and installation featured an Absolut bottle prominently in the art. Admittedly, every potential vodka drinker is not an art devotee. (And maybe that is not such a bad thing for art.) So the question becomes, Where else do you go to snare the culture vultures?

Absolut chose fashion — in many respects, a more mainstream, middlebrow audience. Obviously, everyone wears clothes, and many of us know who the designers are, even if we do not buy their labels.

Not surprisingly, designers are enthusiastic. (The artists opened the door for this.) And they find the requirement to put an Absolut bottle on a dress, boot, or swimsuit to be merely a creative challenge. Soon, Versace, Galliano, and Gucci are eager to participate — and not for the money, but to share the stage with Absolut.

Fashion, too, offers the opportunity of actually branding our consumers. For instance, when DKNY (Donna Karan New York) was hired to design Absolut gloves one Christmas, the brand then delivered a half-million pairs directly to the readers of *New York* magazine inside the magazine.

We faced a different challenge when we decided to approach writers. We like to think that writers are artists whose métier is words. The problem then is a visual one: how to portray the Absolut bottle without the benefit of the Absolut bottle.

The solution: Create a story in which an Absolut bottle, a cocktail or an image that resembles an Absolut bottle has some role. We invited leading novelists — known by the reading public but not overexposed — to create these stories, from scratch. The agency then custom-illustrated each story, based on its particular theme or story line.

It shouldn't be surprising how many different ways the bottle could appear in these stories, given this structure. One could pour the bottle, place flowers in it, play Spin the Bottle. But we were relieved that the writers were more creative than that — which is exactly why we asked Dominick Dunne, Mary McGarry Morris, Doug Coupland, Sebastian Junger, Tracy Chevalier, and others, in the first place.

What Does All This Mean?

Absolut connects with consumers considerably beyond the experience of consuming a martini or a cosmopolitan. It occupies a space in their minds when they go to a museum or gallery. When they listen to music. When they read a book. When they dress to the nines. Or when they engage in absorbing, participating in, admiring, rejecting, criticizing, laughing at, crying over, intellectualizing, and embracing what is referred to as America's biggest export — entertainment and culture.

ABSOLUT WARHOL.

Facts: The Swedish retail sector has witnessed a tenfold increase in the number of brands over the last 10 years. Since 1980, Swedish media investments per capita have risen 450 percent. The cost of maintaining an established brand has risen 100 percent in 5 years.

During the spring of 2000, the 10 largest dot-com companies spent $200 million on advertising, resulting in an average awareness figure of 3.4 percent.

In the United States, there were 20 soft drink brands available in the 1970s, compared to 87 today. The number of jogging-shoe brands has increased from 5 to 285. The amount of contact lens styles available has increased from 1 to 36. The number of PC brands has gone from 0 to 300. Fewer than 10 percent of Americans believe advertisements. The number of campaign recalls has never been lower.

9. STREET-LEVEL LEVEL DISRUPTIONS

To create a communication piece in sync with the times, you might think that we would abandon the old-fashioned way of working. We would no longer need two people in a room writing a script, turning it into a storyboard, choosing a director, and then spending months and millions of dollars to craft a 30-second commercial as though it were a piece of art.

The reality is that we are still using the same devices that we were 20 years ago. It is time to change the rules and do "something else." How about diving into the real world? How about creating real-life events that involve people in the streets? How about filming them in action and making a commercial out of it? For us, it is not so much the ads that are important. It is the idea, and that "something else" that counts.

We are not particularly interested in advertising. It is just one of several tools we use. What we are interested in is the opportunity to get people going, to reach people who zigzag their way through advertising messages without ever being affected by them.

Basically, we have to start by admitting that people are fed up with advertising. The risk involved in conventional advertising is, quite simply, too great, and it is getting too expensive to do things the way we are used to. While it usually requires courage to question convention, we now have to ask ourselves if we dare not to. We need to create ideas that have more substance than a 30-second TV slot.

Perhaps we should call them self-propagating ideas, ideas that spread, big ideas that may include TV commercials as important constituents, just as they may include music videos, football tournaments, stickers, or letters to the editor as other important constituents.

Because if what we do does not get legs and walk away on its own, if it does not make the news, if it is not talked about at coffee breaks, if it does not live on, if it does not get under people's skin and into their hearts, if our efforts only succeed in producing halfhearted smiles, then we have to admit that we have failed (and pull ourselves together and do better next time).

Talking to the Young

Some time ago, we were assigned the task of marketing **MTV**'s European web site. The site had been altered to include interactivity with most of the shows on the TV channel, making MTV in general a more interactive phenomenon and blurring the boundaries between TV and the Internet. Of course, it would be stupid to use conventional advertising for a brand that has a built-in ability to carry on a dialogue with people.

Our strategy for MTV has always been to side with the viewers when it comes to advertising. The channel adopts as critical an attitude to advertising as to young people in general. It uses new and unpredictable ways of reaching out to them. Everything we do is measured by this yardstick. Does it break with convention? Does it push the limits of communication? Because if it does not, it is not good enough for MTV.

When we were asked to market www.mtve.com, we came up with a creative brief that made an interactive pact with our target group. We wanted them to help spread MTV's web address, so we sketched out a win-win pact that would allow MTV to benefit from young people and young people to benefit from MTV. It was never a question of selling the channel to young people, or trying to be cool, or promoting the new web site with the help of ads.

The creative team came up with at least 10 totally different ideas based on the brief. These ideas were not primarily to be aimed at any certain media, but were to be more of a general approach style. There were to be no sketches of ads, no storyboards — only a description of the core of the idea. In this case, the core of the idea might be to buy advertising space on pets or to pay people for striping their cars with "www.mtve.com."

One of the new ideas was to buy only one billboard in the whole of Sweden, rewarding the people who traveled to see it. Another idea took inspiration from the age-old prank of sticking a sheet of paper with the words "kick me" on somebody's back. We all know the kind of attention that can be generated by such signs, and yet no brand was, to our knowledge, using them as advertising space. The conclusion was that if MTV could relay its message on the backs of unsuspecting people, this would guarantee attention.

We felt it crucial not to try to ingratiate ourselves with the target group with the help of a cool or youthful appearance. This was a multinational business looking for people to perform a certain task and we wanted to be honest about it. We wanted to be totally transparent, so we got rid of everything in the advertisements that might be interpreted as striving to be cool or youthful.

The result was half a million yellow stickers carrying the message, "Watch out! www.mtve.com," with instructions on the reverse side for how to stick them to people's backs. In addition, we created ads and TV commercials in which MTV sought the help of young, outgoing people. The ads were modeled on typical job advertisements. A reward was promised to those who fit the bill and completed their assignment. For example, if you put a sticker on a parent, you were awarded a movie ticket. If you put a sticker on a celebrity, you were given a chat board and a cellular phone. If you managed to put the sticker on somebody who would appear with the message on a rival TV channel during

prime time, you were given the free use of a Volkswagen Beetle for six months. Many advertisers have looked at this campaign and questioned its appeal to young people. It is not really visually interesting, consisting mainly of lots of information and a few black-and-white pictures. This campaign is a disruption in the world of youth advertising. In fact, it questions advertising as a phenomenon. We are convinced that growing numbers of people survive the advertising war thanks to a hitherto unsuspected self-preservation mechanism. If you grew up with dozens of TV channels, learned to channel-surf before learning your multiplication tables, are familiar with the latest PlayStation games, have seen every film on the top-10 list before it was released on video, and know the name of every new pop star, then you probably also have the ability to watch an ad for no more than a millisecond and decide instantly whether it contains anything worthwhile. Maybe this campaign did.

At any rate, this campaign resulted in a huge pile of letters addressed to MTV, containing photos of unsuspecting teachers, police officers, parents, and celebrities with stickers on their backs. One of Sweden's most popular artists appeared on the news without suspecting that he was sporting a large, yellow sticker. Good or bad, it also led the mtve.com server to crash.

Kicking Conventions Out: The SBAB Case

When we met **SBAB** bank for the first time, the company was a small player with big ambitions in the mortgage business. Their aim was to give the mortgage giants — the big banks — a run for their money.

The banks had a lot working for them. They shared 90 percent of the market due to the lack of competition. The convention was that mortgages are difficult and complicated things that only banks understand. Banks spoke about competence and figures in ads simply because it happened to suit them.

But SBAB has something the big banks lack. Their mortgage rate is almost always lower than that of the banks. The company also has an energetic desire to side with the average person on the street.

Our strategy therefore focused on challenging the banks.

There was also a set of conventions in our own sphere. Advertisements for challengers were nothing new, and most devices had been employed on more than one occasion. A simple declaration that we were going to challenge the banks would not cut it. We would have to do it for real.

Our solution was to challenge the banks to a football tournament. The reasons were numerous: Football is as alien to the world of banking as it is close to the heart of the man in the street. Football is the people's game. No sailing boats, no golf clubs; just an open space and a ball. It is a team sport that is won and lost together. Everyone has played it and everyone knows the rules. It was a challenge that could be expected to surprise and create interest. And last but not least, it was show, not tell.

The big idea was the football challenge. The advertising was only the consequence of that. The campaign itself was different from anything we had done previously. We were used to working in laboratory-like conditions, shooting hundreds of scenes to get a commercial right. This time we could not predict the outcome. When we pointed this out to SBAB's CEO Christer Malm, he replied calmly, "Isn't that what being a challenger is all about?"

We prepared ourselves for all the scenarios we could think of. If the banks turned up and SBAB won, there would be a triumphal procession for the small challenger. If SBAB lost, they would still be regarded as the sympathetic player, a lot better at mortgages than at football. If none of the challengers turned up, the banks would automatically seem stiff and conventional.

We sent a letter to the directors of the four big banks. That same morning, we announced the challenge by publishing this letter in the major daily papers:

Challenge.

SBAB hereby challenges the banks to a football tournament
to be held at the Stockholm Stadium. While our main intention
remains to give you a good beating on the mortgage front,
a challenger is a challenger, whatever the field.
Kickoff is Saturday, 29 April at 1:00 p.m. See you there!
Yours sincerely,
Christer Malm
CEO & left back

Later that evening, a TV advertisement was shown in which Christer Malm, wearing a football jersey and sitting at his desk, addressed the banks directly: "SBAB is a housing loan company that nearly always charges a lower interest than the banks. But now we're not only going to challenge the banks when it comes to low-cost housing loans...SBAB hereby challenges Sweden's

top four banks, Handelsbanken, S-E-Banken, Merita-Nordbanken, and Förenings-Sparbanken to a game of football. The tournament kicks off on Saturday, April 29 at 1 p.m. at Stockholm Stadium. See you there. If you have the guts."

Now the challenge was truly on. We waited anxiously. How would the banks respond? Would they respond? After a few grueling days, we began hearing rumors. One such rumor told of a famous bank director standing at his office door, yelling, "What the hell are we going to do about this?" Another claimed that the banks had met secretly and decided on a general boycott, while a third rumor had it that another advertising agency had created a countercampaign that was rejected by the banks' boards.

Anyway, there was no turning back. SBAB put together an internal football team for the cup, assuming that the banks would take on the challenge. During a training session, we produced a few TV commercials — and two weeks after the initial challenge, we were back on air.

These commercials featured the SBAB team in training, showing that the little mortgage company was serious about the challenge and was getting ready for the match. There was the SBAB team in fitness training, doing shooting exercises with Sweden's most famous international goalie, running, jumping, having pep talks. In one of the commercials, the team manager gave the players the bashing of a lifetime: "Right, listen up everybody. If you want to beat the banks, you have to shape up. Now show me some attitude!" The overall message was simple and very sincere: "Come on, banks! April 29, at the Stockholm Stadium. If you have the guts."

As game time drew closer, things were heating up. We decided we wanted our own team song, just like any other football team in search of glory. We wrote a song and recorded the SBAB footballers singing it with strong and vibrating voices. We also made a TV spot out of the event and broadcast the SBAB team song commercial a few days a week before match day.

We were ready, but still there were no committed opponents. Therefore, we prepared a final commercial showing SBAB alone on the pitch, telling the world what chickens the banks were. But everything changed. Two days before match day, one of the banks accepted the challenge. All our hopes, fears, and conversations by the coffee machine came to a head. The match was on.

When the day arrived for the big match, the entire staff of SBAB came out in force to the Stockholm Stadium, once the venue for the 1912 Olympic Games. Employees were transported by bus from the head office three hours away. Enthusiastic supporters in red-and-white caps and T-shirts filled the stands, waving red-and-white flags. Tickets were handed out in the city center and airplanes with streamers flew overhead. TV reporters filmed the proceedings, and the bank's players were looking quite pale as they lined up for kickoff.

The SBAB team fought heroically, but in vain. The final score proved a disappointment to the small mortgage company. Goliath beat David 5-1. Still, from a communication point of view, the outcome was great. We could now make a commercial telling people that the diminutive challenger had had to surrender to its giant opponent on this occasion, but that the challenge would go on. An 80-second TV ad aired two days later:

Commentator: "Hello, and welcome to Stockholm Stadium on this wonderful spring day for the big football match between housing loan company SBAB and its competitors."

(In the changing room)

Manager: "Right, lads. Finally, it is the match against the bank. The odds are against us, but we're going to give them a run for their money. Are you up for it? Let's get 'em!"

Commentator: "And here comes SBAB for their showdown with SEB, the only bank that accepted the challenge. And it is time for the kickoff, and SBAB have got off to a flying start and...oooh, he's hit the post! What a start to the match! The crowd is going wild. And here comes S-E-Banken, and it is 1-0 to the bank, and it is 2-0. Glum faces on the SBAB bench despite a sterling performance from the SBAB defense. But here's a chance, and he scores! A superb goal there by Marcus Adolphsson. But despite doing everything in their power to turn the match around, SBAB lose by 5-1."

Reporter: "Before the match you told the team to concentrate on football, not housing loans."

Manager: "Yes, that is right. But the problem is they are highly professional and put a lot of effort into keeping our interest down. Getting them focused on a game of football is not easy."

Reporter: "Any comments?"

Managing Director: "I would like to take the opportunity to congratulate the bank. They deserved the win but they'll never beat us when it comes to housing loans. You can be sure that we'll continue to challenge the banks."

So, Christer Malm got the last word. It seemed fitting since he commenced the challenge some four weeks earlier. All of us involved in the campaign, from advertising agency to mascot, were exhausted.

It turned out that people had taken a liking to our red-and-white team. SBAB's overall awareness figures rose dramatically from 56 to 82 percent, the number of mortgage applications rose 650 percent, and market share doubled. And as important, people realized that they understood far more about mortgages than the banks claimed they did. This enabled people with houses, villas, apartments, holiday homes, castles, or cabins to save a great deal of money — and get rid of the bank for good. For us, that is probably the biggest score of all.

The Creative Opposition

We have created a special method for coming up with ideas, such as the ones for SBAB and MTV — a method that we have employed from the start. We cannot say that it will work for others or that others can even implement it. It may be that it has to evolve along with your company.

We do not have a creative director here. We are, of course, aware of the advantages of such a function: It is a way to promote good ideas, make demands, and provide leadership and inspiration. At the same time, we are convinced that really great ideas can be hatched only in an environment that permits stupidity. The problem with having a creative director is that he or she is in a management position, and thus reinforces a hierarchy that encourages creative minds to keep quiet rather than appear stupid. That is not a good breeding ground for bright ideas.

In our experience, too many creative directors put a damper on fresh, young, innovative talent, taking the credit for ideas that others have hatched. And although we are aware that there are many talented creative directors out there, we decided at the outset that we could live without them. Instead, we work with what we call creative opposition.

Creative opposition means that the responsible team presents several different ideas to other creatives. For instance, we initially had 10 ideas for MTV, ranging from tattooing its Web address on people's foreheads (and paying them for the advertising space) to, as we already said, buying only one billboard in all of Sweden. The ideas are, of course, based on the creative brief and are, at the initial stage, nothing more than general concepts. The opponents then comment on each idea and come up with their own recommendation.

In the final analysis, it is always the responsible team that chooses what to present to the client, often selecting several possible alternatives. As yet, however, no team has ever decided to go ahead with an idea that the opponents really disliked. This is probably because discussions are held at an early stage before any of the ideas have acquired special status or prestige.

For us, opposition serves as a shot in the arm when we get stuck, an inspiration when we are being narrow-minded, and a stimulus when we become complacent. It develops our view of advertising and provides an idiot-proof antidote to any tendency to be conventional.

How to Make Advertising That Doesn't Look Like Advertising

The two campaigns mentioned here — the sticker campaign and the football challenge — have not won any advertising awards. The SBAB campaign was short-listed on one or two occasions, but our guess is that the advertising industry in general considers it odd. It does not look like advertising. It does not feel like advertising. It was not made by a famous director with a huge budget. The core of it consists of balloons, tickets, and cheerleaders rather than funny, 45-second spots. And it does not have a joke at the end. Maybe we just do not know how to do these things properly. But we cannot help but think that advertising is a lot more interesting this way. New tools to use. New spaces to fill. More hearts to win. And we are quite confident that this industry, whether it likes it or not, will have to look upon advertising in a less conventional way in the future.

10. TACTILE
DISRUPTIONS

Rather than relying on the senses of sight and sound, tactile disruptions work at the level of physical tangibility; they can be touched and held, and therefore they engage the recipient more completely. To appreciate exactly how and why this is so, let us take a look at the whole concept of pattern disrupt. Disruption, by definition, is a cognitive event that breaks our pattern of expectation, resulting in a shift of awareness that takes us out of mental automatic pilot and into conscious engagement with the object of attention.

Pattern disrupt

Interestingly, Edward de Bono describes creativity in similar terms. "Creativity is not a matter of inspiration, craziness or gimmicks," he insists, "but a form of logic — the logic of asymmetric patterning."

DIƧRUPTION Here is a simple example. Take the word *disruption*, which was turned into a logo by reversing the *s*. Going against the grain of our conditioned expectation in this way does two things. We consciously engage the logo to search for an explanation for why the letter *s* has been reversed. And it creates a new entity that conveys much more than the meaning of the word — so much so that it captures virtually the entire world of ideas around which this book has been written. Perhaps, then, disruption is the little big bang from which new ideas emerge. Or maybe a new idea is nothing more than a fresh old idea?

®evolution This logo for a brand consultancy called Evolution is another example. By placing the registered trademark sign ® at the front of the word instead of at the end (a disruption of expected sequence), we create a new symbol — a new combination of words and ideas, a logo suggesting that brand development and transformation can be radical, too.

PR**ID**E Pride, the South African Gay Rights movement, wanted a logo that provided a sense of self-affirmation. So we highlighted the third and fourth letters in the word, a basic disruption of the pattern of expectation that neatly captures the organization's philosophy: identity through pride in what you are.

This poster campaign for divorce mediation attorneys takes the idea a step further. The firm specializes in negotiated settlement, which is a lot less painful than litigation. This proposition is communicated in a series of posters that disrupt the pattern of expectation in a disturbing manner. The posters are physically torn in half, directly through the visual. In one poster, the visual is a family photo of sentimental value. In another, the kid's dog. And in a third, a Porsche. Offering an alternative to the soul-wrenching route of litigation, the tag line reads, "It does not have to be this way." A similar idea — perforating the company stationery through the middle — turns business cards, letterhead stationery, and compliment slips into unexpected and therefore compelling pieces of communication that reiterate the concept.

The Martial Arts Metaphor

The martial arts provide some striking metaphors that capture the principles of disruption. The whole system of outmaneuvering one's opponent is based on the idea of pattern disrupt. Through both physical and psychological posturing, the practitioner strives to create an expectation of sequence, or an illusion of predictability, in the opponent's mind. The moment of attack breaks the pattern of expectation. It is unforeseen and therefore goes undefended. Judo extends the concept, and even hints at how to overcome message complacency by working hands-on with the momentum of the pattern of expectation. When an opponent pushes forward, you avoid the conventional reaction to push back. Instead you go with the energy, allowing the momentum — the very force of the opponent's movement — to be his downfall, a kind of nonaction described by a master of the art as "the path of getting out of the way."

If communicators can accurately identify the issue zones where the pattern of expectation is strongest, where psychological momentum is at its most forceful, then the response to Disruption will be most dramatic.

Tactile disruptions came about through the pressing need to achieve business results. The pieces themselves are the result of having challenged some of the most fundamental conventions of all. For example, the notion that if you really want to get the job done, advertise. On the contrary: If your starting point is the belief that a brand is the sum total of consumer perceptions accumulated over time — the result of many consumer experiences at many points of contact — then you have to concede the possibility that the most influential encounter with the consumer is not necessarily the one that takes place in front of the television or while the consumer is reading a newspaper or magazine.

The other challenge to entrenched thinking has a historic precedent. In the early 1960s, Bill Bernbach thought it would be a good idea for copywriters and art directors to work as teams rather than separately, as was the norm back then. By turning convention on its head at such a fundamental level, he triggered a creative revolution that produced advertising that is still used some 40 years later, as an example of creative brilliance.

Drawing inspiration from Bernbach, we have encouraged graphic designers and copywriters to work together on a project basis. The fruits of this unlikely collaboration have been a lot more than ad slogans set in brody-esque type. They are hard-working pieces that pulsate with a mix of sheer aesthetic fun and good conceptual thinking.

Surviving the Trash Can Factor

The sweeping sociopolitical changes brought about by South Africa's new democracy had a profound demographic effect on its cities. Johannesburg's municipal art gallery, for example, suddenly found itself at the wrong end of town, wedged between an ever expanding minibus

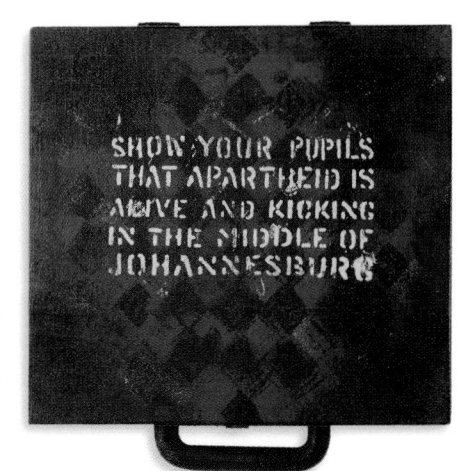

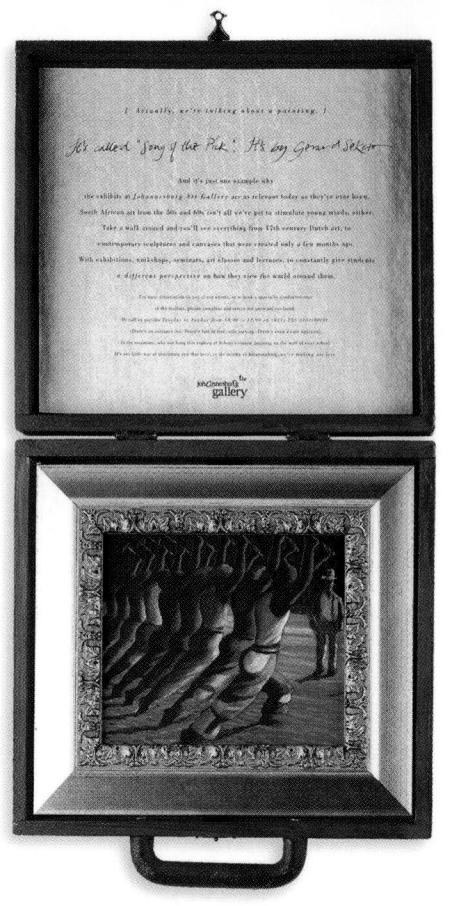

taxi rank and an informal street market. In an attempt to draw visitors back to its deserted halls, the gallery's curator commissioned an advertising campaign. A decision was made to target schools, in the belief that this would achieve two things: One, an ongoing stream of visitors could be provided, and, two, the gallery could win much-needed support by playing a cultural and educational role in the lives of young people. Both were achieved with unparalleled success. There was nothing unconventional about sending invitations to schools. However, when both the school principal and the art teacher received hand-painted wooden boxes with the words, "Show your pupils that apartheid is alive and kicking in the middle of Johannesburg," screen-printed on the lid, this controversial claim got their undivided attention.

Inside the boxes they found framed replicas of an apartheid-era work painted by the famous South African artist Sekoto. Entitled "Song of the Pick," it vividly captures the dramatic but painful choreography of a pick-wielding road gang at work. (If you listen closely, you can hear the song!) The remainder of the contents required less attention: a personalized invitation to the teachers and their classes to come and experience the apartheid years through the eyes and hearts of South African artists.

"The Apartheid Years" was just one way to experience the gallery and its fine collection. A similar mailing offered a tour with a sculptural perspective. This particular mailing was captioned, "There's an old Junkie in the middle of town; isn't it time your students went to see him?" The wooden box contained a printed and framed replica of a turn-of-the-century piece depicting an old Swazi man smoking a pipe, entitled "The Dagga Smoker" (a local term for the indigenous herb commonly known as cannabis). A third mailing featured a provocative series of a naked woman and carried the message, "Improve the minds of the boys at your school. Introduce them to a naked young girl." It got the recipients' undivided attention.

If it can be picked up and opened, it can be thrown directly into the waste-basket. So surviving the "trash can factor" has always been an important objective of our tactile disruptions. A good way to disrupt this response is to make the piece too large and unwieldy to dump. That is exactly what was done with a piece designed for Conservation Corporation, an ecotourism and game park management company that offers time-shares at exclusive lodges throughout Africa. The response to this unique piece was extraordinary. Every one of the recipients called to find out more, and the entire offer, some 80 million Rands' worth of time-shares, was sold in record time.

The target audience was 1,000 senior executives from South Africa's lead-ing corporations. Not an easy group to reach because their mail tends to be intercepted by their secretaries.

The piece — an oversized, 600mm x 300mm wooden folder — was deliv-ered in a white canvas bag with leather straps. You removed the brochure from the bag by unbuckling the straps, then you had to untie leather thongs to open it — a task requiring a certain amount of dexterity. By now the recipient was fighting an irresistible urge to find out what this rough wood-en folder contained. The desire to open it was enhanced by the intriguing message on the front: "The greater St. Lucia wetlands have been saved. Whole families of elephants have been rescued from the cull. The Desert Black Rhino has been given a new lease on life. Now something is being done about the most endangered species of all." On turning the page, this species was revealed to be South Africa's ailing currency — conveyed by means of an actual 1-Rand coin stuck to the middle of the first page.

With our local currency losing approximately 20 percent of its value per annum against the dollar, paying for time-shares at exclusive African lodges in dollars was becoming increasingly prohibitive. In contrast, this was a one-off opportunity to purchase a corporate time-share at an affordable Rand rate.

Spectacular photographs of each venue with full details of the facilities and their location in the respective countries covered the pages of the brochure, which disrupted the expectation of how a brochure should function. Printed on an earthy, recycled stock, each page was individually held in place by tri-angular steel corner fasteners, reminiscent of those old photograph holders found in leatherbound albums.

It could be argued that the offer alone was good enough to elicit the out-standing response. Clearly though, by providing a disruption that ensured its survival past the wastebasket and forced tactile involvement with the object and its contents, the client's business objectives were achieved faster and more effectively.

Something you can touch and feel

By definition, a tactile disruption must be palpable, something you can touch and feel. But there is another kind of disruption that we can nevertheless refer to as tactile, despite the fact that it is also clearly a media disruption. This ranges from disruptions of the usage of space — such as siting a parking spot on an impossible incline marked "Reserved for Nissan X-TRAIL" — to theatrical antics that catch the public unaware as they go about their day-to-day business.

A real estate program was recently launched less than half a mile from the most chic area in Berlin. The cost per square foot, however, was much less than that in the posh district. The launch campaign underlined the foolishness of continuing to live in the most expensive area.

Body outlines were drawn in chalk on pavements throughout the neighborhood, in the same way police draw a line around the body of a suicide victim. Large Post-it Notes were stuck to the ground with the message, "This man committed suicide when he discovered the price per square foot just half a mile from here." The message was signed by the real estate agent. In nightclubs we handed out free condoms bearing the message, "You won't need this if you leave this neighborhood. Just half a mile from here, you can have an extra bedroom..."

Ideas such as these were multiplied throughout the duration of the campaign. The campaign itself cost practically nothing. Not a dime was spent in media, but it was widely reported in TV news coverage. Needless to say, the real estate sold within a few weeks.

Physical Interaction

When you are asking shoppers to give donations, humans are not necessarily the most effective solicitors. Imagine that you are about to enter a supermarket when a tail-wagging dog holding a brochure in its mouth walks up to you and urges you to take it (definitely not for the tactilely defensive). Who better to appeal for funds for the guide dog society than dogs themselves? Not only do these canine representatives disrupt and challenge your sense of doggy reality, they also succeed in making you bond emotionally with the cause as you respond with a gentle stroke to the dog's head, followed by a small donation handed to the human assistant.

Disrupting people's boundaries in a way that forces them to engage a world they would rather ignore, a world outside their comfort zone, is a powerful way to convey your message. For example, you are confronted by a dirty, emaciated drug addict dressed in rags, staring at you hopelessly through bloodshot eyes. She slouches on the floor at the feet of a crowd of Saturday night moviegoers, alongside the line for tickets. Beside her is a sign that reads, "Smoke crack and you will end up like me." This desperate excuse for a person was, in fact, a professional actress, ingeniously made up to look like a crack addict who had hit rock bottom. People had difficulty processing the conflicting thoughts that flooded their minds. Everything about her presence destabilized and disrupted the pattern of expected behavior. Was she for real or not? If so, how come no one helped her? And why did that other person hand out leaflets about the dangers of crack? Could all this have been a setup?

The second idea in this campaign was a body bag suggesting the shape and form of a real human body, left lying on the pavement outside clubs recognized as venues where drugs were peddled. The message emblazoned on the front of the bag made its point with cutting cynicism: "What serious crack users are wearing this season."

The ideas put forward in this chapter suggest that when you are forced to interact physically with a piece of communication that disrupts your pattern of expectation, it will engage you in a way that simply cannot be matched by conventional media communications.

This raises the question of whether tactile disruptions can take place in print or on television or radio. Of course they can. For example, when you tear open a sealed magazine insert to sample the latest fragrance, you connect with the message on a far deeper level than if you were to simply read about it. The communication becomes an event in which you physically participate and of which you become the cocreator — on more than just an intellectual level.

Cocaine Help Line, a free drug-counseling service, received thousands of calls for help from a magazine ad that had a small envelope stuck to the page. Anyone who had ever bought cocaine instantly recognized the envelope as "a gram of coke." Further compelling the reader was the tag line, which posed the question, "Know why it is called a line?" On opening the envelope, the reader discovered a real fishhook — the hook at the end of the line. By offering a powerful physical metaphor for the addictive nature of the drug, the reader connected with the message in a way that went far beyond anything that could be achieved by a two-dimensional execution.

Radio and television are a little more challenging when it comes to tactile disruptions. After all, it is a lot more difficult to hold onto something intangible that exists for only a few seconds in time. However, when we begin to explore the possibilities of interactive television and other digital media, we find ourselves with a virtual tactile realm capable of involving us as completely as the three-dimensional one we live in. The moment you choose an option and click through, you are physically involved.

Disruption, by definition, challenges the recipient's pattern of expectation. It forces cognitive involvement and leads to closure of the intended message. Tactile disruption, however, adds a mysteriously powerful dimension, suggesting that the most seductive way to touch someone is to ensure they can touch you back.

11. DISRUPTION ON-LINE

The digital, interactive world is inherently disruptive, the single most desta-bilizing phenomenon experienced in communications in a long time. Interactivity is changing the rules of engagement from push to pull, from few to one, from leaning back to leaning forward, from intrusion to permission. Consider these changes:

Convention	Disruption
Broadcast	Narrowcast, 1-to-1
Push	Pull
Your time	Their time
Scheduled	On-demand
Lag time	Real time, transactive, instant gratification
One-way	Interactive
Advertiser to customer	Customer to customer (P2P)
30-60 seconds	60 seconds to 60 minutes-plus

Customers can now get closer to brands than ever before. They can interact and experience brands directly; and they can gain immediate new benefits, on a one-to-one, often customized, basis.

Digital communications have disrupted the once evolutionary idea that "The medium is the message." Now the medium is *both* the experience and the benefit.

The Internet and other digital channels are not simply new advertising media, so rather than take the conventional approach and try to figure out how we "advertise" on the Internet, we need to disrupt the process. We need to figure out how we can create unique, interactive brand experiences. The process operates like a spiral: building the interactive brand experience from the brand's fundamental off-line proposition and values, the customer experiences a unique, immediate benefit, which enhances and often changes the brand image on-line, which spirals back out to the brand off-line.

Consumers thus experience and become involved in a brand in bold, new ways. As Benjamin Franklin said: "Tell me and I will forget, show me and I might remember, involve me and I will understand."

Through digital media, a customer connects with a brand in a more substantive way, forming a more committed relationship with the brand.

In the conventional broadcast-push world, traditional advertising ideas matter. In a digital, interactive world, unique experiential ideas matter. An experience takes place and a connection is made, leading to a monetary and/or information transaction in real time, collapsed time, the customer's time. To determine these new opportunities and the most appropriate strategy to drive interactive, experiential ideas, we begin by asking the question: What role should interactive play in the Sales Path and the Customer Relationship Path?

A typical Sales Path is made up of the following phases, taking a consumer from prospect to customer:

Awareness	Interest	Desire	Research	Trial/Demo	Customize	Purchase

A typical Customer Relationship Path continues from the Sales Path and can be made up of the following phases, leading to a one-to-one customer relationship:

Tracking Delivery	Customer Support	Enablement	Tell friends	Upgrade	Buy in the brand family	Buy again

Both of these paths have to be customized to the category and placed within the context of the brand and campaign idea to ensure the seamless interlinking of the digital and nondigital campaign elements. These paths are used to assess where, in the sales and customer relationship life cycle, the experiential program opportunities lay.

The Customer Sales Path

| Awareness | Interest | Desire | Research | Trial/Demo | Customize | Purchase |

The first phase in any Sales Path is to create awareness, interest, and desire in the brand and its offering. This is where most traditional advertising starts and finishes. Interactive technology adds the all-important dimension of involvement. To achieve these gains, we need to move beyond traditional ideas about banners, logos, and design, and think instead about the unique experience the brand can offer.

Federal Express transformed itself when it allowed customers to track their packages on-line. That experience now makes up a key part of what FedEx is all about, on- and off-line. The medium is the benefit in this instance, and has spiraled outward to change the image of the FedEx brand.

An interactive brand experience is multidimensional. It is more than just a messaging and identity effort; it is also the degree to which you ensure a positive user experience, optimize ability, and incorporate technology that addresses key user needs and leapfrogs the competition.

The conventional approach of associating a brand with an experience involves sponsoring an event, or a place, or a face. Absolut has disrupted the convention of sponsoring fringe music and film events by creating inter-active brand spaces with web sites like Absolut DJ and Absolut Director. There, visitors mix dance cuts with musical samples provided by turntable notables like DJ Spooky on the Absolut DJ site. Likewise, visitors cut their own videos from an array of snippets on the Absolut Director site.

These Absolut brand spaces are engaging consumers with the Absolut brand in a dimension never before possible, thereby extending the brand and con-necting with individual consumers through a highly creative personal Absolut brand experience. Connecting directly rather than by association.

Miller Lite also uses interactive technology to create a unique brand experi-ence and benefit. The essence of the Miller Lite brand is camaraderie, which, in the past, had been communicated passively in commercials involv-ing friends having fun while knocking back a few beers. Miller Lite crafted e-mail software that allows users to signal their friends when they're headed out to the corner bar. The slogan: "When the light is blinkin', get ready to go drinkin'!" The Miller Light pager has transformed the brand value of camaraderie into action.

| Awareness | Interest | Desire | Research | Trial/Demo | Customize | Purchase |

The next phase in the Sales Path is the research phase. Interest has been sparked and now the consumer does a little research into the category and/or the specific brand offering.

Procter & Gamble has disrupted the conventional approach of allowing technology to help consumers match a product to their needs. They have taken the "research" opportunity one important step further. Its site, Physique.com, not only helps customers choose products, it also allows them to select the look they want and receive the step-by-step instructions they need to achieve it, with recommended Physique products to create it.

Awareness	Interest	Desire	Research	Trial/Demo	Customize	Purchase

Depending on the category, consumers often want a demonstration before they commit to a purchase, and the digital media can help them do just that. From requesting a Nissan 200ZX test drive on-line to requesting a free sample of Nivea's Age-Defying Creme, the web can deliver a "try before you buy" experience for almost any product or service. Conventionally, packaged-goods food brands have used tactics such as offering tantalizing recipe ideas and dollar-off coupons to stimulate trial. Betty Crocker has disrupted this conventional, often fragmented approach, by creating a utility that answers the question: "What's for dinner?" thereby extending the brand beyond products into the realm of service. "What's for dinner?" helps a customer plan a week's worth of meals, then print out a meal planner, complete with step-by-step recipes and a shopping list for all the ingredients (including, of course, all the Betty Crocker branded ingredients needed). The help does not stop there: the customer can also print out dollar-off coupons for Betty Crocker products, thereby taking some of the risk out of trying them.

Awareness	Interest	Desire	Research	Trial/Demo	Customize	Purchase

The Internet is also disrupting the conventional view of production. The idea of "any color you like as long as it's black" was permanently laid to rest when the Internet began to offer customized production of a single item. In other words: mass customization. Dell disrupted the PC industry by creating a whole new business model and brand proposition around mass customization. Now even Barbie dolls can be customized, at Barbie.com, with different wigs, skin tones, eye colors, and accessories. General Mills created a customized on-line breakfast cereal site—mycereal.com. For about $1 a serving, on the site, consumers can custom-blend breakfast cereals from more than 1 million possible combinations and have their creations shipped from General Mills in two to four days.

Awareness	Interest	Desire	Research	Trial/Demo	Customize	Purchase

Digital technologies can also play an important role at the Purchase phase if a brand disrupts the notion that purchase is about sales transacted on-line. PlayStation took preorders for its much-anticipated PS2 launch on its web site. PetSmart, an on-line pet store, runs a "You sit, we fetch" auto-replenishment home delivery service that is managed on-line; the transaction and delivery take place off-line.

The Customer Relationship Path

Tracking Delivery	Customer Support	Enablement	Tell friends	Upgrade	Buy in the brand family	Buy again

An Economist Intelligence Unit report ("Managing Customer Relationships," 1998) notes that customer profitability is likely to be the second most important measure of business performance by 2002.

Customer value is both the value created *for* customers — such as tailoring messages, products, and service — and the value created *by* customers, which is the segmentation and targeting of the most attractive customers.

Of course, digital technologies play a key role in cost-effectively tailoring one-to-one communications, mass customization, and the sophisticated segmentation of customer databases.

Let us look at a few digital success stories that are increasing customer value along the Customer Relationship path.

Tracking Delivery	Customer Support	Enablement	Tell friends	Upgrade	Buy in the brand family	Buy again

Say you are jumping into a taxi on your way to the airport when you receive an SMS (Short Message Service) message from Qantas airlines telling you your flight has been delayed for two hours. Instead of killing time at the airport, you decide to spend it in your favorite café: you have benefited from better service during the tracking and delivery stage of the Customer Relationship Path. Qantas will also deliver your complete itinerary to your mobile phone via SMS, thus preventing the last-minute paper scramble before a trip.

And then there is the actual delivery of products and services via digital technology. Digital technology is disrupting our notion that music is delivered on a CD, that a book has a cover, and that education takes place in a classroom.

Tracking Delivery	Customer Support	Enablement	Tell friends	Upgrade	Buy in the brand family	Buy again

Once the product or service has been delivered, the crucial customer support phase begins. Conventionally, Kimberly Clark has associated its Huggies brand with parenting by using advertorials and sponsorships involving third-party parenting information. The brand has benefited via association. Using the web, Kimberly Clark has disrupted this approach by creating its own Parentstages.com site as a virtual compass that helps busy parents quickly navigate their way through the wealth of parenting information available on the web. The brand is now benefiting beyond mere association and, by acting as the aggregator, has positioned itself as the authority on parenting information.

Tracking Delivery	Customer Support	Enablement	Tell friends	Upgrade	Buy in the brand family	Buy again

Traditionally, the only time a brand has contact with a customer after the sale is when something goes wrong and customer support is required. Disruption in the Enablement phase addresses the question: "How can the brand help a customer get more out of his or her purchase?" That is, more productivity, more efficiency, more excitement, more value, and, ultimately, greater customer satisfaction?

Sony has created Imagestation.com to help customers get more out of their digital still and video cameras. On-line tutorials teach how to edit digital images, how to create an on-line photo gallery, and how to upload an unlimited number of still images and video. Imagestation.com thus enables customers to be more creative with Sony products, reinforcing the brand's innovative image.

But interacting with a laundry detergent brand? Tide has created a site that receives tens of thousands of visitors a day who consult a simple device called The Tide Stain Detective. The Stain Detective recommends Tide and competing products to help customers eliminate the consequences of fabric mishaps. In this way, the site gains credibility and enhanced brand leadership status as the expert in stain removal.

Tracking Delivery	Customer Support	Enablement	Tell friends	Upgrade	Buy in the brand family	Buy again

"Telling friends" these days is more aptly known as *viral* marketing, and it really does work. In the past, word-of-mouth advertising has been a hit-or-miss exercise, as it relies on consumers to do all the work of passing along a message for little direct reward.

In contrast, viral marketing, made possible by digital media, has disrupted this approach and turned word-of-mouth advertising into a highly strategic affair. (Refer to The PlayStation Experience overleaf on the viral campaign for the Chase the Express launch game in Australia).

| Tracking Delivery | Customer Support | Enablement | Tell friends | Upgrade | Buy in the brand family | Buy again |

The final three stages in the Customer Relationship path involve directly leveraging the customer relationship into further sales. This is where interactive, digital technologies really shine, because they are able to finally deliver the promise of the three Rs: the Right Message/Offer to the Right Person at the Right Time.

Ticketmaster.com disrupts convention by e-mailing messages to consumers after the sale, rather than before. When Bruce Springsteen scheduled 15 shows in New Jersey as the kickoff for a U.S. tour, fans purchased tickets on-line through the Ticketmaster.com box office. But rather than simply thanking customers for their purchases, the company launched a three-message campaign.

The first message was sent shortly after the ticket purchase, and it began with the conventional follow-up: "Thanks for using Ticketmaster.com to buy your tickets for Bruce Springsteen's upcoming U.S. tour launch..." Then it went on to provide links to relevant web sites, including Tour Talk and the CitySearch New York Visitor's Guide.

The second message, sent three days before the performance, contained directions to the stadium, a seating chart, a recap of the first leg of the tour, tips for what to do if tickets were lost or stolen, and more links to related sites, such as Matt's Bruce Springsteen Discography. This message was not solely informational; the e-mail also featured links for purchasing four Springsteen CDs.

The third message, delivered right after the show, featured a play list for the particular show the individual saw, links to message boards, and a short review of the tour from *The New York Post*. It also featured tour merchandise available for sale on-line.

In summary, the medium is no longer the message. The medium is now the experience and the benefit. Thanks to the capabilities of digital media, many famous brands are creating unique, interactive experiences that offer an immediate and distinctive brand benefit/service to the customer.

Building a brand is no longer a linear process of ever increasing brand awareness. The process now operates like a spiral. Building the interactive brand experience from the brand's fundamental off-line proposition and values, the customer experiences a unique, immediate benefit, which enhances and changes the brand image on-line, which spirals back out to the brand off-line. The disruption comes in thinking in nonlinear loops...how does this lead to that and how do I make people want to go there, click through, sign-up, ride to...experience something and involve themselves, not just think and feel something.

Australia On-Line: The PlayStation Experience

Disrupting Word-of-Mouth Advertising

Viral marketing, made possible by digital media, has disrupted the conventional word-of-mouth advertising approach, which was conventionally a hit-or-miss exercise. It relied solely on customers doing the work of passing a message along with little direct reward. In the on-line world, however, the actual experience of participating in a viral campaign is the benefit to the customer and the pass-along is the benefit to the brand.

In September 2000, Sony PlayStation launched a new game in the Australian market called Chase the Express. It was an action/adventure game set on a train hijacked by terrorists, aimed at hard-core male gamers between the ages of 18 and 24. To generate on-line traffic to the game's mini-site, "overts" were developed — combat men who were hard-coded into select sites and gave the appearance of being soldiers parachuting, rappeling, and running across the page. It was one of the first times overts had been seen in the Australian market, and the enticing nature of the graphics generated a click-through rate of more than 4 percent. Clicking through from the overt advertising, consumers got a chance to play a mini-game that represented the story line of Chase the Express, in which the characters that appeared in the overt advertising dropped into the mini-game as part of the game play.

Visitors to the mini-site were invited to participate in an e-mail game of faking their own abduction, which again emulated the Chase the Express game play. Participants e-mailed friends and called on them to visit the site, whereupon the friends were given the opportunity to register and help "rescue" their friends. More than 18,000 unique visitors went to the site — the largest single response to any small tactical Sony software campaign. Three times more people than expected registered on the database to play the game and roughly 50 percent of them were completely new registrations. Nearly half of the registrations came from the overts. The viral aspect of the campaign resulted in thousands of friends visiting the site to take part in the game, 88 percent of whom registered on the opt-in database.

Launching Sony PlayStation 2: Nonlinear Loops between the Off-Line and the On-Line Worlds

In November 2000 Sony launched its much-vaunted PlayStation 2 in the Australian market. But not before 80,000 Australian gamers were co-opted to help Sony PlayStation spread the word. While the main TV campaign for the PS2 launch was masterminded by our London agency, we worked to set the scene for the explosion of PS2 on the market.

Launching the PS2 campaign was a spiral process involving both off-line and on-line communication. The challenge was to ensure that each element of the campaign led to the next and that consumers were involved in a complete brand experience.

It began with a teaser campaign featuring a "?" with a flashing dot, which started to appear around the country weeks before the official launch of the console. Metrolites, billboards, and posters were used to enhance the visibility of this symbol. The mysterious symbol attracted the attention of passersby everywhere, manifesting itself in beach sculptures, pavement graffiti, stickers, pole posters, and massive illuminated balloons in capital cities — the full 360-degree avalanche.

We also developed a direct-marketing

postcard and e-mail broadcast that were sent to existing customers who had already purchased PlayStation 1. It was also sent to those customers who had given us their e-mail addresses and whom we had incentivized to go to a web site at www.chosenone.com.au. The incentive to go on-line was the opportunity to win a money-cannot-buy prize — a ticket to the official PlayStation 2 launch party in Australia.

Once at the web site, customers were invited by the immersive graphics and soundtrack to fill out a registration form in order to enter the drawing for the exclusive prize. They were then given the opportunity for another entry by providing the e-mail address of a friend. The site would then e-mail this person with the message that a friend had just visited the site, and they should go there in order to also have a chance at the prize.

Instead of using an opt-out box saying, "No," we used an opt-out box saying, "Sorry, I don't have any friends." Once players provided the information, they received a thank-you in the form of a free downloadable launch screen saver to get them to spread the word through a form of viral marketing. The entire concept let a select group of people in on the secret, giving them a sense of privilege as they spread the word to others.

The e-mail broadcast proved a phenomenal success, with 30 percent of e-mail recipients entering the competition, while the direct-mail component had an 11 percent response rate. Tens of thousands of people downloaded the screen saver. The viral aspect of the campaign resulted in 64 percent of entrants e-mailing their friends, with more than 3,000 of these referrals also entering on-line.

But the on-line aspect of the campaign was far from over. Each day the screen saver clock clicked closer to the launch date, having automatically set itself after it was downloaded to run off the computer's internal clock. To pass the time, elements of the screen saver could be used for rudimentary games such as a gravity ball, while each day a new soundtrack would accompany the graphics — becoming more frenetic and louder with time.

Finally, on November 30, in sync with the retail launch of PlayStation 2 and at the same time as the TV commercial debuted on the air, tens of thousands of our core target audiences' desktop computers around the country sprang to life with the message, "Welcome to the Third Place." The screen saver then launched into a 2-minute promo of the games to be released at the same time as the PS2 launch.

For those who somehow might have missed the message, an additional 50,000 gamers in the opt-in e-mail database were sent an announcement e-mail, driving them to the PS2 mini-site, which presented all the news on the console, games, and peripherals. The mini-site included two new registration screens that further added to Sony's customer database.

At the reveal stage, the first PlayStation 2 to come into the country was packaged with a certificate of authenticity and auctioned on Sold.com.au, with the proceeds going to charity. It sold for $7,000. Following the launch, strategically placed banners and buttons brought a further 40,000 visitors to the PS2 mini-site, with 49 percent registering.

Sony PlayStation customers granted the company unprecedented access to their personal details — freely offering them each step of the way — and allowing Sony to interact with them on the nearest thing to a one-to-one basis.

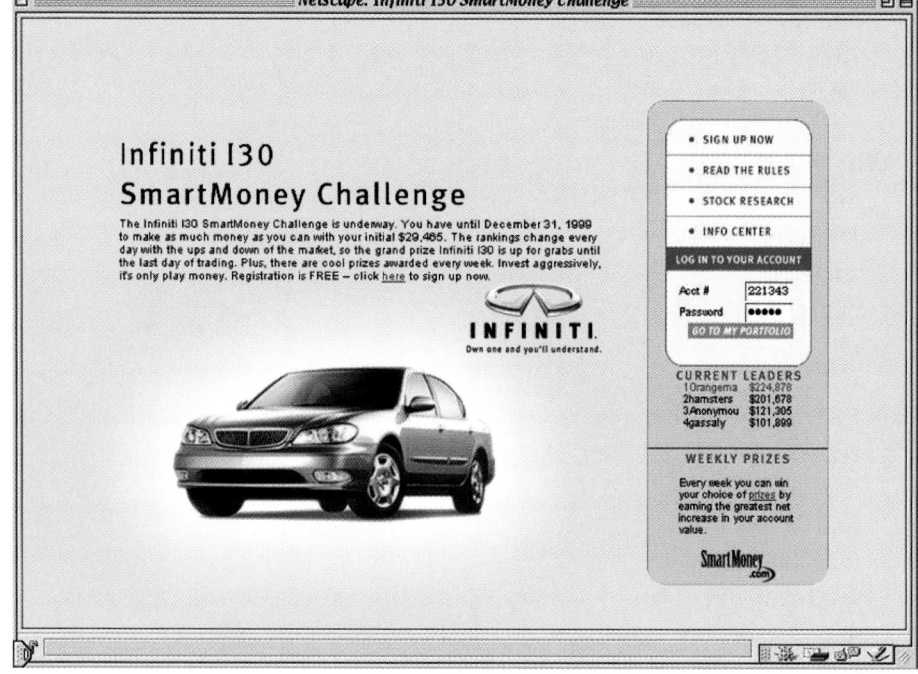

Infiniti I30
SmartMoney Challenge

The Infiniti I30 SmartMoney Challenge is underway. You have until December 31, 1999 to make as much money as you can with your initial $29,465. The rankings change every day with the ups and down of the market, so the grand prize Infiniti I30 is up for grabs until the last day of trading. Plus, there are cool prizes awarded every week. Invest aggressively, it's only play money. Registration is FREE – click here to sign up now.

INFINITI
Own one and you'll understand.

- SIGN UP NOW
- READ THE RULES
- STOCK RESEARCH
- INFO CENTER

LOG IN TO YOUR ACCOUNT

| Acct # | 221343 |
| Password | ••••• |

GO TO MY PORTFOLIO

CURRENT LEADERS
1 Orangema $224,878
2 hamsters $201,678
3 Anonymou $121,305
4 gassaly $101,899

WEEKLY PRIZES

Every week you can win your choice of prizes by earning the greatest net increase in your account value.

SmartMoney
.com

12. DISRUPTION, INTERRUP-TION, PERMISSION

In a digital age, when viewers can choose exactly what they want to watch and when, we can obviously no longer interrupt them as we did in the past. Given that the word *disruption* seems to imply "interruption," the question becomes, "Is the concept doomed to die a premature death?"

The Death of Conventional Wisdom

The Americans have a saying that goes, "It is easier to apologize than to ask for permission." Long the secret credo of traditional advertising, the challenge for marketers and their advertising agencies has always been to make our interruptions — whether commercials, posters, print ads, or mailings — relevant and likable enough that consumers did not mind, but rather looked forward to the intrusion of the next commercial break.

For nearly 20 years, advertising agencies, competing for new accounts, cited case history after case history demonstrating their ability to create intrusive and distinctive communications that would break through the clutter. Our skill in interrupting a consumer's currently held attitude or behavior was thought to be one of our most important assets.

Truthfully, the scenario described in the previous paragraph was 10 years, 400 channels, and thousands of magazine titles ago. A time when the big networks in any country ruled the airwaves, and the penetration of personal satellite dishes, broadband cable, and computer on-line access was still two spaces to the right of a decimal point. But you would not know it from the behavior of most marketers today, who cling to practices designed for an outdated scenario.

Hunters & farmers

The old scenario of marketing was ruled by conventions that focused on acquisition and trial, in a game that assumed infinite growth. Bound by these conventions, marketers are more concerned with their total market share (as hunters would be) than with their share of customer and lifetime value (as farmers would be). And while phrases such as "lifetime customer value" have become a regular part of today's politically correct, marketing-cognoscenti banter, it has only been in the last year, with the slowing of the economy, that the infinite growth game has stalled and the true limitations of the conventions have become exposed. Desperate to break the vicious cycle of growth at any cost, marketers have grown eager to embrace an alternative vision — one in which they come to intimately know and serve their customers.

However, few marketers can identify their customers, much less quantify their value and understand how to escalate those customer relationships to improve their value over time. Unfortunately, even our tools of measurement seem prehistoric at times, and revolve almost solely around today's volume moved and not tomorrow's value created.

When Jean-Marie Dru wrote his first book, *Disruption*, Netscape had just staged a successful IPO, billions of dollars were flooding the capital markets, and pundits were predicting a new age in which the Internet would supercede all other channels for communications and transactions. The key prediction of that book still rings absolutely true: "While hypoth-eses fly and interpretations abound, there is only one certainty: We are all going to become experts in constant conversation." The choice of the word *conversation* is no accident; rather, it was a hint at the framework of a major disruption to the conventions of marketing — specifically: Do not interrupt the conversations customers are having; include customers in the conversations themselves.

From Dialog to Permission

Today, marketing executives enjoy pontificating about having "dialogs" with their customers. In fact, the concept is so widely accepted, it is considered a marketing truth. But few marketers are actually maintaining such dialogs. Why?

1. Because it is not as easy as we first thought; it requires listening and response to be considered genuine.
2. It can be quite expensive, depending on your brand franchise or portfolio.
3. It requires ongoing participation rather than a series of discrete campaigns.
4. Most important, it requires the fundamental surrender of power from the company to the customer.

It was not until a few years later, in 1999, that Seth Godin gave us the vocabulary for this new paradigm in his book, *Permission Marketing: Turning Strangers into Friends and Friends into Customers* (Simon & Schuster, 1999). Godin described the new marketing challenge as one in which we moved the customer or prospect up the "permission ladder," from stranger to friend, from friend to customer.

Godin clearly outlined the rules of permission marketing, as well as the new responsibilities and ethical standards that companies and brands would need to adhere to in order to succeed:

• Permission is nontransferable.
• Permission is selfish.
• Permission is a process, not a moment.
• Permission can be canceled at any time.

In order to appreciate the caliber of this Disruption, compare these standards to the conventions of traditional or "interruptive" marketing.

If permission is nontransferable, what does that mean for those practices we have built around decision sciences and predictive modeling to better push, cross-sell, and up-sell our new products and services to our customers? It means marketers must operate with a new level of integrity, and that a brand's elasticity has a direct correlation to attaining continuous and additional permission for access in customers' lives over time.

If permission is selfish, what does that mean for the conventions we follow for the development of new products and services that require a certain volumetric to succeed? It means that marketers must look at how to personalize the product, the transaction, and the overall ownership experience. It means that success is not quantified by volume but by the cumulative collection of satisfied individuals over time.

A process and not a moment

If permission is a process and not a moment, what impact does this have on the way we measure success? It means that marketers must truly develop continuous-tracking feedback loops, rather than making projections from intermittent snapshots of the marketplace.

And, finally, if permission can be canceled at any time, what does that mean for the integrity of alignment between a company's communication and its behavior? It means that marketers must see both as systemic and that no inconsistency or breakdown is too small or inconsequential. It also means that a failure that leads to a customer revoking permission does not merely return a company to zero, but to a subzero position that can be extremely difficult to recover from.

In summary, if one of the qualities of a true disruption is the degree of re-invention it causes inside a category, discipline, or marketplace, then permission marketing proves to be an excellent example. However, the magnitude of this disruption means that marketers must recognize that this is a complete change in the atmosphere, not just a change in the weather. Additionally, while it was the promise of the Internet and its purported infinite scalability that led many marketers to their interest in permission marketing, we must remember not to categorize the principles to the quadrant occupied primarily by e-marketers, but rather to look for its power across the marketing landscape.

Permission Crosses Channels

The principles of permission marketing are not limited to the opportunities enabled recently by the Internet, but can be applied even more broadly to today's multichannel world. We have found that every aspect of the brand relationship must be aligned and consistent across every channel — from communications to transactions and, ultimately, to the ownership experience.

When a company engages its most valuable customers, the rewards are high. The customer moves up the ladder to emerge as a brand advocate and becomes an active participant in designing the brand's future. Therefore, a brand must constantly ask for, and earn, permission. And, in return for that permission, a brand must deliver on its promise, in every channel, every time.

Saturn, a General Motors car division, is frequently held up as the role model for successful new-age brands. Not only did Saturn embrace the shift in power from company to customer but, by inventing a car-buying process that gave consumers greater control and eliminating the discomfort and power plays despised by most car buyers, they earned permission to have a different kind of relationship. When asked about their relationship to the company and the brand, Saturn owners regularly respond that they feel like they are part of a family. They believe that their local Saturn dealer is looking out for their best interest by keeping their car running safely and smoothly. The Saturn owner relinquishes no control to the Saturn dealer in the relationship and there is a high level of trust between the two. This is a 180-degree difference from the responses elicited about the average car dealer, categorized by most respondents as one of the least trusted occupations and often described as operating only in their own self-interest.

Quite simply, on-line and off, Saturn keeps their promises, which, in turn, keeps earning them greater permission to offer additional products and services to the citizens of their brand community.

But, what if marketers cannot recast or reinvent their entire company the way GM did with Saturn? Can you teach an old dog new tricks? What if your product has a sales cycle that lends itself to intermittent contact? Is it possible to engage your customer meaningfully outside of the purchase process? We believe that it is possible, and we offer the following example of our client, Infiniti Motor Corporation.

The Infiniti Division of Nissan North America, is a luxury-car manufacturer, competing primarily with Mercedes, BMW, and Lexus for market share. In 1999, Infiniti was scheduled to launch the new I30 model. The market was heavily saturated with a wide array of models from each manufacturer, and advertising spending for the luxury segment in which it competed exceeded $600 million in the United States alone. There was a distinct need to extend an invitation to new members of the Infiniti brand and to extend the relationship that current Infiniti owners already had.

Marketing conventions suggested that the average luxury-car buyers were not interested in a brand relationship except for the three months they spent actively engaged in the purchase process. This resulted in a marketing strategy that required that we interrupt Infiniti prospects with our messages on a regular basis, in order to make conquest of them when they arrived in that three-month-long "sweet spot." A new permission component was added to an already integrated campaign of television, print, and direct response, all based on this strategic platform: "Infiniti. All the Best Thinking." This permission-based device challenged the conventions by engaging luxury-car buyers with the Infiniti brand regardless of whether they were currently in the market to buy.

The device, developed in collaboration with *Smart Money* magazine, was a highly involving on-line stock portfolio game called the I30 Challenge. The premise: The game gave each registered player $29,465 (the value of a new I30) to invest and manage over a period of three months. The player with the highest-valued portfolio at the end of the game would win a new Infiniti I30.

The result was an environment in which members actively engaged with the Infiniti brand, giving the manufacturer more and more personal information over time, as well as escalating those members up the ladder of permission from stranger to friend, and from friend to potential customer.

More than 60,000 players visited the site, with almost 20,000 registering in the first week and playing throughout the three-month period. Registration required answering 20 initial questions consisting of demographic and car purchasing behavior. Additional questions that were asked throughout the course of the game, as well as the participants' game-playing behavior, helped us develop a better understanding of this group of exclusive and valuable customers.

Here is what happened: The game attracted more affluent consumers than previous direct-response outreach, with over 62 percent of all players reporting higher income. The game reached mainly conquest targets, with 74 percent of all players not currently in the Infiniti franchise. This meant that we were not just cultivating our existing customers, but also actually engaging entirely new ones, a goal not previously achieved via traditional direct mail. Of all registered players, 76 percent were luxury-car intenders and were predisposed to buying imports rather than American brands. However, the best news was that each visit to the game averaged 10.7 minutes and total user time averaged 494 minutes per player, comparing favorably to the highest-profile information and entertainment sites. This meant that, on average, each player engaged in a significant session with the Infiniti brand approximately 49 times over a period of three months. The program contributed to a successful launch in which sales surpassed objectives by 50 percent, and the engagement strategy has extended the penetration of the Infiniti brand into a new community and gained that community's permission to market its models and services in the future.

Which Came First, the Permission or the E-mail?

Never does the topic of permission marketing create more frenzy and promise more than when one is having a conversation about e-mail. Whether you understand all the principles or not, everyone seems to want to jump on the e-mail bandwagon as swiftly as possible. There are a couple of reasons for this.

$5 per thousand

First, it is hard to argue with the math. Consider this: According to Forrester Research, a direct-mail program to a company's in-house mailing list will cost $761 per thousand, whereas an e-mail to that same in-house customer list will cost $5 per thousand. The average direct-mail response rate for a successful program is 2 percent. Whereas the e-mail response rate for successful campaigns hovers around 10 percent. Even those who are not followers of the permission marketing mind-set argue that the return on investment alone makes even poorly planned and executed e-mail programs worth doing.

However, new research indicates that the pendulum may be swinging back the other way. On-line users have gotten over the initial excitement of hearing, "You have got mail," knowing that it too often means sifting through nothing but junk. According to *eMarketer*, 22 percent of all e-mail received today is marketing related and only half of those e-mails are permission based. Furthermore, over half of these originate from a customer opting in or, more accurately, not opting out. This fact is starting to drastically affect behavior.

210x3-5 emails

In a new study conducted by Forrester Research, typical consumers, who on average receive 210 e-mail messages of all kinds each month, are now half as likely to make a purchase as a result of an e-mail pitch as they were just a year ago. Multiply that total e-mail number of 210 by 3 to 5 to get the range of the number of e-mails received by the average professional, and it is clear that the days of the e-mail hyperlink quickie sale are severely numbered.

Conversely, those brands that have the highest level of success with respect to e-mail are those that are not attempting to convert e-mail recipients from stranger to customer in one encounter, but rather are building a relationship over time. Amazon.com, whose collaborative filtering provides excellent referral opportunities to buy more works by the authors you love, is one good example. The experience is on par with that of using a personal shopper or, more accurately, a thoughtful friend — one who happens to notice that your favorite author has just published a new book and offers to pick it up for you. Another example is a brand that helps develop your personal competence over time, like personal finance software maker Quicken, which sends e-mail tutorials to registered users offering valuable software tips for designing and running personal finance reports just in time for tax season. Both companies have built their businesses and their brands on customer feedback and participation. Not only are both companies believers in, but they are also true practitioners of, permission marketing.

It is clear that the reinvention of marketing in its totality, including all the new eCRM (electronic customer relationship management) efforts that this Disruption has enabled, is still very much in progress. However, one thing is clear: In the future, smart marketers will leverage their customers better. They will understand how e-mail fits into an overall multichannel strategy, and they will see and use e-mail as a cost-efficient and long-term loyalty builder and brand experience manager rather than merely as a cheap acquisition method.

Permission, Preferences, and My TV

In the past five years, there has been a great deal of discussion with respect to narrowcasting, individually addressable cable boxes, and interactive TV, and while they are on the horizon and are important, nothing has rocked our world like TiVo.

For those who do not know about it, TiVo is a digital personal video recorder that, over time, can learn your preferences about programming and shows, harvest them for you regardless of the time of day, and deliver them to you as if you owned your own personal network. The bottom line: Regardless of when you come home, there is always something on TV that you want to watch. You liked what you saw on that premiere episode? Just push the season pass and you will get more of the same. Losing interest in that four-year-old sitcom? Jettison it simply by changing your rating to thumbs-down from thumbs-up.

Your own personal network

We have long been accustomed to setting preferences with our software. Think of TiVo as the preferences setting for your digital cable system. Rather than 600 cable and 50 PPV channels, you now can have just the channels you want and lots of suggestions about the types of programs you like best. And it keeps getting better, with more filters and wish lists being introduced every day. Whereas once you would use the remote to channel-surf when you lost interest in a show, now you use it to rewind, pause, or fast-forward your recorded or live programs. Watching conventional broadcast television in the conventional way, on the network's terms, is now an agonizing — but unnecessary — experience.

The power of TiVo to the marketer did not come clear until the launch of the recent BMW Films campaign, developed by Fallon. I routinely use my TiVo to fast-forward through commercials that air during my favorite programs.

Enter the BMW Films campaign, a series of six short films by famous directors, each of which features a unique getaway story line and stars a particular model of BMW sedan, coupe, or roadster. Being a highly digital diva, I downloaded the first of the films and the player from the Web when the buzz began about the campaign. I thought that the campaign was clever, and I archived the films and sent them to friends — contributing to the viral effort BMW was hoping for. I enjoyed the experience, although I found the small screen and inferior sound on my computer a poor brand experience.

Then, magic struck. Three weeks into the on-line campaign, I was delighted to see a 30-second letterboxed BMW spot on my TV with a TiVo rating prompt. I gave the commercial three thumbs up and the very next day my TiVo had collected and delivered to me the full six-minute film to be enjoyed properly on my home theater system. The Disruption? Using TiVo, BMW had asked my permission to interrupt me with a quick question, "Do you want to see the whole film?" I had given BMW permission to become a star in my roster of entertainment choices — as a program, not as an interruption to a program.

This example serves as proof that permission marketing can apply to any and all channels. BMW's permission marketing effort, so well designed and so well executed, took the king of interruption marketing — television — and served up Disruption at its finest.

Church with Red Ribbon, 2001
Bricks, stucco, stained glass, metal ribbon
Courtesy of
The Museum of Contemporary Art,
Los Angeles

13. DISRUPTIVE MEDIA PLANNING

As men and women go about their daily routines, thousands of messages are thrust at them on television, in the newspaper, on the radio, just about anywhere and in any way imaginable. The number of media choices today is more than thirtyfold greater than it was just a decade ago. This media barrage makes it increasingly difficult to capture consumers' attention and establish a meaningful dialog.

In addition, consumers are more sophisticated than ever. Messages that are blatant, condescending, arrogant, or even irrelevant are automatically eliminated from consideration. In these cases, media placement does not even matter. However, when you have the right message, disruptive media planning becomes a critical component that can make the difference in terms of being seen, heard, and remembered.

So, this begs the question: How does a marketer stand out and make an impression that is truly lasting and not just sensational for the moment?

One of the key issues is to keep the linkage of the media strategy to the creative process. In most of Europe and increasingly in Asia and the Americas, the media side has been separated from the agency creative function. Clearly, there are enormous economic benefits in media independents. But great creative work has to be linked to great media thinking. The two sides have to work as one in support of the brand.

The other key demand on media planning today is for increased effectiveness in media spending. Conventional media plans can be supported by conventional research and metrics. As you will see from the cases that follow, you sometimes cannot get research to justify some media channels. Who can give you an estimate of the consumer impact of bananas? But when you feel that the brand, the medium, and the creative message have bonded, then no research should be needed. Emotions guide decisions as much as reason does. Let us take a look at how disruptive media planning, in conjunction with focused creative work, can help make a more meaningful connection by capturing the consumer's attention and becoming part of the brand's message.

Making the Media Placement Unexpected

The first 15 minutes of a television program are the most critical to the television networks. Simply put, if viewers do not sample the first 15 minutes of a television program, then they will not sample the remainder of the show. There are no second chances.

Creating tune-in for those first 15 minutes is the challenge for the ABC television network. And the amount of competitive clutter is enormous. All networks use spot radio. All use *TV Guide*. All have on-air TV spots. And all have the same overriding message: "Watch our shows!"

Disruptive media planning is something we use to break through this enormous amount of clutter. This means using media that are unexpected and unconventional for a television network, enabling ABC to communicate with potential viewers at a safe distance from other networks. Although generally less broad, they often generate more buzz (and sometimes publicity) than traditional mass-reach media vehicles. ABC's advertising does not totally abandon traditional methods. Rather, an effort is made to augment the number and type of vehicles used with unique show-specific or brand-specific media. Obviously, this works best when the creative matches the media.

Here are some examples:

Brand-specific media for the ABC "Yellow" branding campaign launch:

Medium: Banana peels in grocery stores

Message: "Another fine use of yellow."

Medium: Yellow bus benches

Message: "Wouldn't you rather be sitting on your couch?"

Medium: New York taxi-top advertising

Message: "Raise your hand if you watch ABC."

Show-specific media:

Purpose: *James Bond* fall schedule

Medium: Martini glass

Message: "Shaken, not stirred. *James Bond*, Saturdays This Fall."

Purpose: *The Norm Show*

Medium: Talking bathroom poster panels

Message: Off-the-wall toilet humor

Purpose: *The Geena Davis Show*

Medium: Supermarket floor graphics

Message: The story of a domesticated socialite

Making the Medium the Message

Our creative brief was simple: Raise the awareness of the Museum of Contemporary Art (MOCA) in Los Angeles by taking the museum experience to the streets. A visually distinct and typical element was lifted directly from the walls of the museum — art labels (black type on white) — and placed in everyday surroundings.

To maintain MOCA's character, we wanted to replicate the sense of discovery and inquisitiveness that a museum evokes by making every single execution unique to its environment. Like the museum and the creative, the media placement needed to be unexpected and engaging, so the museum message was placed on dry-cleaning hangers, paper coffee-cup bands, and gas-pump handles. Using these vehicles, we were able to demonstrate that art can be found everywhere, even in ordinary things and experiences. Also, because the creative featured black type on a white background, potential media ideas included eggshells, Chinese food takeout cartons, and tablecloths.

Billboards were individually selected using two criteria: physical location with commentworthy surroundings and high-traffic areas likely to experience congestion. This provided an opportunity to make a thought-provoking statement, while giving people the necessary time to experience it. The billboards disrupted the conventional design format by breaking with the industry rule (created for obvious reasons) of using eight words or less. In this example, media placement was literally part of the message.

In a short time, MOCA's unaided brand awareness increased significantly due to the word-of-mouth buzz generated by the campaign and public relations. Phone inquiries about membership tripled in volume and, based on the results of a brand tracking study conducted by Hall & Partners, the public's perception of MOCA's attributes went from "it does not relate to me" and "it is stuffy" to "it is cool, witty, and innovative."

Impact Is Key: Go Big or Don't Go

In all forms of media, whether domestic or international, the Apple strategy remains constant: Impact is key. Go big or don't go. In the use of print we employ a cover strategy. Spreads must run predominantly on cover 2/page 1 and all single-page units can run only on back covers. In television we employ a premium "prime-only" strategy, whereby each individual show on which advertising is being considered is hand-picked through discussion between Apple and the agency. The same premium strategy is carried through in our outdoor campaign by hand-selecting highly visible and unique locations in our key markets.

We continually strive to partner the Apple message with media that enhance its brand identity.

For example: *Frasier*, yes; *Weakest Link*, no. *Time*, yes; *Maxim*, no.

Spectacular outdoor sites, such as the side of the Louvre in Paris and the Hotel Figueroa in Los Angeles, are selected, and we are often the first user of such sites.

Apple is showcased in fewer locations, shows, and magazines, but it is featured with a higher frequency, with the intention of creating a bond with consumers in the key media vehicles that they find important in their lives. It is much harder work for the agency. But the effort of combining the creative message with the right context massively increases the impact of each dollar spent.

In all these cases, we have gone back to the basic building blocks of communication. The medium is part of the message. And then the creative work multiplies the impact. One plus one should equal more than two in all good disruptive media plans.

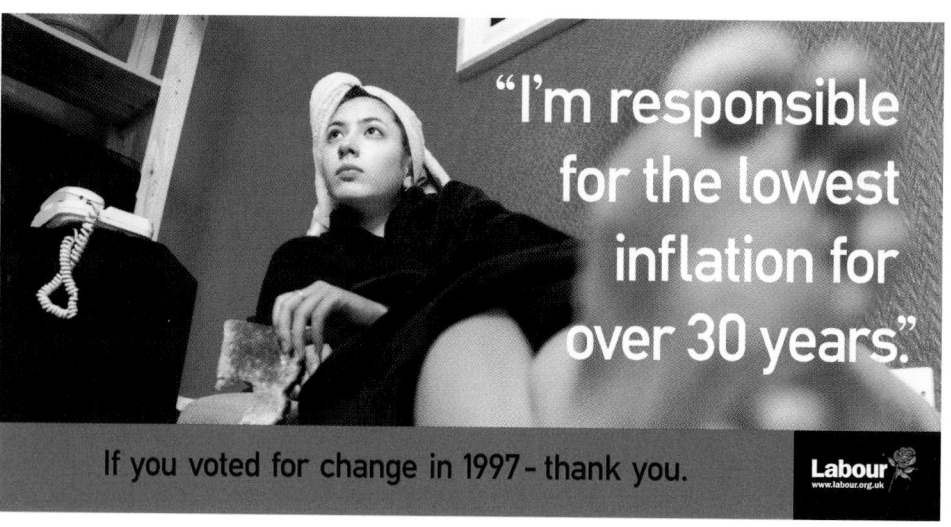

14. DISRUPTION IN POLITICAL ADVERTISING

Whatever occupation you are in, there is always something to disrupt. Everyone comes to this realization sooner or later. Even politicians are starting to see the light!

Politics, political communication, and, particularly, political advertising are riddled with — and hamstrung by — convention. Political advertising is still held captive by conventions that the rest of the advertising world has largely escaped.

From the advertiser's perspective, dramatic changes have taken place in people's consumption patterns and level of sophistication over the last 30 years. From a political viewpoint, people's attitudes toward, and their relationships with, politics have also undergone huge change.

The Decline of Interest in Politics

Consumers have become more complex and less easy to predict. The era of being able to pigeonhole people on the basis of demographics and life stage has gone. Consumers no longer fit into neat, easy-to-understand categories, and they actively resist marketers' attempts to force them into such boxes. The world that marketers and advertisers now face is immeasurably more complex and difficult to navigate successfully than that of 30 years ago.

Likewise, the political world and the relationship of the voter to political parties has also changed. The unquestioning identification of voters with a single political party is in steady decline, with the result that voters are more volatile and less easy to predict than ever before.

Just as demographic labels no longer tell marketers everything they need to know about consumers, job class and geography no longer constitute a clear predictor of political allegiance. In Britain before 1980, you could be 80 percent certain that an automobile factory worker would vote Labour and a London lawyer Conservative. Between 1980 and 1997, they were both more likely to vote Conservative. Now, both are likely to be voting Labour. These shifts in the allegiance of specific groups can also be seen in the United States, where, for example, many traditional Southern Democrats have switched to the Republican Party.

Diminished party identification

This diminished party identification has combined with a trend toward declining involvement with politics in general. The impact of this can be seen from the turnout in recent elections. Turnout in the British general election of 2001 was the lowest for 83 years, at 59.5 percent. The turnout in the U.S. presidential election in 2001 was 51 percent, despite it being the closest race in years.

Breaking with the Conventions of the Past

Faced with massive changes among consumers and in their consumption habits, marketers have had to become innovative in their approach. They must constantly work harder to communicate with, and reach, the public. Most advertising today is unrecognizable from that of the 1970s. How many advertisers are using the same language and techniques that they used 30 years ago? Very few, and, among those who are successful, even fewer.

Political communication, on the other hand, is stuck in the conventions of the past. It ignores how people have changed. The phrase "hard-working families"' was used by Richard Nixon in a television broadcast in 1968, Bill Clinton used it in 1992 and 1996, Tony Blair in 1997, and by 2000 both Al Gore and George W. Bush were claiming that they represented and would work for the "hard-working families of America."

Of course, people are still working hard — if not harder than before. But when a phrase becomes conventional, it is shorn of real meaning; it becomes wallpaper — a lesson advertisers learned a long time ago. There is a better way to describe the public, a way that actually means some-thing rather than sounding like a bland platitude. Such uninspired communication is one of the reasons why people are growing increasingly disconnected from politics and politicians.

It is no coincidence that the most successful contemporary politicians around the world are those with the ability to reach beyond the political sphere and connect with a wider public. Bill Clinton in the United States, Tony Blair in Britain, Gerhard Schröder in Germany, and Junichiro Koizumi in Japan all connect with voters in ways that go beyond the conventionally political.

They do not easily fit into existing categories. They are all natural disrupters. They do not fit the conventional pattern of politics. Rather than appealing to a single, homogeneous core group of supporters, they are skilled at building a diverse coalition of voters, often from beyond the (shrinking) traditional borders of their party. These coalitions are built as much on an emotional connection to the leader as on any rational policy platform.

These politicians make such connections through the force of their charisma and natural communication skills. Their advertising also tends to be better than that of the political sector as a whole, but it still fits within the conventions of the sector. To take the next step toward halting falling political involvement, these politicians need to disrupt the conventions of political advertising.

There are only two memorable forms of political advertising:

The negative attack

This is exemplified by Lyndon Johnson's 1964 "Daisy" commercial, which used the image of a little girl, followed by that of a mushroom cloud, to highlight the nuclear risk of electing Goldwater. Other examples include Saatchi & Saatchi's classic 1979 poster, "Labour is not working," 1992's "Tax bombshell," and George H. W. Bush's infamous "Willie Horton" TV ad that painted Michael Dukakis as soft on crime. This was brutal negative advertising, attacking an opponent's record, character, or anticipated future performance.

There is a clear parallel between negative political advertising and one of the earliest commercial forms of advertising: the Unique Selling Proposition. Examples include advertising based on the message that "X has more widgets than Y" or that "Z cannot get out tough stains like A."

The positive TV panegyric

Started by Dwight Eisenhower's 1952 "The Man from Abilene" ad and raised to a new level in the U.K. with 1987's "Kinnock the Movie," this approach was also used by Bill Clinton to huge effect in 1992 with "The Man from Hope." These commercials introduce a candidate to a mass audience in terms of the candidate's upbringing, values, and character. They do not address issues and they do not say what the candidate has achieved or would achieve if elected. The very best of these can be moving and involving; however, all too often they are saccharine, unbelievable, and easy to ignore. The positive panegyric mirrors the second wave in advertising development, which occurred in the late 1960s and 1970s, when brands discovered that USPs were not enough. Instead, they concentrated on emotional selling propositions (ESPs), such as Coca-Cola's "I'd like to teach the world to sing," which essentially say, "Buy X because you like us."

Both the positive and the negative forms are now mired in convention. Familiar as the result of more than 30 years' use, they just do not seem to work as well as they used to. Yet, politicians persist in following the conventions of these two types of advertising, as if commercial advertisers likewise used only these two kinds of advertising. Can you imagine how boring and ineffective such advertising would be?

Political advertising needs to change. It needs to disrupt in the same way that the best politicians are disruptive. It needs to connect with voters on their terms. It needs to innovate and find new modes of communication beyond the USP and the ESP, as the rest of the advertising world has done. Fortunately, there are some emergent examples of disruption.

Disruption in practice 1

The power of saying thank you.

Convention Politicians always claim all achievements for themselves.

Disruption The achievements of a government are the achievements of the people who voted for it.

Vision Become the party of a reinvigorated democracy by speaking through the people of the people's achievements.

All over the world, politicians spend a lot of time claiming what they have achieved, in speeches, TV broadcasts, and print. The result is, of course, that we do not believe them. They tend to overclaim or spin the figures to make themselves look good.

In November 2000, the British Labour Party ran a campaign that broke every political convention. It was positive but not a panegyric. It did not claim the credit. It was not about politicians, and it did not involve politicians talking down to the public. It was disruptive.

The "Thank You" campaign dealt with the achievements of Labour's first four years in government. It communicated to a cynical electorate what had changed since the election of 1997. Instead of trying to claim achievement

"Thanks to my dad the NHS now has 10,000 more nurses."

If you voted for change in 1997 - thank you.

Labour
www.labour.org.uk

for the Labour government, it allowed the people to speak for themselves to the people. It gave the credit to the people rather than the politicians.

The key disruption was the recognition that the achievements of a government are also the achievements of the people who voted for that government. When did you last see a politician give someone else the credit? These were groundbreaking, unexpected, and disruptive communications that achieved a significant turnaround for the Labour government.

Disruption 2

The power of wit and satire.

Wit "The alliance of levity and seriousness by which seriousness is intensified" (T.S. Eliot).

Convention Politics deals with serious issues, so political advertising must be serious.

Disruption Serious issues do not need serious advertising.

Vision Strengthen the connection between party and voter through shared humor of adult-to-adult communication.

In 2001, the Conservative leader William Hague lacked clear politics of his own — he harked back to the Conservative leader Margaret Thatcher and her policies of the 1980s. Indeed, Thatcher was out campaigning on his behalf for the first time since she left office. The perceived threat to the public was real and very serious — but the most effective approach to the advertising did not need to be:

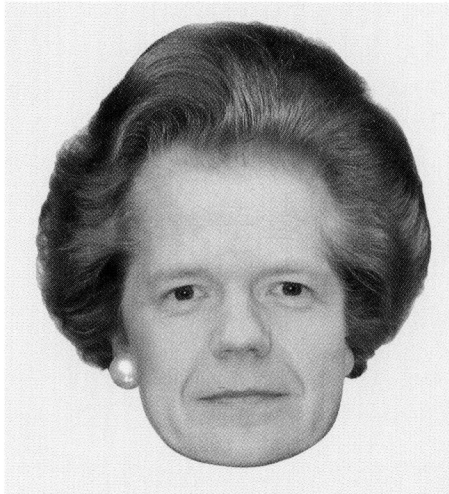

Be afraid.
Be very afraid.

Vote **Labour**
www.labour.org.uk

This was iconic political advertising that seized the political agenda and linked the history of the Conservative Party to a threat against the future. The combination of William Hague's face and Margaret Thatcher's hair grabbed headlines and started conversations. It was reproduced on the front page of three (conservative) national newspapers.

Satire such as this engaged voters with the communication and provided an amplifying vehicle for the serious message that Hague was the heir of Thatcher and Thatcherism. The charge, in and of itself, was serious; however, the satire made it stronger, more powerful, and more memorable. A humorous image says more than a hundred speeches.

Rather than rehashing old arguments or performance, this ad took the political argument and reframed it for today's voters — voters who are engaged by humor and take out the serious message.

Disruption 3
There are alternatives to open attack.
Convention Attack opposition policies using advertising.
Disruption Subversion can be more powerful than attack.
Vision Make the Liberals the party of common sense amid an absurd world.

Doris Day

Finally, political advertising does not need to be conventional advertising. In Canada's 2000 elections, Jean Chrétien and the Liberal Party used disruptive humorous campaigning to undermine the opposition's credibility.

One of the key policy pledges of opposition leader Stockwell Day was the ability to trigger a referendum on any issue, provided that 3 percent of the electorate wanted it. Chrétien and the Liberals, in conjunction with friendly media, set up a special web site in order to sign up 3 percent of the Canadian electorate in favor of Stockwell Day being forced to change his name to Doris Day if he were elected.

The idea took hold, and the Liberals started rallies and broadcasts with "Que sera, sera," as recorded by Doris Day. They achieved the necessary 3 percent support, highlighting the weaknesses of the pledge and ridiculing Stockwell Day in the process. This was campaigning taken beyond the ordinary, with extraordinary impact. Jean Chrétien won comfortably, and Stockwell Day's credibility was ruined.

These examples demonstrate the rewards of breaking the conventions that define and confine political advertising. Unlike far too much political advertising, they recognized the changes that have occurred in the past 30 years. Like the best of the advertising world, they have used innovation to seize the advantage. Given the parallels between the early USP/ESP advertising and current political advertising models, will we see political advertising follow other marketing innovations and strategies? Might we see political challenger brands, organizational selling propositions, niche and cult parties, personal selling propositions?

Who can say? Roll on the next election.

15. DISRUPTION IN EMERGING MARKETS

Emerging markets have a lot in common with each other. Very often, the concept of individualism is close to nonexistent. People in these markets rarely strive to be different from each other, never mind challenging the way the majority behave. In other words, these markets are a long way from being ripe for Disruption.

Therefore, applying disruptive thinking in Asian markets represents a significant challenge. Disruption is fundamentally at odds with the conservative values that underlie behavior in the Confucian societies of Japan, greater China, South Korea, and Singapore. Ng Aik Kwang, in his controversially titled book *Why Asians Are Less Creative Than Westerners* (First Edition, 2001), comments, "...in the Confucian society of the East, conservative values which emphasize the importance of tradition, conformity and security will serve as the...channel of behavior for the Asian."

Exploring why China seems to have forgotten Zheng He, its greatest adventurer hero, *Time* magazine argued, "One explanation, surely, is that the Chinese typically do not revere adventurers. This is a society that for centuries was dominated by a Confucian ideology that ascribed overwhelming virtue to orderliness. Everyone had a prescribed role to play according to his social status; everything fit into its rightful place. Only then was civilization thought to thrive."

Challenging 2000 Years of Confucian Teaching

Confucian society is dominated by the "six relations," which govern all aspects of social life. As they are themselves based on the relationship between parent and child, at their foundation is the concept of filial piety (which then becomes the moral code determining relationships between rulers and subjects, teachers and students, and even among friends).

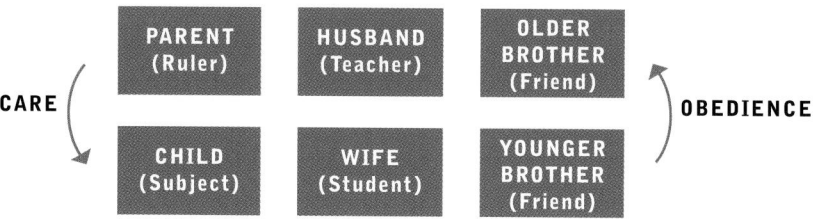

Filial piety, and its corresponding value, obedience, to a large extent negates the ability of people to challenge established thinking. And this, in turn, limits the Disruption opportunity.

"Japanese society has a strong heritage of people working together and learning from each other to unite the organization to help meets its goals. However, it can have a serious weakness because sometimes this heritage can kill the disruptive — that is, the breakthrough — idea."

Professor Shoji Shiba, Massachusetts Institute of Technology

In these markets, Disruption thus runs up against a significant Confucian cultural barrier. In addition to an unwillingness to change the rules, Confucian thinking is also past-positive (as opposed to future-positive). There is a strong tendency to revere the old. As Confucius himself said, "I am a traditionalist, not one who creates new things: I am faithful, a lover of the old."

Confucian thinking has had a significant impact on the practice of marketing in these markets. It has resulted in a short-term focus on immediate sales (rather than branding) and a follow-the-leader mentality.

Sales versus Branding

Branding, as it is practiced in other markets, is not a priority. Here the marketing challenge is distribution, pricing, and product. Name awareness is important. But developing an emotional connection with customers to ensure future loyalty? That is something that is not always understood, let alone needed. This is particularly true in fast-growing markets such as the Asia Pacific.

For many years, these markets enjoyed fabulous economic growth. Per capita income rose. New brands were launched and were snapped up by aspirational consumers. There was no need for sophisticated communication or business practices — you just had to make sure people were aware of your brands and that they were readily available.

Here, innovative thinking to create new market space was not something marketers needed to think about. The new market space was an economy growing at over 8 percent per year. "Launch it, and it will sell" was the rallying cry of marketers across the Asia Pacific region, thus reinforcing a historical marketing modus operandi.

Copying is safe

Follow the Leader

The tendency was, therefore, to use tried-and-true strategies and executions. If a specific approach works for the market leader, then why not use it as well? The fact that this just works to reinforce the position of the market leader is not something that is well accepted or even recognized. Copying what everyone else does is safe: How can you be blamed for doing something that has been shown to work by your more successful competitors?

In China, the two leading FMCG brands are Procter & Gamble and Unilever. The P&G advertising formula (functional problem to "scientific" solution to emotional resolution) is now widely copied — and not only by Chinese brands within the traditional personal care category, but also in the categories of infant nutrition and health care.

In Singapore, this follow-the-leader mentality is called *kiasu*, which Dr. Kwang defines as follows: "If so many people are going after the same thing, then it must be good, or else why are they going after it?" *Kiasu* thus becomes self-fulfilling: The value of going for something itself becomes the reason why that something is worth going after.

Disruption: The Appeal of Process

However, one should not underestimate the value of an open-ended, process-driven exercise. With Disruption, no specific model is force-fitted into a business problem. No one is expected to buy a specific solution. Rather, they are asked, in a risk-free but highly creative environment, to arrive at specific conclusions. This is a winning proposition for any marketer.

Five factors underlie why the Disruption process can eventually be successful in these conservative markets: theoretical rigor, cooperation, challenge, inspiration, and creativity.

A Rigorous Process

The extensive prework involved in preparing for a Disruption workshop is immediately apparent to all participants. A formal agenda is set. Participants are divided into teams. Time is allocated to specific exercises that drive the process. The theory and process of Disruption are introduced through an extensive presentation outlining the need for Disruption, highlighting cases where Disruption has been successfully applied, and detailing the methods and exercises from which, with luck, a breakthrough idea will arise.

Disruption workshops are split into three sections: convention seeking, agreement on how the conventional system works, and, finally, visioneering (whereby participants use a variety of tools developed to inspire out-of-the-box thinking). For most marketers, the convention-seeking part of the workshop is highly revealing.

"It is surprising that there is a convention that drives the marketing and customer communication in the telecommunication field."
Angela Ho, Marketing Manager, New World Telephone.

A Cooperative Process

In Confucian-based societies, a high value is placed on group harmony and teamwork. There is a strong culture of cooperation and joint responsibility. While it is rare to find individuals willing to take on the risk of doing things differently, one can be sure that a group of people who are strongly motivated to find group consensus will sometimes arrive at key decisions based on a thorough investigation of the system. This is the reverse of more individualistic societies, where participants tend to arrive at specific personal conclusions and then use the stimulus material to justify these positions.

In these conservative markets, Disruption workshops work extremely well because, by their nature, they are cooperative ventures. They involve senior people from both the advertising agency and the marketing company. The Confucian value of establishing harmony within the group helps in successfully building bridges between the two sides. While the process might be slower, there is less arguing and the conclusions reached are jointly owned.

An Inspiring Yet Challenging Process

A Disruption workshop can guarantee that the conventions governing a specific market will be revealed and challenged. At a minimum, it is thus an alternative market and competitive review. However, the revealing of the conventions of a category naturally leads to the idea that these conventions need to be challenged.

"The theory of Disruption challenges our conventional mind-set. It confronts us to think outside the box, form innovative strategic directions of the business or a specific brand, and implement actions that will challenge the competition. It's the foundational basis for our business thinking and organization re-alignment before the branding of our company and products."
Kee Fui Kon, Product & Development Manager, Selective Herbicides, Syngenta, Asia Pacific.

A large number of cases prove that Disruption is a process that works, and also establishes the desire to emulate the proven success of disruptive thinking in the development of strategy.

"My impression is that large companies like ours run the risk of developing a resistance against innovation and change mainly because of fear of cannibalization of current business. People need to be convinced about the value of risk taking, trying new approaches."
Kaspar Mueller, Syngenta, Asia Pacific.

A Creative Learning Process

Out-of-the-box thinking is not something that most people have an opportunity to do. Even in Japan, where total quality management (TQM) has been identified as a key management methodology that helped the country compete with the West, middle managers often found that none of the truly radical ideas put forward in these TQM sessions were ever implemented. Instead, true to the principle of *kaizen* (small improvements), it was the small, noncontroversial cost-saving or quality-improvement idea that found rapid support and was thus implemented.

The opportunity to think outside the box in a nonrisk environment is highly attractive. Disruption grants permission for people to go beyond conventional thinking, to challenge their assumptions, and extend their thinking unconstrained by their company's formal systems and culture. But it is the nonrisk format of the workshops that provides enough comfort for this to take place. Disruption has significant appeal for many marketers in these conservative markets. But there is a difference from the appeal it has in Western markets. The attraction is the Disruption process itself. Here Disruption appeals because of its ability to bring cross-disciplinary people together to think about specific issues and problems. Thus, when introducing the idea of Disruption, it is important to develop a different rationale from that which is common in markets where revolution, differentiation, and win-lose scenarios are part of the marketer's psyche.

Presenting Disruption in Conservative Markets

The three key benefits of Disruption in conservative markets are better resistance to rising competition, proven effectiveness, and market/industry relevance.

Competition

Developing markets are increasingly subject to global competition. China's recent entry into the World Trade Organization (WTO) is just one example of the threat of increasing competition. We can expect a similar situation to that experienced in Mexico with the North American Free Trade Agreement (NAFTA):

"After the Free Trade Agreement, many of our clients here in Mexico began facing stiff competition from the ever expanding array of international companies trying to enlarge their piece of the pie by expanding into Latin America. And unless local accounts are equipped to play on the same terms, they are going to lose in the long run."

Jeanne Vaughn, Strategic Planning Director of our Mexican agency.

Marketers in conservative markets can no longer rely on government protection. These marketers have seen the successful introduction of brands by major packaged-goods companies and have noted the seeming inability of local producers to compete in the higher-margin area of their markets.

In addition, it has become evident that the clutter in these markets is massive (and increasing). In China, for example, media research has shown that the average consumer is exposed to double the amount of advertising that would be experienced by the average German consumer. Virgin Atlantic avoided utilizing outdoor media for its Shanghai launch campaign because the environment was seen to be too cluttered, and thus difficult in which to really make an impact.

The only way to get around the problem of clutter is to develop unique communication that can stand out, to invent a new advertising medium — as Virgin Atlantic did when they painted the traditional green-and-white Star Ferry red.

Effectiveness

"I think there is a need to quantify the benefits you have tracked with your clients. Such data or information substantiate the real value of Disruption."

Kee Fui Kon, Product and Development Manager, Selective Herbicides, Syngenta, Asia Pacific.

Disruption case studies are showcased that help "in convincing us about the value and 'implementability' of Disruption," according to Edgar Juan Surtida III, president and CEO of Syngenta in the Philippines. The fact that real-world cases can be presented demonstrates that Disruption is not just more theoretical marketing consultant babble. It is a proven process that has delivered results to clients around the world. And these cases are from well-known brands that have strong validity and authority in communicating the benefits of Disruption.

When applied to specific situations, it is often necessary to highlight the ineffectiveness of the current approach. Many marketers know quite well that the way they are currently engaging the market, while being safe, is not necessarily effective.

"Disruption opened our eyes to how the industry as a whole was thinking and behaving particularly towards its customers. It made us realize that there are many improvements our company could make in the way we think and interact (manifested through our marketing, branding, and communication activities) with our customers that could help improve our competitiveness," adds Surtida.

Relevance

It is necessary that participants have confidence in the theory and process of Disruption. International cases are highly effective in establishing the value of Disruption. While PlayStation, Apple, and Absolut are inspirational examples of disruptive thinking, an overreliance on cases from western countries can lead to problems of relevancy in conservative markets.

We recently developed a commercial for **Bic's Orange** razor for use in emerging markets. In the film, we see a dad kissing his little girl good-morning. She is lying with her back turned to him and says, with her eyes still closed, "Good morning, mom." There is a universality to this simple scene, which underlines the softness of the dad's skin. The commercial has since been exported all over the world, from non mature to mature markets, and has become a relevant case history for everybody.

In the case of **Shangri-La Hotels**, we were able to demonstrate, by challenging category conventions, how Disruption as a process can help identify a more relevant proposition for a brand.

Its key target audience, the frequent business traveler, resented the lack of differentiation among the top hotel brands. Moreover, for them, traveling on business was an arduous and not always pleasant experience.

By focusing on the emotional side of the experience, rather than on hotel hardware, Shangri-La gave itself a relevant and unique proposition, linked to the myth that Shangri-La is a place of elegance, harmony, privacy, and peacefulness: "Shangri-La — a tranquil haven in a frantic world."

Ahead of the Competition

Without exception, Disruption has delivered real value to clients in these conservative markets. And indications are that, with globalization, the economic downturn, and an increasing dearth of marketing talent, the attraction of Disruption will only increase.

As Keith Smith, our regional chairman for Asia Pacific, says, "As the economic realities of the twenty-first century continue to hit the Asia Pacific region, the reality of having to find new market space will become increasingly important to those brands which want to survive and prosper."

Disruption, rather than representing a threat, is seen as an opportunity to get ahead of the competition. Given that many of these markets are a branding blank slate, Disruption provides the opportunity for local brands to develop the power to beat the new international entrants at their own game, thereby attracting a new consumer, who is increasingly freed from the conservatism of Confucian thinking.

(For more on Disruption in Asia, refer to Exhibit B page 297.)

Religions and Brands

The fundamental difference between the brand-savvy markets of the West and the lagging markets of the East can be traced back to religion. The older religions of the East bear little resemblance to the newer Middle Eastern ones: From the perspective of the newer religions, the guiding principles of Hinduism are at best a loose philosophy, with Buddhism subsequently adding a bit more structure. These philosophies influence the perceptions about economic wealth and achievement. The older religions offer an explanation for every condition in life, but do not attempt to impose notions of right and wrong. These binary notions are the cornerstones of newer religions. It seems that the newer the religion, the more work-friendly it is, hence the success of the Protestant work ethic.

Inclusive and Exclusive Religions

A single set of guiding principles creates assimilation. People are brought together with a common set of objectives into a homogeneous market. Add common purpose and rootlessness, and what you have is a very fertile land in which to sow the seeds of brands. This is how America became a brand in the nineteenth century. In the East, a common purpose is imposed artificially from outside, by invading rulers, oppression, or Communism, and the religion is free to be interpreted by all cultures it comes into contact with. Hinduism varies from India to Nepal and Indonesia; Buddhism is fragmented from Tibet to Thailand and Japan. The common roots, however, mean that divergent sects rarely go to war with one another.

Brand theory, much like the Christian Church, is founded on the principles of exclusion — things you need to do to earn membership. Oriental philosophy, in contrast, is inclusive by nature. You can remain a Hindu without ever visiting a temple; on the other hand, you can only be born into Hinduism. There are no clear guidelines for converts. Confucianism similarly was developed as a philosophical practice devoted to easing the trauma of living rather than as a religious belief. Five hundred years before the birth of Christ, Confucius tried to find the best way for a society to be run, in an attempt to unite a China split by warring feudal lords. His concept of harmony, represented by the interplay of the yin and yang, sought to explain that everything had its equal opposite, making for a natural balance. At a political level, it urged citizens to work for the development of the state, while the state had a duty to care for its citizens. Today, we see manifestations of the same principle in the apparent homogeneity of Singapore and Taiwan. Why did South Korea's chaebols diversify? Because when staff's tasks were made obsolete by automation, the company had to find other things for them to do.

These older cultures have developed social systems to give members a sense of belonging. Family name, class, clan, and culture offer a sense of belonging that trad-itionally left little room for brands. And, while the religious principles of exclusion worked well in the brand's orig-inating cultures of the West, they restrict-ed its abil-ity to travel to Eastern markets. Such has been the experience of that universal brand, the Catholic Church, in this region. Left to their "better product" school of advertising (my God is better than yours), future brands would have had a tougher time entering the older lands of the East. That they did, to the extent of people looking up to the West as a better way, is tribute to a master dis-rupter in history.

Khakis in an Indian Summer

Together with cricket, the English language was the foundation on which the British Commonwealth was built. The British rarely imposed it on the conquered lands. English, rather like the wearing of trousers, was adopted by natives as an aspiration, a way of being as smart, as civilized, and as successful as the British settlers. The English language had a profound effect on the diverse cultures of the Empire. In the Indian context, it upset the carefully constructed social ladder. Being English was seen as being better than a Brahmin, thereby relegating the language of the Brahmins, of knowledge and wisdom, Sanskrit, to second place. Where the missionaries failed in seeding themselves into an existing order, the British succeeded in supplanting a fifth higher level in the caste system. The ruthless propagation of a brand is born of such insensitivities.

We said earlier that brand theory is founded on the principles of exclusion. However, to be globally successful, we know, brands need to leave enough room for local interpretation. The English language did just that. Today, from Manila's Taglish to Singaporean Singlish to the Indian Hinglish, the language has allowed users the flexibility needed to keep a brand going. The Oxford English Dictionary does its bit. It incorporates pidgin words in an inclusion strategy. English is now the lingua franca of 85 percent of the Internet, leaving the French to worry about their grammar.

Disruption at Work

Similarly, we recognize local interpretations of the same brand battles.

Pepsi entered India at the turn of the 1990s, around the time when the country was abandoning its adopted road to self-reliance, marked by low but manageable levels of economic growth, and socialism. In time-honored Pepsi fashion, it rallied behind the youth and aligned itself with the optimism that capitalism brought. They called it "the right choice." Ironically, Coca-Cola had been ousted from the country in 1977 for being symbolic of the ills of capitalism. When Coke returned in 1993, Pepsi responded by reframing its rival as the disagreeable face of socialistic thinking. The turning point was an ad Pepsi released on the day Coke relaunched itself. In typical Pepsi fashion, they urged Indians to try a Coke that day. By law, Pepsi was required to acknowledge the use of another company's brand name — they did this to glorious advantage.

"Coca-Cola and Coke are registered trademarks of the Coca-Cola Company. Pepsi is the choice of a new generation." Coke became associated with the red tape that had held the country back for so long. And that was not all. When Coke figured that Pepsi's investment in cricket was paying it rich dividends, it went about outbidding them at the 1996 Cricket World Cup. Coke became the official cola. On that occasion, whatever mileage they were hoping to get out of the sums invested came to nothing at the very first match of the tournament when a riot of blue balloons went up from the stands proclaiming, "Pepsi. Nothing official about it."

Order, Chaos, and Something in Between

Mohandas Karamchand Gandhi's biggest disruption was to rally Indians under the banner of their own religious heritage, and let the British watch helplessly as their engineering of Indian society got re-engineered. As a classical disrupter, Gandhi defamiliarized the idea of protest from an industrial world's perspective of "striking" to "a day of fasting and prayer." And, in reframing the argument, he became the biggest brand to come out of India, an influence on all struggles for freedom and self-determination.

Gandhi started out with the same establishment stamp as his peers, but, between his sailing England to study law in 1888 and his return in February 1931 to discuss the terms of the Delhi Pact, he had transformed himself into an individual figure with all the attendant quirks of a modern-day brand. Gandhi became the politically correct face of positive anarchy. His approach is a lesson to all marketers seeking to enter the diverse Asian market. He chose the lowest common denominator — salt, a vital commodity in a hot climate — and challenged the British salt-making monopoly. In terms of revenue, salt was insignificant to the British, but, symbolically, it united Indians of all creeds and castes. Who could have imagined the impact of such an action? But then Gandhi was not just an opportunist, he was a visionary.

Maybe long-term visions are easier to come by in the East, where time moves ever so slowly. As Zhou Enali apparently replied when asked what he thought of the French Revolution, "It's too early to tell."

In pursuit of scale,
luxury brands are democratizing
downwards via the inherently
disruptive behaviour
of brand stretching.

In pursuit of margin,
mainstream brands are diversifying
upwards by the equally
disruptive behavior
of reframing their business models.

16. THE LUXURY OF DISRUPTION

Limited by scale, encumbered by history, managed by intuition, luxury brands are generally dismissed as tangential, if not irrelevant, to serious thinking about the serious business of brand management. As the conventional wisdom would have it, luxury brands epitomize the reactionary — old-school, old-fashioned, and, quite often, old-world. It is hardly surprising then that in discussion about innovation and creativity, let alone Disruption, luxury brands are conspicuously absent.

Brands Behaving Well

But does the conventional wisdom (and the caricature of luxury brands it perpetuates) hold up under scrutiny? What if luxury brands were the rebellious ones, the radicals and the revolutionaries that actually behave the most creatively in creating brand value? At a time when brand owners are wrestling with complex issues of generating shareholder value through brand innovation and innovative branding, might not luxury brands, at their best, contribute to a best-practices model for brands behaving well?

Pushing this notion further, what if luxury brands were the great protagonists of our times, furthering the cause of disrupting the conventional models that frame the conventional thinking about brands and branding?

At least, according to *The Economist*, the time for such disruption may well be sooner rather than later: "Of the 74 brands that appear in the top 100 rankings in both of the past two years, 41 have declined in value.... Even in America, home to nine of the world's ten most valuable brands, it can be a shockingly old-fashioned business. Marketing theory is still largely based on the days when Procter & Gamble's brands dominated America, and its advertising agencies wrote the rules. The result is that many of the world's biggest brands are struggling. If they are making more and more noise, it is out of desperation."

Brands have become a company's most valuable economic asset, and the most valuable brands are those that behave well. If, as the economic logic goes, "building a relationship with customers secures future earnings by engendering customer loyalty at a premium price," it is not surprising that Vuitton, Chanel, Moët & Chandon, and Rolex are now cited among the world's most valuable brands. Could it be then that brand owners may well have as much to learn from the behavior of Armani as from General Mills, from Ferrari as from General Motors, from Chanel as from Procter & Gamble?

Disruption Is a Verb

Jean-Marie Dru describes Disruption as being "at once a method, a way of thinking, and a state of mind." In challenging us to challenge the constraints of convention, it would have us look beyond, and think outside, the boundary lines of our familiar — all-too-familiar — territory.

Yet Disruption is not simply a matter of seeing through a new lens, or even thinking with a new logic: It is a way of behaving with new actions. Adopting an attitude that embraces change and encourages originality is necessary but far from sufficient: "Disruption is powerful only if it takes action and only if that action moves the brand toward its vision."

Disruption is vision-driven behavior, and that behavior comprises creative actions that create value. Brands are creative not because they speak the language of "lateral thinking," "thinking out of the box," or "thinking like a challenger" but because, fundamentally, they behave creatively, both operationally and in relation to their customers.

The Liberty of Disruption

It is argued that not all brands have the luxury of behaving creatively — for a brand with long-established equities and well-established franchises, disruption, and the presumed chaos that ensues, is risky business. Or that, while perhaps appropriate behavior when radical innovation might be required,

Disruption cannot or should not drive brand management as standard operating procedure. Again, the presumption is that it entails too great a risk factor.

One could counter with the disruptive notion that in the hyperdrive global village that we inhabit — in which news, gossip, fashion, advertising, if not brands themselves, cross borders as quickly as they once crossed the street, creating a surface culture of instantaneous sameness and a psychology of accelerated expectations — no brand, or none with great expectations, has the luxury of not behaving creatively.

Luxury brand owners do not have the liberty of behaving otherwise. Sustaining their brand value — economic, emotional, experiential — has always mandated sustained disruption. They must lead customers; they cannot follow consumers. They must imagine a future of their own creation; they cannot conform to one derived from the outside. They must remain a discovery; they cannot become predictable. Often they must break what is not broken; they cannot risk the complacency of simply protecting the status quo.

Chanel's vision remains visible even as Karl Lagerfeld, who has directed Chanel for 18 years, keeps the brand looking ahead. As the *Sunday Times* of London observed, "Lagerfeld avoids the problem of complacency by constantly renewing himself...surrounding himself with the young and the irreverent...with young guns Prada and Gucci snapping at its heels, the company must move forward."

Perhaps that is why 91 years after Coco Chanel opened her Chanel Mode in Paris and went on to disrupt, literally, the way women dress, the House of Chanel is still alive and very much kicking — with Chanel #5 still the best-selling perfume in the world and "everyone from young London to bourgeois Paris to loaded Middle East...wondering what goodies the fashion house will offer for the autumn." (Jeremy Langmead, *Sunday Times Magazine*, UK October 2001.)

Dogmatic to their brand vision, luxury brands cannot afford to mortgage their future brand value to present brand dogma. It would not be an exaggeration to say that a luxury brand behaving well is always operating at an inflection point — when the prevailing rules of engagement need to be re-evaluated and reframed, and new brand behaviors created and enacted.

At their best, luxury brands create their own inflection points; they do not watch and wait for one to appear on the horizon. Managing a brand at an inflection point is serious business for any brand owner — particularly at a time when a Darwinian "innovate or die" ethic is such a prominent feature of the corporate agenda. For luxury brands, managing at the inflection point is their business, according to a creative logic of their own design.

The Creative Logic of Luxury

Luxury brands are driven by a creative logic, relentlessly pursued, that frames their very business model. In his book *Selling Dreams* (Simon & Schuster, 1999), Gian Luigi Longinotti-Buitoni, former CEO of **Ferrari** North America, cites creativity as the single most important success factor for companies in the "dream" business, "the business of maximizing the added value to finance creativity." Elaborating on the value (and values) of creativity, Buitoni maintains, "Companies cannot rely on market studies or customer clinics to decide what to do. . .to surprise the customers' imagination you must prophesize what they will want tomorrow. . .inspiration must come from within the company. A company must develop at all levels of the organization a culture that actively promotes original experimentation."

Understanding brands as behavior and branding as an organizational activity constitutes a disruptive notion. As a vision-realizing and value-creating process for the entire organization, the creative logic of luxury brands implicitly ruptures the virtual Chinese Great Wall between marketing, the de facto keepers of the brand, and all other organizational disciplines and activities concerned with enacted brand management.

Reversing the logic
of classical marketing

While intensely customer-focused, a luxury brand is a creative-centric brand — internally, driven by a creative culture, inspired by a creative vision, and externally, enacted by creative behavior. As such, the inherently disruptive behavior of luxury brand management effectively reverses the logic of classical marketing, which locates the consumer at the center of the branding universe.

The notion that brands are best built with the voice of the consumer as the principal architect has long been a tenet of the orthodoxy of marketing best practice. By the starkest of contrasts, the architecture of the brand is bred in the organizational bone of luxury brands, not as a creation of the consumer and captive of marketing, but as an organization's sense of self and collective behavior.

With sophisticated marketing methods and research technologies being deployed, yielding a steady-state stream of data, there are promissory notes of "mass customization" and "one-to-one marketing." Yet, this begs the question as to how far a brand should go to make itself in the image of the consumer. At what point does a brand become, not a vision for what can be, but a reflection of what is?

On a more pragmatic level, can the reason for the extraordinarily high new-product failure rate be that marketers are looking to the wrong people (consumers) to make the creative leaps necessary to envision possible futures for a brand, or possible brands for the future? In other words, have brands become so fixated on reflecting the consumer's sense of self that they have lost sight of their own?

In pursuit of the innovation necessary to drive growth and profitability, brand owners might do well to focus a bit less on what the consumer sees and, instead, as Buitoni would have it, to look within for inspiration. Perhaps borrowing a page from Ferrari, arguably the most powerful automotive brand in the world, GM is looking to do just that.

When Robert Lutz, who championed the Viper at **Dodge**, was named vice chairman and head of product development, it was, as the *New York Times* suggested, "with a mandate to reinvigorate the GM design process...to shake the company of its overall stodginess." The move represents a significant organizational discontinuity for a company that "has been known for a reliance on a strategy borrowed from consumer product companies called brand management. In it focus groups and marketing largely dictate how vehicles will appear."

Lutz subscribes to a radically different logic, more akin to that of luxury brands. He says, "I see us being in the art business, art, entertainment and mobile sculpture which coincidentally also happens to provide transportation.... I am not anti-research but I like to have the big idea first and then test it as opposed to using testing, testing, testing to try to come up with the big idea.... Over reliance on research is like trying to drive by looking in the rear view mirror...."

One has only to look at the generic vocabulary with which brands present themselves to detect the insidious impact of marketers "staring too long in the rear view mirror" through the eyes of consumers. With everyone asking the same questions of the same people, is it any wonder that communications, if not products themselves, would blur into a banal tide of homogeneity? An ironic twist of fate that branding, originally devised to decommoditize products — to literally brand a product with a distinctive mark — is returning brands to commodity status.

Far from disrupting old conventions in the pursuit of new possibilities, the excessive cult of the consumer is a reactionary force stifling creative brand behavior. As Dru admonished, "There are limits to being consumer-led.... If you ask consumers what you should do, which product you should launch, expect to get a conventional answer. The unquestioning respect for what the consumer has to say has in fact become an excuse for continued conservatism."

This is not to say that luxury brands are ignorant or dismissive of customers. If anything, the newfound obsession with continuous relationship marketing and other variations on customer relationship management is an old-school practice of luxury brands for whom customer loyalty (and enthusiasm) is among their most valuable assets. Creative brands need a well-defined audience and need to know that audience well, and empathy with its aspirations, values, and behaviors is prerequisite to successful luxury brand management.

Ferrari does not enjoy a 60 percent loyalty rate among its owners because it does not know its customers. In knowing who its customers are and what they want, Ferrari never loses sight of knowing who and what it wants to be. Among all the clients with whom I have worked, none has been as close to the customer as Ferrari — and none has as tenaciously been driven by an internal creative logic. To be customer-focused is not to be led by the nose of the consumer.

Luxury brands behave differently.

The Grammar of Luxury

Luxury is a notoriously relative concept and defining luxury, a notoriously difficult task, susceptible to personal bias and subjective judgment. On one hand, luxury is equated with extravagance, the conspicuous, if not the ridiculous; on the other, it is identified with excellence and cultivation, if not the sublime. That said, regardless of orientation, most definitions default to price-point generalizations and related notions of scale and scarcity.

Yet, to describe the fault line between them by reference to relative price, scale, and availability is as seductive as it is obvious, but ultimately fails to capture the more significant (because more actionable) distinction in brand behavior. To reiterate: Brands are behavior and luxury brands behave differently.

One way of understanding how luxury brands behave (and how such behavior might be relevant to brands and branding in general) is to think in terms of the grammar that informs their behavior. In 1994, Damian O'Malley, my partner at Brand Architecture International, first suggested the concept of

The Grammatical Brand™ — a new brand model predicated on the notion that a generative set of rules implicitly guides all elements of brand behavior. As with the rules of language or games, understanding a brandgrammar™ could then help to decide when a brand behaves well, or badly, when an action adds to brand value and when it diminishes that value. And, as with the rules of language, a brandgrammar must enable the brand to meet unforeseen or novel situations, if it is to be useful.

While each individual brand engenders its own unique grammar — the specific rules governing the behavior of **Armani** are obviously quite different from those for Versace — it is possible to reveal the shared deep-structure grammar by which luxury brands behave — a grammar that is inherently disruptive:

▶ Relentlessly pursuing a *radical conservatism*, they keep one foot firmly grounded in the past while the other provokes their future.

▶ *Inherently playful*, they experiment and innovate in a perpetual game of what-if and what-can-be to avoid predictability.

▶ *Embracing complexity* as a virtue, they recognize that brand value is an emergent system of interwoven behaviors that constitute the total brand experience.

Pursuing a Radical Conservatism

Luxury brands are protagonists of the future with a long memory. Not content to simply ride waves of past success or present trends, they want to create the future tense. They do not just think ahead of a curve of predictable trajectory, they think around corners to places that must be believed to be seen. In this way, creativity is inherently optimistic. When queried as to which of his cars was his most beautiful creation, Enzo Ferrari consistently would remark, "The one I have yet to build."

The big (relatively), iconic (absolutely), and ambitious (always) luxury brands achieve scale and stature not by inertial commitment to conventions of the past and insecurity of the untested what-ifs of the future, but rather by a double-helix strategy of embracing their past while provoking their future. The former without the latter is self-indulgent nostalgia, which ultimately damns a brand with the faint praise of respect without relevance. The latter without the former is visionless hype that may well attract 15 minutes of fame for a brand, but is hardly likely to create sustainable premium value over time. One has only to recall the pathology of dot-com advertising to see the difference between the fame earned over time and fame bought with noise — just as great brands are built over time, not bought overnight.

In the radical conservative world of the luxury brand, any disruption premised on wholesale rejection of the past is tantamount to branding suicide. Great brands do not forget, and the great (and most valuable) icons of luxury — Chanel, Hermes, Rolex, Mercedes, Tiffany — are still trendy after all these years because their sense of self is framed by a remembrance of things past, even as they navigate themselves forward.

If all brands are, in part, memories, luxury brands are the ultimate memory palaces. Many take the notion of a memory palace literally, building museums to keep their legacies of what was, as inspiration to what can be: Bass Ale, Ferrari, Girard Perregaux, Cartier, Steuben, to name but a few.

Sustaining her own brand of disruption within the fashion world for 20 years, Vivienne Westwood expressed how this radical/conservative juxtaposition propels creativity: "It is the very opposite of conservative to seek inspiration from the past for ideas, otherwise you are just swallowing the propaganda of the age in which you live." It would seem that for Ms. Westwood the only tenses that matter are the past (from which she draws) and the future (which she creates).

Playing in the World of Disruption

Nietzsche defined maturity as "having found again the seriousness one had as a child at play." For all their seriousness of purpose, children at play never seem to confuse dogma for truth, convention for certainty, and inertia for success. They have the luxury of living creatively. Play is essentially a creative act, and Disruption is inherently a playful behavior, insofar as it improvises, speculates, experiments, and creates. Informed by rules, play must allow for the unanticipated, the unconventional. It risks, it learns, it reframes behavior as it moves.

It is when one stops playing and assumes the pose and posture of things cast in stone that one stops learning, stops being creative. A luxury brand that forgets how to play risks becoming caricature. Think **Gucci** before CEO Domenico De Sole and designer Tom Ford reinvigorated the Gucci brand. Of the iconic House of Chanel, the *Times of London* said, "What is remarkable is how they have managed to avoid letting the legacy of women so famously uncompromising and startlingly successful become an albatross around their neck."

But play is purposeful as well. In behaving according to a grammar, it is neither ruleless, nor visionless. There is a point to the game, and creativity is not to be confused with an anything-goes attitude or, worse, the oft-applied phrase in brainstorming sessions, "there are no bad ideas." For brands behaving well, there are good and bad ideas, just as there are good and bad moves in a game of chess.

Having worked with the likes of Giorgio Armani, Jean-Paul Guerlain, and Gian Luigi Longinotti-Buitoni, I can say without hesitation that they would find the notion that there are no bad ideas unintelligible. Creativity is not for the lazy or the faint of heart; it is willful behavior requiring integrity, clarity, and self-control. It knows where it wants to go and goes where it wants to go.

Embracing the Virtue of Complexity

Brands are complex, and branding is a complex process. Even a soap powder is no more just the powder in the box than Guinness is just the beer in the glass, or Rolex just the dial on the face of a watch. Levels of brand complexity vary by degree, but are not different in kind.

If there is a difference, it is that luxury brands embrace the complexity of the brand experience, not as a vice to be shunned but as a virtue to be valued. They recognize that a brand's behavior is an experience of irreducible complexity — multidimensional, multilayered, and often polysensual — and it is this very complexity that instills desire and justifies price.

Less is never more

And as with a *grande complication* watch that tells us quite a bit more than the time of day, the pleasure it affords is often derived from the complexity itself. For luxury brands, less is never more. Satisfying the emotions, reason, aesthetics, memory, all at once, is not a simple task, and does not admit of simple solutions.

It should be said that this is by no means an argument for the sort of gratuitous or *fausse complication* espoused by brands lacking in authentic experience. Nor is there anything inherently wrong in the urge to simplify, particularly when the motive is greater clarity of thought and precision of action. But, when reducing complexity for the expedience of reduction, oversimplification becomes an exercise in bad faith. Defining brands as an espoused list of generic functional attributes ("crisp, clean, refreshing" come to mind for beers) and anthropomorphic personality traits ("convivial, accessible, current") might simplify advertising briefs but has little to do with the real world of enacted brands, let alone inspiring great creative. Somehow one doubts that Frank Gehry worked to a brief of "sturdy, stylish, and big," when envisioning the Guggenheim (a remarkable brand in itself) at Bilbao.

When Dru states, "We must refuse to accept simplification and the banalization that ensues," it is a challenge to the conventional logic that equates simpler with better, simplest with best. "For advertising people accustomed to simplifying, that is a rather disruptive thought."

Managing a virtuous, if complex, circle of discovery, desire, and demand, luxury brands are accustomed to just the opposite. As creative brands, they (and their customers) expect, if not demand, that they defamiliarize and recomplexify themselves as a matter of course — and all the more so, the more ubiquitous they become.

The very architecture of luxury brands dictates that they remain works in progress whereby even radical innovations can be accommodated without compromise to the integrity of their vision. Even highly successful icons the likes of Chanel and Vuitton, cannot afford to indulge in the inertia of a closed system, in which customers come to believe they know the whole story. They need to reinvest themselves with the shock of the new — both in product and presentation — if their mystique (and value) is to be sustained. The predictable is antithetical to the creative, and, again, the grammar of luxury is creative by design for both creator and customer alike.

Self-control of the retail experience is yet another embrace of complexity. The new religion of environmental marketing is old philosophy for many luxury brands, for whom their behavior at retail is inextricably threaded through the enacted brand experience. Because the pleasure principle by which they operate often applies as much to their purchase as to their consumption, luxury brands like to build rooms of their own in which the brand experience can be brought to life in context, and its past brought to light in the present.

Consider the new **Hermes** store in Tokyo's Ginza district, commissioned to envision "the story of the company's 165-year journey from its origins in saddlery to today's temple of luxury." The store itself is a measure of an embrace of complexity, as well as a radical embrace of the past — "La Maison Hermes is not just a retail fantasy, but an exhibition space for contemporary art, a museum, a cinema and the ultimate manifestation of the contemporary luxury goods market...a multi-layered shopping experience." (Art of Glass, *GQ* [British Edition], 2001).

Of his glass-brick "vertical water" vision, architect Renzo Piano said: "Ultimately glass is a metaphor of Hermes, it is a material with a deep memory...it is the limit between the rational and the sensual that I would like to transgress." Transgression of such limits in relentless pursuit of a creative vision is precisely the sort of complex behavior that propels luxury brands forward.

Disruption at the Premium Nexus

"I was told that an impassable gulf divided the Rich and the Poor. . .governed by different laws by different manners with no thoughts or sympathies in common; with an innate inability of mutual comprehension." as stated by Benjamin Disraeli.

The "impassable gulf" could well fit most marketers' description of the distance dividing luxury from other brands. But the gulf is narrowing in ways significant to the future of brands and branding:

In pursuit of scale, luxury continues to open its lens toward a more "democratic elitism" via the inherently disruptive behavior of brand migration — to new markets, products, and platforms.

In pursuit of margins, mass brands continue to aspire ever upwards toward a more elite democracy positioning via equally disruptive business and brand behaviors of acquisition, extension, and/or reinvention.

With the proliferation of "bridge lines," fashion affords a notable example — and Armani has long provided a case study in democratizing a luxury brand through sustained disruption. Since opening his own design boutique in 1975, Armani has developed into a US$ 1 billion brand with global reach and influence.

Perpetually at play with the boundaries of the brand, Armani is a model of successfully navigating the fault lines between aspiration and accessibility, between past and future. Take the creation of A/X Armani Exchange, which brought Armani sensibility to basics in the early 1990s, giving impetus to the "simple chic" phenomenon, or the move to the Web with armaniexchange.com in 1996, ahead of all other major designers. The opening of Armani Casa in Milan, New York, and Los Angeles takes the Armani brand experience still further — into the realm of home design. The next disruptive act with which to migrate Armani is rumored to be hotels. It would appear that the master of the classic cut is also a master of the creative leap.

Queried back in 1991 as to what the future of fashion would be, Armani responded, "If I were a prophet I would be able to answer you. But I am not. . . . I truly believe, however, that items based on good design and high quality will be in demand, otherwise we would be living in a homogeneous society.... It is a question of time to learn how to go from a high brand to one of a broader scale." In creating their future, creative brands tend to be their own self-fulfilling prophets.

The automobile sector is another tangible expression of the emergent premium nexus, as automakers, be they American, Japanese, or European, converge in the apparent promised land where volume and margin collide. The Japanese are fond of creating entirely new brands — Nissan's Infinity, Honda's Acura, and Toyota's Lexus. The Europeans introduce new models. Mercedes has lowered the price floor without lowering its prestige pedestal, while Renault seeks to leverage its new high-end cars to try to move its company image upscale.

Volkswagen's plans for a US$75,000 entry to compete with Mercedes S-class is perhaps the most telling, if not the most extreme, case of convergence — iconic of simplicity, of utility, of frugality, the venerable VW must now learn to behave according to the grammar of luxury. As *Motor Trend* commented, "Lexus developed new and often exclusive dealership arrangements, including special training on how to manage the relationship marketing process and high customer service expectations that are so much a part of retailing luxury. VW will have to step up to compete."

It is also apparent that convergence is by no means limited to high-fashion or high-ticket sectors. The world of consumer goods is increasingly populated with premium brands whose behavior has more in common with luxury than with mass brands (and whose brand management might be better served by the creative logic of luxury than by the classical practices of soap-powder marketing).

Häagen-Dazs, once a regional U.S. luxury ice cream, has emerged as a US$1 billion multiline brand marketed in over 30 countries. The luxury brand that helped to disrupt an entire category in the 1980s, both with product-based pleasures and with pleasure-based advertising, continues to be a creative force for the entire sector. When Häagen-Dazs enters a new category such as sorbet or gelato, other companies generally follow.

With its acquisition by Unilever, **Ben & Jerry's** ice cream, and its signature brand of idiosyncratic flavors and equally signature brand of experiential marketing, is following suit. With its legacy of hard-core classical brand management, Unilever would hardly qualify as a usual suspect for Ben & Jerry's.

But, as Walt Freese, Unilever's chief marketing officer for Ben & Jerry's Homemade, explains, "Unilever executives have been actively supportive of our mission and in fact want to learn from us." According to *Advertising Age*, in selecting Freese, "Unilever was looking for somebody who had expertise in 'experience marketing,' a depth of consumer relationship that goes beyond a positioning statement.... Freese hopes to drive the brand through new platforms beyond line extensions and to expand internationally and into new channels."

When the mega-marketers begin to sit up and take notice of the potential inherent in adding premium players to their portfolio, one is likely to see some formidable bridges being constructed over that once seemingly "impassable gulf."

In this brave and disruptive new world of convergence, at the premium nexus, understanding the brandgrammar of luxury may well be an imperative for all those concerned with building great brands. If, as Scott Bedbury, senior vice president of marketing at Starbucks, once observed, the common ground of all great brands is "to be the protagonists for each of their entire categories. . .it raises the bar, it adds a greater sense of purpose to the experience," then luxury brands may one day be judged as the great protagonists of our age. A disruptive notion indeed.

DISRUPTION

TOMORROW

In a foreseeable way, the fourth and last part of this book tackles the future. We have applied Disruption to the future of our business. It is our hope that it will inspire you to apply Disruption to the future of yours.

Over time, we have had the opportunity to rethink the Disruption process and the role of each phase. Initially conceived as a system to help challenge conventions, we have repositioned Disruption's focus to identifying and creating new visions. In Disruption's infancy, Vision served as a road map with a preestablished and clear destination. Now, visions are not intuitively known in advance. The goal of our work with conventions is to help us imagine and create new visions.

As a result, we have evolved our thinking on the role of conventions – they are no longer exclusively negative. Instead of being prejudices, they can lead to insights — human truths that we bring to light concerning the everyday life of people. **Richard Monturo**, head of our planning department in Los Angeles, explains in Chapter 17 how we unearth these hidden insights that often escape us. Moreover, he shows us how brands gain in substance when they embrace new visions springing from profound insights.

Chapter 18 is devoted to what we call "Connections." Over the past 20 years, in countries such as France, South Africa, and Holland, we have been working toward a convergence of resources that enables us to maximize our effectiveness. From direct marketing to internal communications, from advertising to design, from public relations to sales promotion, and from sponsoring to nonprofit marketing, event marketing, and consumer magazines, we set out to make group companies work together in a synergy that simply makes sense.

Part of this process implied moving beyond the traditional strategy, and understanding that the key is to manage interactions between the various disciplines. In the final stages of aligning the different companies, one imperative is to find transversal ideas. You could call them media-neutral or, better yet, media-infinite ideas. They bounce from one discipline to another and the resulting effect increases the power of the idea tenfold.

The time has come to adopt a more scientific approach, to approximate less and become more methodological. This is the goal of Connections. Connections planning, a discipline that seeks to identify and optimize every point of contact between a consumer and a brand, was launched from our New York office under the aegis of **Carl Johnson**, our worldwide COO, and **Nick McLean**, the worldwide head of this new department. Nick wrote this chapter.

Where Disruption is a method to help define the future of a brand, Connections is a way of thinking to make sure we have the ideas and the means to get there. The goal of this initiative is to better connect the brand with the consumer, touching on all the possible connection points (from advertising to street events, from television shows to loyalty programs, coming full circle back to advertising). In other words, the goal is to define how we connect the different disciplines, and how and when to use them. In the future, every part of the relationship between our clients and their customers will be our business.

Isaac Newton said, "There are more people who build walls than there are who build bridges." With Connections, we build bridges.

In the end, this new form of planning will help disciplines interact with one another in ways we have never seen before.

Both of these initiatives — Disruption and Connections — enlarge our field of intervention. The combination of these two disciplines changes our business approach from top to bottom.

So, naturally, we conclude with the role of the agency. This is the subject of Chapter 19, written by **Damian O'Malley**, one of the founders of our Brand Architecture company, and **Robert Birge**, worldwide director in charge of group development.

Robert Birge, renegade of Boston Consulting Group, joined us several months ago to help redefine our business model. We briefed him with the help of a (particularly immodest) quote from Jerry Garcia, the late leader of the Grateful Dead: "You do not merely want to be considered just the best of the best; you want to be considered the only ones who do what you do."

Robert and Damian discuss how Disruption and Connections can be used as points of differentiation from our competitors. In combining these two disciplines, we move one step closer to being "the only ones who do what we do."

"We don't see things
as they are,
we see things
as we are."

ANAÏS NIN

17. INSIGHTS

How do insights help in disrupting conventional thinking and behaviors? How can insights lead one to imagine disruptive visions? In this chapter, we examine the role insights — into consumer thinking and behavior, category definitions and dynamics, business models and revenue streams, product attributes and benefits, and brand associations — play in disrupting conventions and creating new visions for brands and businesses.

To do this, we will need to clarify the distinction between a true insight and mere data or observations masquerading with this name tag. We can then demonstrate the catalytic role that an insight plays in creating Disruption. We will follow up by looking at some up-front activities that can facilitate doing the homework necessary to discovering those profound and actionable insights that are so helpful to making Disruption an organic process.

Raw materials for disruptive visions

Without the power of a profound insight fueling it, Disruption would be little more than contrarian thinking without an endgame. Insights are the raw materials for disruptive visions, and, as with most raw materials, better-quality materials assembled with precision and craftsmanship will ultimately yield better-quality finished goods. What is true for great cooking, fine tailoring, luxury cars, and even great music (from classical instrumentation to hip-hop samples) is also true for brand strategy and the communications that result.

This may seem a hopelessly retrograde Industrial Age thought for a creative practice in a knowledge-based economy. But some things do not change. Creating truly disruptive thinking, whether cultural or commercial, requires similar or greater attention to quality and detail. Otherwise, it is "garbage in, garbage out" for your brand, and your business.

An Introductory Rant: Stop "Duh" Insights

Insight is a word that gets floated about quite liberally in marketing circles, often applied to bits of trivia about people, products, categories, businesses, or brands that say nothing new or offer no deeper meaning about what is already common knowledge. We call these the "Duh" Insights — those upon which weeks and months of market research, analysis, brainstorming, and countless people-hours are exerted, but are so obvious and superficial as to be unworthy of the term "insight." Many of the "duhs" that we have encountered are either generic statements of condition about people or category-sell attributes. For example:

People "Duhs"

- People lead increasingly busy lives.
- Teenagers are rebellious.
- People want to be empowered.
- Employees need to watch out for the boss.
- Men and women are different.
- You are your (clothes, car, makeup, house, brands, any category at all).

Category "Duhs"

- Clothing should be comfortable.
- Technology increases productivity.
- Technology leads to a better future.
- Alcoholic beverages are a social lubricant.
- Soft drinks are refreshing.
- Food should taste good.
- Car buyers are increasingly concerned about quality.
- Finances are important and serious.

This is not to say that one cannot create great brand ideas using these statements as a foundation. Much of the best marketing, communications, and advertising take many of these seemingly ordinary facts and twist them in a new way in the execution. However, the burden is placed on the talents of creative professionals to convey a basic fact in a new way, rather than having it leaping from a rich insight at the outset.

Using the "garbage in, garbage out" philosophy, this kind of generic, bland thinking more typically leads to generic, bland marketing communications, especially when the "Duh" Insight is parroted right back to the consumer with the only connection to the brand or product being the logo. Consider these environmental pollutants that give the practice of marketing a bad name:

- "Me and the guys in our favorite place" beer commercials.
- "I am" statements affirming one's self-esteem.
- Tabletop fast-food footage spliced with "bite and smile" people (lately, due to microsegmentation, replaced by the same guys from the beer ads).
- Outrageously hip young people doing idiosyncratic, "extreme" things.
- "I love my car more than life" acts of devotion.
- "Glass and metal" technological or financial "cities of the future."
- Indirect, obtuse connections between a product and "your busy lifestyle."
- Anything in which the future has been fetishized as a utopian paradise, "enabled by solutions."

You have probably seen some of these before. You may even have asked yourself, "What were they thinking?" Perhaps "they" were not thinking at all. In their defense, coming from someone who has been guilty of some of these sins, the likely scenario is that many marketing professionals do not have the time or the resources to dig deeper through the information pile and excavate the true insight.

The True Insight: A Deeper Version of the Truth

If the "Duh" Insight is superficial and assumptive, there is a level of thinking just beyond that looks into specific, profound truths about people, categories, products, businesses, brands, or all of these, in a fresh and stimulating way. We call this the *True Insight*.

The True Insight is not some egghead academic factoid that you need to be a rocket scientist to figure out. In fact, one should be wary if highly specialized language is used to dress up the obvious. It is not some obscure piece of trivia that has no relevance to everyday life.

What the True Insight is all about is the surprising, "how did they know that?" revelation of the hidden truth that we all know, but often are not able to articulate or acknowledge. It is unique, it is revelatory, and it is extremely compelling in its adherence to the truth about the human condition. In his first book, *Disruption*, Jean-Marie Dru wrote about the use of consumer insights as a source of inspiration:

"Consumer insights are observations about life. They are a little like stolen moments, fleeting forays into real life, revelations of the way people think or what they do.... If an advertiser accurately portrays what you are feeling or thinking, you are already won over. We are always drawn toward those who understand what makes us tick."

As relevant as this is even today, we do not mean to imply that the True Insight comes solely from study of the consumer. Insights can come from anywhere there is something new to be learned and something interesting to be communicated. This is a mistake many marketers have made in the last few years, relying only on consumer insight to drive strategy, without giving equal attention to insights into the business, brand, product, or category.

Your strategy is showing

The result is an increasingly annoying school of "consumer psychobabble" advertising and marketing language, in which consumer insight becomes a substitute for something to say about the brand. If you can imagine what the focus groups were like while looking at the communication, then consumer insight has taken way too much of its share of the total message. The inside joke says it all: "Pardon me, but your strategy is showing."

From the creative revolution of the 1960s well into the early 1990s, a more complete view of sourcing True Insight was the norm. Doyle Dane Bernbach found disruptive insights in apparent business or product weaknesses — VW's car, Avis's market share, Chivas Regal's price. Visa took its business strategy of ubiquitous distribution from a common perception to universal acceptance — for card and for card carrier.

More recently, corporate values are as much a source of insight as the consumer, and they are often more differentiating. Apple, Virgin, The Body Shop, Southwest Airlines, and IKEA are all examples of values-driven brands that subsequently found they shared those values with consumers. Did they conduct exhaustive polling to determine their brand visions? No, they dug deep into their souls and expressed their own values with sincerity and conviction. As people identified with those values, they identified with those brands.

The True Insight is not confined to brands and marketing. On the contrary, today's popular culture often gets there far ahead of marketers. Shame on us for falling behind, but there is something to be learned from their astute examples of being right on the pulse of the culture (I apologize in advance for the exclusively American examples, but I am an American planner doing American advertising for American people, so I am a bit more comfortable working from my homeland):

- The American family, who shines on the surface while hiding deep interior flaws, is dramatically depicted in films like *American Beauty* and *Ordinary People*. In a more comic vein, *The Simpsons* and *King of the Hill* are honest explorations of real family issues, even as TV cartoons.
- The African-American experience — long exaggerated or exploited in advertising — finds a richer, multidimensional voice in everything from rap (deemed by Chuck D of Public Enemy as "the CNN of black America") to Spike Lee's film work to the variety TV show *Showtime at the Apollo*.
- The dehumanizing consequences of rank-and-file corporate America are sent up hilariously in the comic strip "Dilbert," the documentaries of Michael Moore, and films like *Office Space* and *Clockers*.
- News stories capture the public imagination through revelation of real-life human drama concerning the likes of Princess Diana, Monica Lewinsky, Elian Gonzalez, and the life-and-death struggles of police and firefighters at the World Trade Center.
- The rebellion of youth is expressed in its purest form in the cultures of WTO protesters, rave and dance music, the Burning Man festival, and the interlinked skateboard, surfing, and snowboarding communities.
- Speaking of communities, the Internet has been a leading force in bringing together borderless organic communities, from the early days of Usenet and MUDs to the Linux development community and public forums such as Slashdot and the one we have developed for the FCUK company in the UK.

All of these examples are notable for their spontaneity and naturalness, avoiding the clichés of presenting the world as we want it to be in favor of presenting the world as it really is. Can marketers do it as well?

Yes, to a point. Because marketing communications combine the desire to connect with people physically and personally with the need to sell the sponsor's product or service, we walk a fine line between respecting the audience's personal space and exploiting insights for financial gain. The best marketing examples of using insight to disrupt conventions succeed because they reflect the right truth relevant to what is being offered without crossing the line into overstating the product's role in that truth or drawing attention to the discovery of the insight itself. (e.g., "See, we know this about you. So buy our product.")

The True Insight in Marketing — Some Examples

As mentioned, disruptive insights can come from the deeper truth about the consumer, the business, the category, the product, or the brand. Some of our favorites (both agency-created and from our peers) include the following.

Insights into the Consumer

- The "Got Milk" campaign took the absence of the product as the source of its immediate value, reversing decades of "milk is good for you" advertising by dramatizing the role milk plays in complementing cereal, cupcakes, peanut butter sandwiches, even cats.

- The New York Lottery's "Hey, You Never Know" advertising changes the emotional focus of the game from the moment of winning, which only a select few experience, to the fantasy of winning, which is universal.

- VW's "Drivers Wanted" campaign connects idiosyncratic consumer attitudes and behaviors with key vehicles, from the slackers and goofballs in Golf ads ("Da Da Da" and "Mr. Roboto") to the not-so-confident grown-ups for Passat ("Five Second Rule").

- Our Paris agency has shifted the market positioning of the TGV high-speed train based on digging deeper into the end benefit of what it delivers to people. From a train to a transport offer. From speed to seamlessness. From saving time to mastering time. In the end, what people want is beyond the functional solution of getting from here to there; they need to be back in charge of their schedule, and TGV delivers that better than air or car transport.

- For Chivas and Martell, the challenge was to appeal to men in their early thirties who feel that whiskey or cognac is old-fashioned and meant for an older generation. These newly grown-up men are in a life-transition period. They have left their wild days behind, are not yet ready to settle down, but are beginning to embrace the realities and pleasures of being mature adults. The insight was about how to talk to these men who have reached that difficult transition age (one foot on each side of the age chasm): seduction and wit for Martell (with an alluring French femme fatale), and complicity, irreverence, and humor for Chivas (with the "When you know" campaign).

- Today, more than ever, people want to be in control, whether it is in control of money, family life, health, or business. For the last 20 years, the usual strategy for low-alcohol beers has been to not focus on the reduced alcohol level, but to insist on its high-quality taste. Real men want real beer. For Lingen's Blond in the Netherlands, we have shifted the focus to something more in line with today's expectations: "Everything under control."

Insights into the Business

- The previously mentioned strategy of turning a weakness into a strength — for example, **Avis**'s number two position or Visa's commonness — continues to find resonance in such campaigns as EarthLink's "Real Internet" (as opposed to the packaged AOL version) and the repackaging of Kmart's "Blue Light Special" from tacky retail ploy to an icon of American thriftiness.
- **Dell** and **Charles Schwab** turned their unique, consumer-centric business models from operational assets to consumer drivers by respectively leveraging ease of doing business and "creating a world of smarter investors."
- In Europe, we have redirected **Danone** from being in the business of marketing healthy products (yogurt, bottled water) to being in the business of health. With the creation of the Danone Institute, Danone has become an advocate of health in the broader sense, opening up new business opportunities and a deeper meaning for the brand with consumers across the continent.

Insights into the Category

- To launch **PlayStation 2** in the United States, we depicted the futuristic world of "PS9," which framed PS2 as the beginning of the future — a fine ad strategy. The category effect is even more ingenious: The classic technology strategy of freezing the market by preannouncing an impending update establishes long-term platform leadership in a category devoted to the latest release, pushing Sega out of the hardware business and setting Nintendo back several years. (Time will tell, however, with the upcoming entrance of Microsoft into the category.)
- **Nissan Altima** borrowed imagery from the luxury-car category (audaciously from rival Toyota's Lexus campaign) to establish quality credentials in the midsize segment. While not a new approach, the attention to detail in the advertising rubbed off on the car itself.
- The gas station chain **Total** observed what would, on the surface, be a "Duh" Insight: that all gas stations are the same. However, the deeper insight was to call attention to this consumer perception overtly in communication as the means to differentiate Total's products and services in France. Thus, parity became the foil to a perceived superior offering.

Insights into the Product

- To demonstrate the Visualizer feature of **Apple**'s iTunes while conveying the breadth of music applications, real Visualizer imagery was backed up with unique musical offerings, all instructing people that creating your own CDs was as easy as "Rip, Mix, Burn."

- The twice-winning Grand Effie campaign for **NYNEX** used puns on some of the more unique categories in the comprehensive NYNEX directory to convey the idea that "if it is out there, it is in here."
- What happens when you discover that skin naturally contains an antiwrinkle constituent that diminishes with time? There is no longer a need to vie with competitors for the latest scientific formula. As the **Nivea** Visage campaign explains, all you have to do is give this natural ingredient back to the skin. This is the magic of Q10 cream, which has become worldwide leader in its segment in the space of a year.
- Automobile tires obviously wear out the more distance you cover. So what is important is not so much the mileage — how many miles you think you can drive — but the fact that the tire's performance (for example, road-holding) declines as little as possible with use. Hence, our tag line in Europe, that reflects the **Michelin** corporate vision: *"Les performances les plus belles sont celles qui durent"* (the only real performances are the ones that last).

Insights into the Brand

- When we were given the task of relaunching **Apple**, upon the return of Steve Jobs, the key to communicating the brand's vision did not come from consumer perception (a troubled company, but one that people wanted to succeed) or category differentiation (the last holdout from Wintel hegemony). It came from the soul of the brand itself — a company that "thinks different" not by making computers, but by making "tools for creative professionals."

The Catalytic Role Insights Play in Disruption

A simple analogy can sum up what we have said so far:

"Duh" Insights are to Convention as True Insights are to Disruption.

Very simply, the deeper you go to get to the truth about the consumer, business, category, product, or brand, the more likely the disruptiveness of your vision for communicating the brand's promise.

We have often talked about Disruption as "creating a larger share of the future" for brands and businesses. It is important here to characterize what we mean by "the future" while we map out Disruption on a time continuum.

We have plotted this continuum starting in the here and now, where the consumer benefit from a brand is largely a degree of relevance, or how it fits into a person's life. As we move along the continuum toward something we call "15 minutes into the future," the brand does not just fit into someone's life, it enhances it in new ways. Further along, in the "near future," the brand does not just enhance someone's life, it changes that life for the better. At the extreme end of the spectrum are brand visions that do not just change individual lives, but that change the lives of many people, for a disruptive impact on society as a whole.

An example of this can be found in the evolution of wireless telephones. Wireless telephones originally found their way into the hands of mobile business people, who often had to get to the nearest phone to do their jobs. In this iteration, the personal mobile phone fit into the routine of mobile professionals who needed to get in touch. This subsequently enhanced the lives of mobile business people who were now able to reach out and were able to be reached. As the technology decreased in cost and spread to consumers, the mobile telephone changed ordinary people's lives by allowing them to converge their personal and professional lives. Ultimately, the concept of a phone changed from it being a location-based to a person-based instrument. The recent use of mobile phones to connect people who were affected by the terrorist attacks on the United States shows the overarching impact the mobile telephone has had on society at large. The insight? That by changing the definition of the telephone from a device at a fixed location to a personal communicator, the wireless phone connects everyone to everything that matters in their lives, not just to what they need to perform at their jobs.

THE FUTURE CONTINUUM. EXAMPLE: WIRELESS TELEPHONY

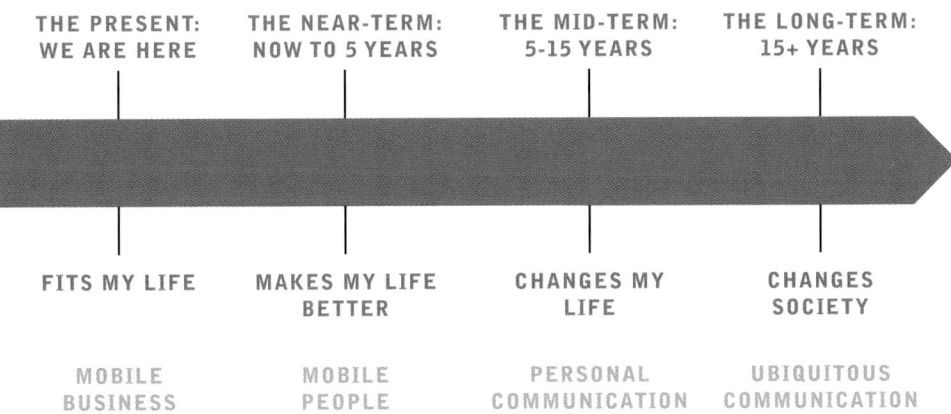

If you can place your brand or product in the context of what it might promise in the future in terms of enhancing or changing individual lives — or changing society as a whole — then the discovery of insights to that end can disrupt the conventions of today toward the vision of tomorrow.

Apple made machines of computation into machines of imagination. PlayStation made children's games into games for your inner child. The catalytic effect of the true insight is as powerful as you can imagine it into the future.

Methods to Help Uncover True Insights

Bill Bernbach once said, "We turn knowledge into insights." At the nexus between strategic and creative expression, the source of insights comes from the collective knowledge of those charged with creating the brand. But let us back up a minute. Where does knowledge come from? How do we know what we know and learn what we learn? These are not Confucian riddles; a clear linearity is present in research and analysis:

THE PATHWAY TO INSIGHT

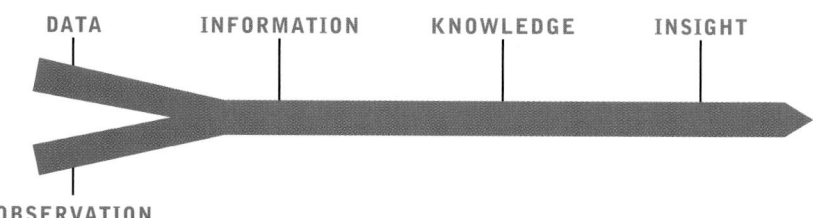

It is a long road from the raw analysis of market research to finding an actionable insight. It is critical that the gathering of data and observations be rigorous and comprehensive. Do everything right, leave no stone unturned, and you start on the right path toward the True Insight.

Unfortunately, many of us stop at the information stage without asking *why* after we have uncovered *what*. By doing so, we are in danger of having a merely linear reaction to the findings. For example, if we start with focus groups to learn that people want their clothes to be comfortable, do we bother to determine what "comfortable" means?

Knowing what and why, the pathway from knowledge to insight requires even greater diligence, expanding into "what we can do about it" and "how can we do it?" In our network, we utilize a toolbox of methods and exercises designed not just to get the information, but to convert it into knowledge and, ultimately, into insight.

Our toolbox is filled with activities and practices we have developed or adapted ourselves and feel comfortable working with, but it is fairly easy to assemble your own toolbox of approaches that move you from data to insight.

Consumer Practices

Many traditional research methods — focus groups, attitude and usage studies, attribute research, segmentation — can be made to be more disruptive simply by using them in systematic combinations. For instance, segmentation combined with ethnographic research into prototypical representatives of the segments can help you make the leap from what is on paper to what is going on in the real world. Examining links and paradoxes among different methods, you can make leaps into consumer behavior and attitudes that isolated methodologies may not uncover.

In addition, many marketers treat their consumers like guinea pigs, as subjects to be examined and manipulated. However, we regard most consumers as thoughtful human beings, so we try to involve them in our development, using collaborative methods for everything from concept statement construction to advertising creative development. As long as you use this kind of consumer-centric input with the proper filters — they are there to inspire, not dictate — you can ensure relevance and maybe even move on to transformation strategy and more quickly and successfully involving the audience in their brand.

Business and Category

Rule number one of looking at the business is to determine the structure and effectiveness of the business model. Where does the brand or the company stand? How do they make money? From where do they source business? How do they sell through product into the channel? What does the purchase cycle look like? How does the company actually operate?

What does success look like?

My favorite question is one that my colleague, Tom Carroll, always exasperates us with when we are in the throes of a communications project (but it really helps): "What does success look like?"

Is the goal share or volume? Category position or segment leadership? Brand awareness or purchase consideration? Push through the channel or pull through the consumer?

If you uncover a disruptive insight, it is critical, if you have any hope of selling it through the organization, to evaluate not just its communications potential but the potential impact on the business. Will the company have to change entrenched practices that it might not otherwise be able to? How can the company maintain short-term revenue goals while creating that share of the future we all seek?

The communications industries have lost a lot of respect in business circles, because fewer and fewer of us have the ability or interest to take the whole view of our practices across the business model. Being professional and being creative are not mutually exclusive. On the contrary, they combine to form the most ingenious communications solutions to vexing business problems.

Product

Contrary to popular belief, the Unique Selling Proposition is not dead. However, the classic definition that relies on a differentiating product attribute to support a brand proposition has outlived its usefulness in a world of product parity, in which a host of competing brands have reached a level of excellence that makes product differences harder and harder for consumers to experience themselves.

In the 1960s creative revolution, the practice of selling whatever minute difference Brand X had over Brand Y evolved into a more holistic approach to what Bill Bernbach advised: "Find a simple story in the product and present it in an articulate, intelligent and persuasive way." Leo Burnett went beyond the simple story, advising his colleagues to look for the "inherent drama" in the product.

Story. Drama. The USP has grown up from its roots in product attributes and "product as hero" to make the product the protagonist in a more complete narrative. Storytelling is how we communicate as human beings. What better way to make products relevant than to bring that human capacity to what is for sale?

Brand

A lot of the activity people undertake to uncover brand insights looks at the consumer's relationship to the brand. We do not need to go into all of the practices that we undertake to characterize what consumers think of brands; they are so common in the marketing profession that we would merely be redundant.

However, it is surprising how little effort we take to uncover insights behind the brand that come from the company that has created it. We believe a company's culture, expertise, and history have as much bearing on a brand as the relationship the company has with consumers. Would Apple be Apple if it were not for Steve Jobs? What makes FedEx so absolutely, positively reliable if not the operational delivery of the promise? What would Absolut be without its Swedish heritage and the simplicity and steadfastness that are engrained in the Scandinavian culture?

We pair all brand work we do with the consumer with a thorough excavation of the values of the company behind the brand. These values, when consistent with those of the brand's audience, can create long-standing common ground between brand and consumer that transcends product and category differentiation or consumer insight.

The methods you actually employ while uncovering insight are based on your own expertise and comfort level. The principles behind those methods — comprehensiveness, ingenuity, and professionalism — are universal.

Summary: The Truth Shall Set You Free

The Convention/Disruption/Vision model is a useful framework for imagining new brand visions. But it is only a framework. The application of deep, rich insights into the relationship between people and brands and the contextual factors surrounding the relationship switches on this static framework into active, vibrant life.

Insights take work. The work can be frustrating, lengthy, and sometimes futile. But for those rare moments when the insight is profound and true, the connection to a disruptive brand vision becomes clear and obvious to everyone on the team. "Duh" becomes "wow" and, for a few precious moments, the practice of marketing moves from science to art. Those are the moments we all work for, and they should be nurtured and cherished.

CONNECTIONS THEORY WHEEL

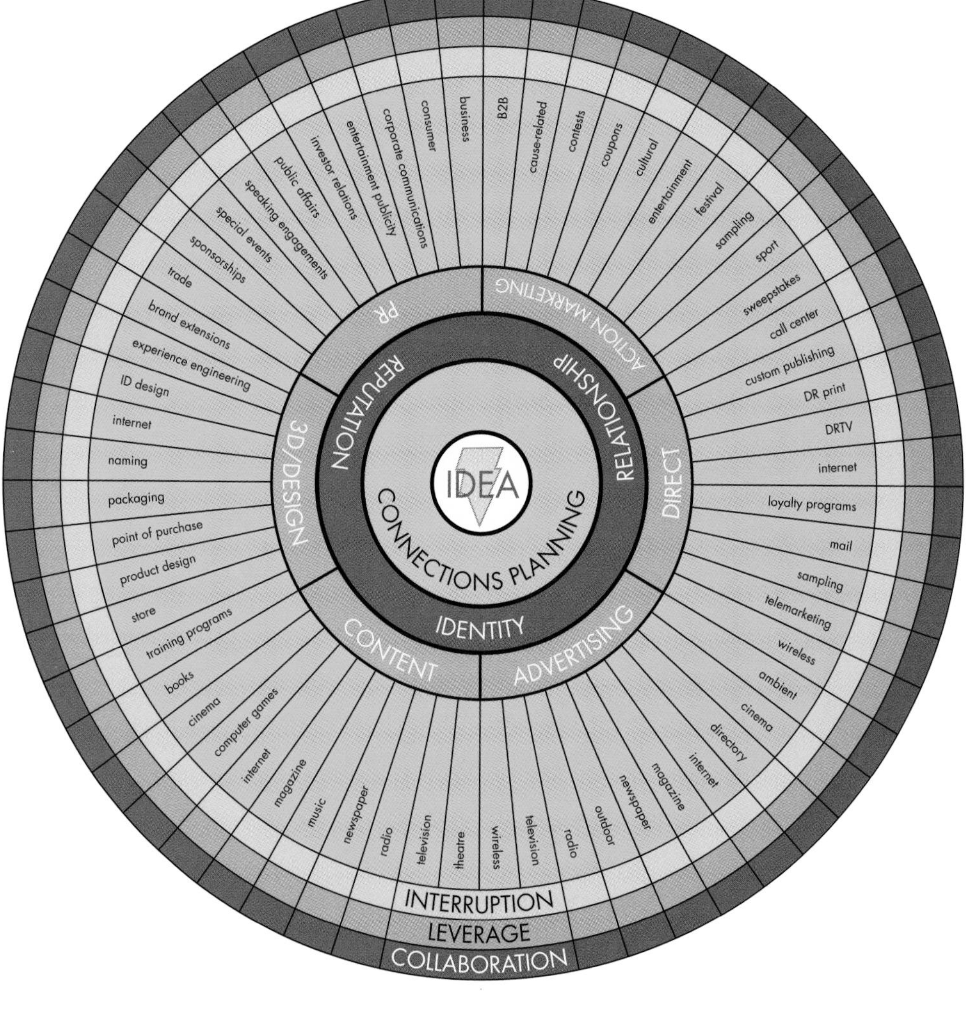

IDEA
CONNECTIONS PLANNING
REPUTATION
RELATIONSHIP
IDENTITY
PR
ACTION MARKETING
DIRECT
ADVERTISING
CONTENT
3D/DESIGN
business
consumer
corporate communications
entertainment publicity
investor relations
public affairs
speaking engagements
special events
sponsorships
trade
brand extensions
experience engineering
ID design
internet
naming
packaging
point of purchase
product design
store
training programs
books
cinema
computer games
internet
magazine
music
newspaper
radio
television
theatre
wireless
television
radio
outdoor
newspaper
magazine
internet
directory
cinema
ambient
wireless
telemarketing
sampling
mail
loyalty programs
internet
DRTV
DR print
custom publishing
call center
sweepstakes
sport
sampling
festival
entertainment
cultural
coupons
contests
cause-related
B2B
INTERRUPTION
LEVERAGE
COLLABORATION

18. CONNECTIONS

Media consumption has changed more in the past 3 years than in the previous 30 years. Accompanying this shift in media consumption have been fundamental shifts in consumer behavior: the way we shop, the way we search for information, and the way we communicate. In short, the way we connect. Despite all this, the reality is that there has been a considerable lack of development in the evolution of the advertising services industry over the last 50 years. Beyond the introduction of account planning at the start of the 1970s, and the separation of media planning and buying into media agencies during the late 1980s, little in the way of structure and process has changed in agencies.

The modern communications agency has as much to do with distributing the big idea as with creating that idea in the first place. In other words, it does not matter how great your message is if no one comes in contact with it. With an increasing palette of choices, marketers are left at a loss: what to use, in what order, and in what way?

The proliferation of channels and the obsession with results-based communication planning requires an immediate upgrading of the tools and processes used by marketers in order to still be able to reach their target audiences. We are proposing the formation of a new marketing discipline called "connections planning," born to disrupt the conventions of marketing and help marketers make intelligent choices in today's environment. In this chapter, we will take a look at some of the conventions of the marketing world and the way that communications agencies do business, with the intent of showing how connections planning will disrupt the theory and practice of connecting with consumers.

Marketing Conventions

Disruption happens every day in every field of endeavor; the world in which marketers operate is no exception. Over the past 20 years, the conventions of marketing have been broken in increasingly rapid succession. The conventions of marketing in the United States congealed by the early 1960s. Postwar prosperity had created a seemingly monolithic population with similar tastes, needs, and desires. Three television networks broadcasted advertising-supported content that kept living rooms occupied across the country every night. Magazine, newspaper, radio, and outdoor advertising continued to feature prominently in American life as it had before the war, with content tailored to the idealized nuclear family: the local newspaper for Dad, *Good Housekeeping* magazine for Mom, pop music on the radio for the kids. Outdoor advertising reached the whole family during outings in the car on the weekends.

The modern advertising agency developed in this conventional environment, as did the modern media department. Agencies were paid on media commission, and the buying and selling of media became a convention unto itself. In the case of television, with a limited number of choices, conventions ruled the day, such as the surefire success of buying prime-time television, the time block after dinner and before bedtime.

The conventions of marketing — a monolithic population, reachable using a few reliable media channels, at the same time every day, with quality content — did not erode over time. They were disrupted.

The question of "who"

By the 1980s, the American population no longer seemed so easy to target. Diversity of race, income, marital status, household composition, and even tastes turned marketing on its head. Probably the greatest single factors in the creation of this newly realized diversity (beyond immigration) were the innovations in database technologies that made it possible for marketers and social scientists to collect and analyze population data like never before. With a new awareness of our individual differences on the grandest of scales, sociologists tried to create new conventions to explain the diversity.

The invention of yuppies (young urban professionals) was quickly followed by more dubious designations, such as buppies (black urban professionals) and dinkys (double income, no kids yet). Audience fragmentation has continued to accelerate to such a degree that PRIZM, the media research company, now uses 15 different social groups and 62 different clusters to describe American consumers. And yet, many media planners at advertising agencies continue to use these standard target definitions to identify whom they want to reach. The question of "who" is becoming increasingly difficult to answer.

"When" is becoming irrelevant.

The advent of the Internet in the 1990s revealed that the media market had always been in a state of disruption, just a slower one. It took radio 38 years to reach 50 million households in the United States. Television took only 13 years. And the Internet took a mere 5 years to reach half of the households nationwide. Technological innovation has made American life asynchronous. Because we can send e-mail anywhere, anytime, work is omnipresent. A 1999 AOL Roper Starch study revealed that 33 percent of all Internet users check their e-mail while on vacation. Personal video recorders such as TiVo (and even VCRs) have made it possible to watch prime-time television anytime. The "when" is becoming irrelevant.

"Where" now means everywhere.

Channel diversification is a result of audience fragmentation and technological innovation. With technological adoption speeding up, the number of content choices for the public grew quickly as well. From the three television channels one could find on broadcast television in the 1960s, there have grown to be more than 200 available to the cable or satellite subscriber today. Magazine racks groan under the weight of titles as diverse as the people they reach, from *Car and Driver* to *Bride* to *Computer Shopper,* there is a magazine for every interest. Channel diversification has disrupted the ability of marketers to consolidate the attention of their consumers easily. The "where" now means everywhere.

The answer to this problem from the media community has been to consolidate ownership. Consolidated ownership is not a disruption in the purest sense. It is an important development based on a conventional view of the marketplace. The conventional view is that we must consolidate the attention of a target audience in order to market to them; the result is one-stop-shopping convenience for media buyers. A television commercial booked on the children's cable channel, Noggin, gets a discounted placement in *Nick* magazine, a sponsorship of a rock concert, and a link to an MTV web site. Why? Because all are owned by Viacom.

But, more often than not, consolidated ownership and selling like this have led to editorial deterioration. This kind of deterioration is also not a disruption, but rather another interesting ripple of channel diversification. With advertising as the major source of revenue, editorial content has at times suffered at the expense of the bottom line. Television sitcoms are churned out using formulas from previous successes. Radio stations have collapsed their playlists into easily typed formats that reach defined audiences that marketers find more palatable. News reporting has become "all crime, all the time" because it is more cost-effective to wait around, listening to a police scanner, than to investigate stories.

In one case, consolidated ownership and editorial decline have actually sparked a disruption: the rise of subscriber-based models. AOL-Time Warner has led the charge in the development of media properties without interruptive advertising. The success of HBO is predicated on the existence of editorial decline; its subscriber-paid content sells only if it is superior to the other choices available on television. Even if HBO spends US$120 million on a miniseries like *Band of Brothers*, it is all worth it when subscriber fees top US$65 million a month. By asking, "What if we don't take advertising at all?" HBO has taken a leadership position in television in the United States. Subscriber-based models make it even harder for marketers to reach targeted consumers; there is no interruptive advertising at all.

With audience fragmentation, technological innovation, channel diversification, consolidated ownership, editorial deterioration, and subscriber-based models, marketing has become a lot more complicated. The "who," "where," and "when" of the big idea are not clear at all. And the conventional tools of media planning are still gasping just to catch up with the ever-elusive target consumer. In a marketplace of constant disruption, marketers cannot successfully use frameworks built for the twentieth century to understand the twenty-first.

Connections Theory

Connections planning avoids many of the conventions of marketing by starting with no preconceptions of how marketing works. The "who" is not necessarily the end user of the product or service, but anybody who needs to know about the big idea, ranging from management, staff, investors, and suppliers to existing customers. Connections planning also avoids the conventions of "where" and "when" by defining connections as anything and everything that exists between a client and its target audiences.

Connections planning is designed to inspire, amplify, and leverage total communication ideas. It is not enough merely to integrate a campaign. The "who," "when," and "where" of the big idea should not be an afterthought. The "who," "when," and "where" of the big idea must be given as much thought as the "what."

The implication of this approach is that connections planning informs the construction, selection, and use of clients' communications across all marketing disciplines: public relations, direct marketing, advertising, action marketing (events and promotions), design, and original content.

The end result is that connections planning determines the most relevant, cost-effective, and advantageous points of contact between clients and their existing or potential customers. This enables us to arrive at the best possible mix, use, and order of connections to change consumer behavior to achieve the client's desired business objectives through the use of results-based, multi-disciplinary planning.

By starting with the idea instead of the consumer, connections planning sidesteps target-obsessed conventions of marketing. Instead, we categorize connections as anything that communicates a brand idea's reputation, relationship, or identity.

By reputation connections, we mean connections that help the brand assert the role that it plays in society (for example, a public relations campaign).

By relationship connections, we mean the connections that help the brand communicate individually with its audiences (such as direct-mail marketing).

By identity connections, we mean connections that help the brand express its beliefs and its voice (such as a television advertisement). The totality of connections can be placed under one or more of these categories.

Connections can be further subdivided into six major disciplines: public relations, design (from in-store to product design), direct marketing, action marketing (including events and promotions), advertising, and content (ranging from publishing to movie making). Each discipline has widely differing processes involved in the planning and creating of connections with an audience. For example, in simplistic terms, PR begins with message definition and follows with media leverage, while the advertising discipline engages in creative development before distributing its creative output through media acquisition.

Each of the disciplines can be, in turn, further subdivided into individual channels; for example, the list of advertising channels typically includes television, radio, print, outdoor, and interactive. Recognizing the current forces of technological innovation and channel diversity, no list of channels is ever complete, as the choice of channels changes constantly.

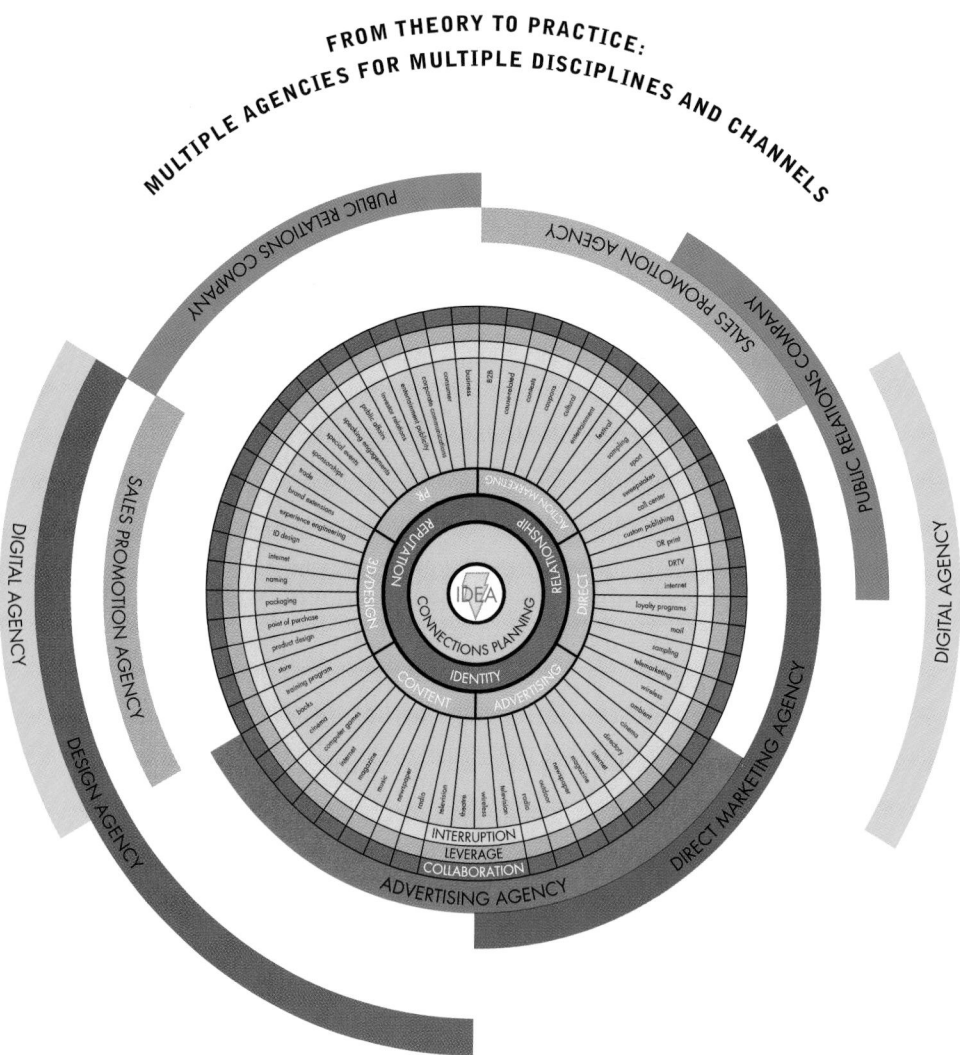

Each channel can be broken down according to its possible uses, which span everything from a passive interruption (for example, a badly placed 30-second television commercial that has no relevance to the viewer) to a sponsorship (a program sponsorship that places the brand in closer proximity to a relevant but separate context) to a mutually beneficial collaboration (a 30-minute TV program that represents the brand's values and immerses the viewer in a relevant entertainment). Deciding the way to use a channel is an important and often-overlooked detail in the planning of communications. It is as important to understand the depth of context as it is to understand the reach of a connection.

Different communications agencies typically think of themselves as specialists in one or more of these disciplines. An advertising agency might think of itself as producing advertising as well as content. An event agency might think of itself as an expert both in action marketing as well as in the design of brand environments.

Therefore, a company involved in connections planning must work early in the process to help inject the correct "who," "where," and "when" into the big idea. It must ensure that the brand idea's reputation, relationship, and identity connections are maintained with each audience. It should stimulate the flow of big-idea thinking between the different agencies, as discipline and channel responsibilities overlap. And a connections planning company must work to increase the depth of connections at every opportunity. But, as we will see, most communications agencies are woefully unprepared for the new demands of connections planning.

"Why," "who," and "what"

Communication Agencies Today

The calculation of the optimal delivery of communications ("when" and "where") tends to be left until the last minute, by which time the "why," "who," and "what" have already been decided upon and often dictate the answer. Companies have attempted to change the situation and to inject some objectivity into the process by introducing new rules. Often these new rules end up as little more than a new language designed to cover up the inadequacies of the same old system.

Media-neutral, for example, has tended to mean that agency teams forget about the reality of "when" and "where," and simply rely on their unconscious channel prejudices, which, of course, tend to be based on the industry norms of the day. More often than not, the unfortunate result is either stagnant cliché or wild, impractical fantasy.

Channel-infinite offers a slight improvement but, in reality, often leads to the creation of a seemingly endless shopping list of multimedia opportunities that come with no clear means of prioritization or selection.

Much has also been made of *integration*. Typically, an advertising agency will create a television or print campaign and integrate the look and feel and message of this campaign into as many disciplines as money will permit. In most cases, this checklist mentality does not result in better sales figures, or even in better work. No one asks, "Why are we doing this the same way, year after year?" Integration has become a convention in and of itself.

What we are witnessing is a major overhaul of once-sacrosanct principles, which, until now, seemed to get us by without as much as a peep from a client. Agencies are being asked to work that much harder in order to answer to the token presentation slide titled "Measures of Success." Suddenly account planners are required to become accountable planners. Putting it simply: Clients want to know where the hell their dollars are going.

At its simplest, connections planning is an attempt at a cure for the channel planning problems facing a global advertising agency at the start of the twenty-first century: problems caused by the structure and processes of advertising agencies themselves, changes to the media landscape, and the inadequacies of integration.

A Disruptive Ethic for Connections Planning

Changing the way that agencies do business requires a framework for doing, or a set of ethics. The ethics of connections planning has three phases (science, art, and technology) that reflect stages of Disruption (understanding conventions, disruption, and discipline). This enables connections planning to be grounded in results, allow for creativity, and take advantage of technological opportunities within the marketing environment.

In the science phase, observation and hypothesis reign. Historical data on audiences and past sales results are modeled and projected to help in the selection of channels. This is a sorting stage that helps lay out a palette of choices to stimulate the creativity of connections planners and defines the communications conventions of the client's category.

The art phase demands that connections planners use creativity to disrupt any limitations in the system. In this critical stage, connections planners work closely with other strategists to help create a framework for the big idea, and begin on possible connections ideas that illustrate how different audiences might experience the big idea. The form and, most important, the order of connections are constructed in this phase: There is a powerful aspect of storytelling in connections planning. Several iterations will be required before a final connections strategy is defined.

The technology phase allows connections planning to be as opportunistic as possible. Connections tactics that allow for message amplification or cost efficiency, for example, are pursued. The addition of this stage maintains discipline within the process.

Connections theory and connections ethics, taken together, define a daunting task for connections planning. Not only must the universe of connections be addressed, but disciplines, channels, and their respective agencies must be coordinated for maximum effect. Connections planning must incorporate scientific observation and hypothesis. There must be room for creativity and storytelling. And it must all be done in a way that takes advantage of the opportunities in the current marketing environment.

Toward a Connections Planning Process

Our experience with connections planning, to date, has enabled us to refine a process that helps us fulfill these requirements. Further, we have developed a set of tools that can facilitate (and improve) connections planning. Applying connections ethics to the work flow of an advertising agency means being part of the creative process. In the agency context, there are four stages to connections planning: from science comes context, from art comes strategy, and from technology come planning and evaluation.

During the *context* stage, connections planning contributes to the overall strategy by analyzing information about how, when, where, and how often the brand currently connects with the consumer. This is done by using a series of connections planning tools. The tools were created to assist the connections strategist at each stage of the planning process.

The primary tools used during the context stage are the *Connections Wheel* and *Mapping Tool* and the *Connections Clock* and *Mapping Tool*. The Connections Wheel and Connections Wheel Mapping Tool assess the money spent on the current universe of channels by the brand and its competitors, and go on to approximate the impact of this spending by channel. These tools are particularly helpful in identifying conventions and opportunities for disruption. The Connections Clock and Connections Clock Mapping Tool help the connections planner understand the relationship between a brand and a target audience, step by step. A third tool is the *Consumer Connections* tool, which illustrates a day in the life of consumer consumption of and interaction with the brand.

While the strategist analyzes the connections currently used by the brand and its competitors via these tools, account planning uncovers audience insights that will help lead to the brand positioning. This stage culminates in a meeting between the two to share information, at which time the account planner delivers an inspirational briefing to the connections planner comprising business analysis, brand positioning, and consumer insights.

The inspirational briefing is the starting point for the *strategy* stage. The connections strategist leverages learning from the context stage and uses additional tools to develop a prototypical connections strategy. The connections strategy is an expression of how best to connect the brand to the consumer. Tools used during this stage include the *Customer Value Calculator*, to define priority target segments; the *Advocacy Chain*, to assess how different target segments influence one another; and a *Migration Matrix*, which assesses where the brand is on a relationship capability continuum. A *Timeline* is then created by merging the Advocacy Chain and the Connections Clock from the context stage to provide a framework.

The strategy phase culminates in a meeting of connections strategists with account planners, account managers, and creatives from all marketing disciplines. This collaborative meeting is intended to synthesize all thinking, leading to a connections strategy. After the meeting, the connections strategist creates a connections brief designed to inspire creative teams from all disciplines. A briefing session, where both the account planning brief and the connections brief are presented, follows.

As the creative idea is developed, the process enters the planning stage. Led by the strategy, a plan is developed using the most effective, relevant, and impactful connections. The planning stage includes building different scenarios on the planning Timeline and assessing the validity of those scenarios with the *Persuasion Sequence* tool. The plan is then reviewed, refined, and amplified, based on the creative idea.

Once the creative idea and plan are complete, the connections strategists brief managers from each marketing discipline. Any additional channel input can be consolidated into the overall plan. The individual discipline representatives then execute the plan.

Evaluation occurs on an ongoing basis during the execution and deployment of the plan. During the evaluation stage, tools used during the context and planning stages can be reintroduced to assess the effectiveness of the plan.

We Are All Connections Planners

Connections planning has been designed as a specific discipline with rigorous processes to be carried out and tools to be used by dedicated staff possessing the right mix of skills, knowledge, and experience. Despite this, I often still find it useful to elaborate on Seth Godin's dating analogy to explain the whole concept. I would like to share that analogy with you now, as a summary of the chapter you have just read.

I have expanded the analogy to involve a friend of mine. It is based on the story of how he met and got to know his future wife. I hope you will recognize enough similarities to your own experiences to empathize with it.

Having noticed a beautiful woman at the far end of the table at a dinner party, my friend made sure that he appeared smart and witty in front of her by attempting to tell a few funny jokes over the coffee and liqueurs (that was the start of the PR part of his plan). Having retired to the sofa, he made sure that they chatted and got to know each other well enough to exchange telephone numbers before the end of the evening (a small piece of database marketing). Having let a suitable amount of time pass — long enough to not seem too desperate but soon enough to show that he was interested — he phoned her (permission-based telemarketing) and invited her to lunch (event marketing). Consciously breaking with etiquette, he, as the inviter, sent her, as the invitee, a handwritten thank-you note (direct marketing), having successfully thought of a ruse to get her to give him her address over lunch.

When she phoned, as he hoped she would (direct-response analysis), he invited her to the theater followed by dinner (event marketing again) on the pretext that he had an extra ticket to the must-see production of the moment (limited-offer promotion). At the theater she was pleasantly surprised and a little pleased to discover that the heroine of the play shared her name (branded content) and over dinner she began to find herself wondering whether she and he shared a common dream of the future.

I will stop there because, of course, by now you will have got the point. He did not use individual marketing disciplines to develop a relationship with the target audience. More to the point, he did not use advertising at all during the early stages of his connections strategy. At best, she would not have believed an ad about him; at worst, she would have judged him as arrogant and almost certainly would never have given him her phone number. That is not to say that advertising did not play a vital role, but to explain that I will have to fast-forward to the end of the story.

Every year since they met, on the anniversary of the dinner party, my friend has presented his wife with a beautiful card containing words that he has toiled over for hours in order for them to adequately express his love (brand advertising). Of course, he also presents her with chocolates, flowers, and an invitation to her favorite restaurant. However, the point is that advertising continues to play an important role in the overall connections strategy.

By telling the story I am not trying to downplay the complexity of connections planning, but I am trying to suggest that it is achievable because we are all inherently successful connections planners already. For most of our lives we have been creating and implementing highly complex connections strategies throughout both our private lives and our professional lives. It is how we attempted to get what we wanted as small children, it is how we dated as teenagers, it is how we met our partners, and it is probably how we have managed our careers so far. The skill came to us naturally and we practice it unconsciously. The problem is that when we are faced with devising and implementing communications for companies or brands, we tend to consciously follow a convention. That convention is better known as *marketing*. This is where Connections Planning comes into its own. It allows us to provide a much-needed disruption of the conventions that exist today in terms of inventing and implementing total communication plans.

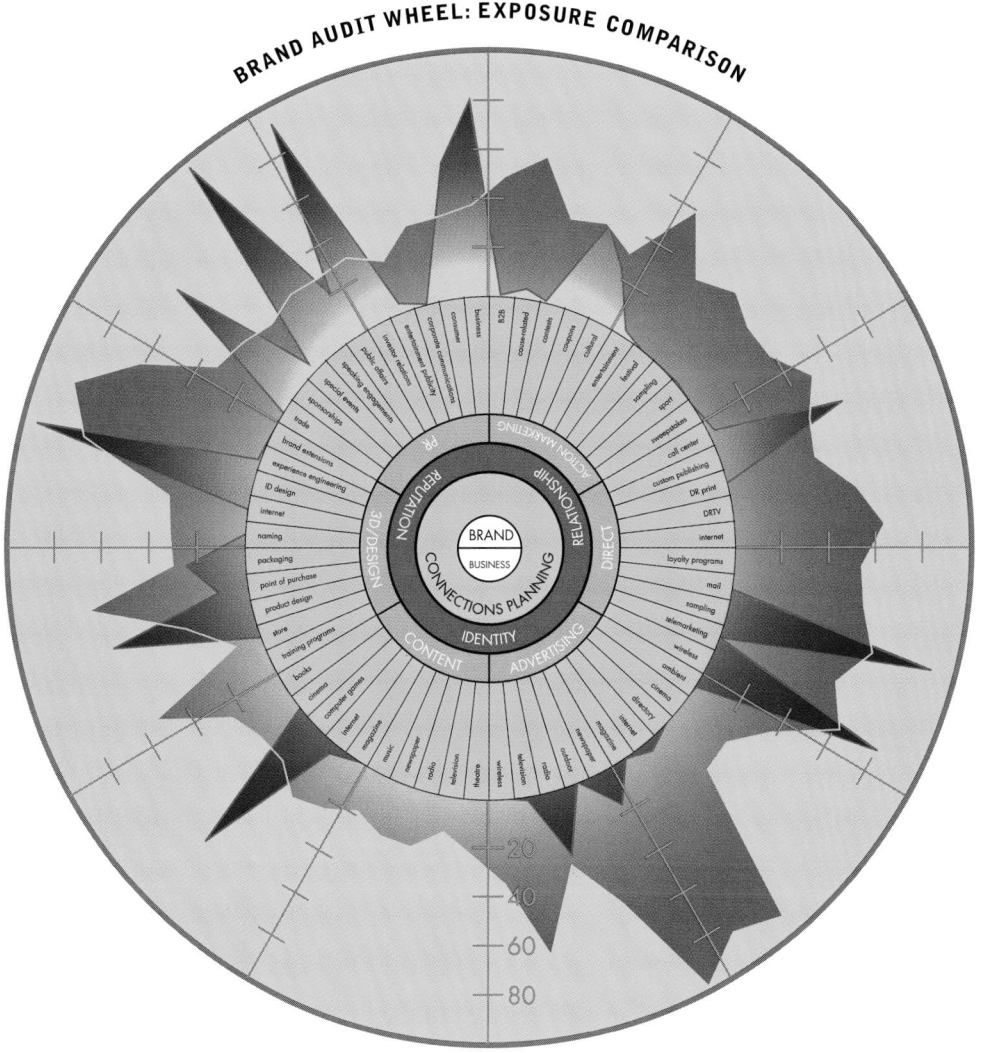

"What made you successful
in the past,
won't in the future."

LARRY HOCHMAN

19. NEW BUSINESS MODEL

God knows, agencies are good at beating themselves up. Or, to put it more positively, they are intensely self-critical. And yet it seems to us that there is a great deal more debate than actual change. This is a problem because there are actual changes in the context in which agencies operate. Some of the changes are structural and demand a response; some are illusory and require debunking. We will examine the changes and try to distinguish between the two.

The response of agencies to these changes has been primarily a defensive assertion of the eternal verities of advertising. Agencies cling to the ideal of the client and agency in symbiosis, of the revolutionary business leader who does not move a muscle without consulting his or her poet/warrior/visionary/seer in the agency. This ideal is so rare that it is useless as a model of agency development. The truth is that agencies have to learn how to sell the value of creativity, of Disruption, to accountants. To do this we have to understand and, if necessary, disrupt our own conventions.

We remain optimistic about advertising agencies. In so many ways they prefigure the management clichés of today — the search for excellence, making a virtue out of chaos, the fluid matrix organization. We have all the pieces; we know the rules; the challenge is to play like a grandmaster.

Changing Contexts

Has the advertising industry lost its luster, as Jean-Marie Dru suggested in 1997? In terms of self-perception, it certainly seems so. Industry leaders like Dru have been making similar observations for the past 10 years. The two most common themes are the incursion of other kinds of consultants onto traditional agency turf, and a concomitant decline in status and influence for the advertising agency, popularly described as being "pushed down the food chain."

An examination of the hard data suggests that we must distinguish between the economic performance of the advertising industry, which, by and large, has been good, and the influence issue, for which there is clear evidence of decline, at least in the United States.

From 1985 to 2000, U.S. advertising expenditures grew from around $95 billion to over $240 billion. From 1992 to 1997, advertising agency revenues grew from $13.6 billion to $16.9 billion in the United States. The recent global collapse in dot-com revenues, however, together with the on-again, off-again recession (at the time of writing very much on again, given the tragic events of September 11, 2001), suggest there will be a slowdown in marketing expenditure.

Both the financial reports of publicly traded holding companies and profitability information from the 4As (which is, unfortunately, confidential) show that the advertising industry has improved profitability over the past 15 to 20 years. Agencies have achieved scale efficiencies through consolidation and the inclusion of higher-margin below-the-line activities into agency groups.

Yet, despite this apparently rosy financial picture, there is evidence that clients increasingly view agencies as less relevant or less in touch with their business. For example, according to a confidential industry study we were allowed to review, 15 years ago the top agency percentage score for the criterion "understands the problems that affect my business" was in the 70s. Today, the top score is in the 20s.

The war for talent provides another indicator of the purported industry decline. In certain areas, particularly account management, advertising agencies seem unable to compete with management consultancies, investment banks, and law firms for the brightest college and business school graduates. In the United States, few advertising agencies bother to recruit Ivy League students any longer. The dearth of training programs, the paucity of top talent in the industry, and the consequent increase in the cost of such talent are common complaints globally.

Let us consider the causes behind the advertising industry's difficulties, real or perceived. This will enable us to contemplate practical and, ideally, disruptive, ways in which advertising agencies could reclaim a leadership position in the business world. While many advertising executives have cited the industry's failure to keep up with management consultancies, we assert that the underlying reasons have more to do with changes in the broader business context in which advertising agencies operate.

Who cares about a brilliant 30-second commercial if you have to wait 30 minutes on the customer service line?

For starters, the growth of consumer services has drastically changed the business context. Unlike those about consumer packaged goods, perceptions about service brands primarily stem from customer experience. Who cares about a brilliant 30-second commercial if you have to wait 30 minutes on the customer service line? To put it bluntly, communication, particularly advertising, has less impact on the brand in a service-oriented world, thus diminishing the strategic importance of the advertising agency.

Of course, it is a cliché to say that the world of marketing has changed dramatically, but let us examine the depth of change from an economic perspective. For example, the long-term supply-and-demand curve of advertising has greatly diminished the attractiveness of mass marketing since the explosion of television in the 1950s. Since ads are not widgets, what is supply-and-demand in an advertising context? We would consider supply as the amount of time consumers are available to receive marketing messages, a function of population growth and average time spent consuming advertised media. And we would consider demand as the level of spending marketers devote to delivering marketing messages — that is, demand for a moment of a consumer's time.

Between 1985 and 2000, the average time spent consuming advertised media (supply) declined slightly. Inflation-adjusted advertising expenditures (demand) grew at an average annual rate of more than 3 percent. Put more simply, for every dollar of advertising spent in 2000, consumer expenditures were approximately $27.60. Adjusted for inflation, this was the lowest figure since 1960. The supply-and-demand curve of television advertising looks even more telling. From 1955 to 2000, per capita consumption of television grew only 15 percent, while inflation-adjusted television advertising spending grew over 450 percent. Obviously, an imbalance between supply and demand leads to price increases, making it now extremely expensive to reach consumers through conventional media advertising.

This, together with globalization, increasing heterogeneity, fragmentation of media consumption, marketing clutter, and the coming tide of personalized mass communication through Web-based channels, has made marketing and marketing communication incredibly complex. This, in turn, has forced marketers to look for more diverse and higher-quality advice, but as dogged purveyors of the 30-second spot, advertising agencies are poorly positioned to provide the objective advice clients seek.

Who is the competition for the position of strategic marketing adviser? We would suggest that the first group that has usurped the agency's historic role is clients themselves, followed by management and brand consultants. The agency business model focuses on execution, not advice. Agencies give advice, but clients pay agencies for execution. As a result, advertising agencies have trimmed in the advice area and consultants have simply moved into the vacuum. And they have moved into this vacuum not out of a conspiracy to displace the advertising agency, but because their clients asked them.

How has the industry responded? Primarily through consolidation and horizontal integration (actually started in the 1970s with Young & Rubicam's "Whole Egg" business model), but there have been few other fundamental, strategic changes. Considering these contextual changes to the advertising industry, how then can we disrupt the industry conventions and reclaim the mantle of the trusted strategic marketing advisor?

Disrupting Agency Conventions

The conventions we have chosen are implicit in the preceding two sections. Here we make them explicit, discuss them in more detail, and then suggest how they can be disrupted.

Convention One
Television Advertising Is the Prime Creator of Brand Value

It is ironic that, as the concept of the brand has become more important to business, advertising agencies, the outside consultant most associated historically with brand creation, have clung to this outmoded view of the way in which brand value is created. We would suggest that this convention is wrong, both in principle and in practice.

The emphasis over the last 20 years or so on giving brands a cash value has persuaded most CEOs that brands are an important intangible asset. Indeed, many commentators have argued that, given the wave of outsourced production by a wide array of marketers from Kraft to Nike, a company's brands are the only assets that now really matter. But, when we dig deeper into what is meant by the concept of brand, we see that the idea now encompasses every aspect of a company's interaction with the customer, from product design to fair trade policies.

Self-evidently for a service brand — a McDonald's, or a Carrefour, or a Deutsche Bank — the quality of the customer experience will be a key driver of brand value. As we said earlier, what use is a brilliant 30-second commercial for customer service if the average wait on a customer service line is 30 minutes? Even for product brands, however, consumers increasingly want to know about the brand behind the brand. The story about the alleged link between Nike and third-world sweatshops was front-page news around the world, a book about the marketing practices of Procter & Gamble was on the best-sellers list. How much damage did Coca-Cola's CEO do to the Coca-Cola brand by reportedly responding to the Belgian contamination crisis by saying, "Where's Belgium anyway?" The idea that branding is a kind of spin control is dead. Everything a company does is branding; brands are behavior.

Where does this leave the 30-second commercial? Everyone in the industry is familiar with the transformational power of advertising — the Apple "1984" spot that ran only once, the Lucozade commercial with Daley Thompson that spawned a new drinks sector, and countless others. But would the Apple creative have worked for IBM? In other words, was it not the fact that Apple had created a revolutionary culture and revolutionary products that enabled the advertising to perform its magic?

On a more practical level, media inflation and increased media complexity have conspired to reduce the effectiveness of any piece of creative, no matter how startling. Advertising has a part to play in brand building, but so do direct marketing, product development, pricing, design, PR, event management, investor relations, and, perhaps most important, channel marketing and staff training. Advertising is but one of the many variables that brand management now has to juggle and, de facto, it has become less central to brand value creation. It is a stubborn adherence to the craft specialization of advertising, and the business model that accompanies it, that has led to the agency's apocryphal journey down the food chain.

Convention Television advertising is the prime creator of brand value.

Disruption Brands are behavior; advertising is but one
of many things that a brand does.

Vision An agency that is genuinely solution-neutral and behaves accordingly.

Convention Two
Agencies Have a Special Relationship with Their Clients and Know the Business from a Privileged Insider Position

David Maister has written an influential book about the advice business, called simply *The Trusted Advisor* (Simon & Schuster, 2000), in which he argues that there are two important prerequisites for a trust relationship: first, that the adviser has unique knowledge or skill and, second, that the client believes that the advice is objective or, at least, disinterested. Let us examine the client-agency relationship using these two criteria.

As we have established under Convention One, the agency does have special skill in the area of advertising, but, as we have also argued, this skill has become less important in the business process of brand value creation. Moreover, we would also suggest that agencies have a partial view of one aspect of a client's business.

In most instances the agency-client relationship is mediated on the client side by the marketing department, which has itself adopted an increasingly narrow role. Few marketing departments have profit-and-loss responsibility and they are, in most cases, removed from the key decision makers in the company. For example, a recent *Economist* survey found that less than 1 percent of the time in European board meetings is taken up by marketing! In effect, many marketing departments have become communication departments, and less than 50 percent of their budgets are expended on advertising.

In most agencies, a specialized department, account management, mediates the agency-client relationship. The account management role embodies a dichotomy: on the one hand, "air traffic control"; on the other, business partners and strategists. Few other consultancy companies would understand the requirement for an intermediary like account management. The fact that the value-add in agencies is split across diverse functions — account management, planning, creative, and media — makes it harder to pin down and makes it very difficult for the client to build up trust relationships with those individuals responsible for the advice.

This is a structural problem for the agency. Some agencies have responded by disintermediating account management and encouraging direct contact between clients and creatives (in fact, in most smaller markets, this is the norm). Others have responded by relieving account management of its administrative function and combining account managers, account planners, and media planners into one strategically focused department.

The concept of a special relationship, has another, more insidious consequence. Inevitably and unconsciously, the prime directive of the agency becomes to protect the relationship — code for "protect the revenue." Once clients sense this, they begin to doubt the objectivity of the advice they are being given and the all-important trust breaks down. In extreme cases, the agency is seen as part of the problem. In no other industry, apart from perhaps the movie business, is the severing and forming of business relationships attended with as much drama and theatricality as in the ad business! It is instructive to look at the business model of strategy consultants for a point of comparison. Companies like McKinsey, Boston Consulting Group, and Bain invest huge sums of their own money in "knowledge creation." These companies, or their alumni, have created — and we use this word deliberately — most of the big, commonplace management ideas. In most cases, they refuse to divulge to clients hourly rates, so that clients evaluate the fee in terms of the quality of the advice they are given rather than the number of staff working on the project. These consultants truly understand their clients; they literally live with them for months on end. Regardless of the criticisms thrown at consultants, the fact is that the number of these top strategy consultants has grown steadily for decades. CEOs pay handsomely for their advice — why? Because it is typically very good advice from people with whom they have built trust relationships.

Agencies invest huge sums in their creative departments — typically the greatest cost center within the agency — but restrict the agency deliverable to advertising, limit direct contact between the client and the creative function, and thus undersell the importance of creativity as a business process to the real decision makers.

Convention Agencies have a special relationship with their clients and know the business from a privileged insider position.

Disruption The only true basis for the agency-client relationship is the quality of ideas that create measurable value, not the remuneration system or specialized departments.

Vision Trust-based relationships.

Convention Three
Agencies Cannot Compete with the Banks, Law Firms, and Consultancies for Top Talent

We have tried hard in this chapter to avoid giving the impression that consultants are somehow out to get agencies. Agencies feel about strategy consultants the way Canada feels about the United States. They obsess about us because they are bigger and more powerful than we are, while, at the same time, we disdain them because they are not as creative as we are. On the other hand, consultancies feel about agencies much the same way the United States feels about Canada; that is, they do not feel much at all. If pressed, they will say perhaps that they admire our creativity, but they certainly do not worry about competing with agencies. On the whole, they have got into the brand strategy area because clients asked them to and, as we have argued, the marketing services industry had left a vacuum there.

One area in which there is clearly direct competition, however, is the talent market. No advice business can survive for long without a constant supply of exceptional talent. If our talent pool shrinks, then the quality of our creative thinking and ideas will decline and, in time, so will our income and profit. Indeed, this may already be happening. It is also worth noting that the competition for talent has grown fiercer on the creative side, too. The dot-com industries have been a major drain on the advertising industry, as has the burgeoning independent television industry. And, yet, on that side of the house we can generally offer creative people better salaries and a more stable working life (yes, it is true) than these other industries. It is perhaps in the strategy and management areas that we have to rethink our offer.

The plain fact is that, when it comes to salaries, it is very hard for advertising agencies to compete with a McKinsey, or JP Morgan, or Freshfields. This is certainly true at the postgraduate level. In the United States, an MBA student may well have invested more than $300,000 in tuition costs and opportunity cost of two year's compensation to gain a second degree; in most cases, they will be in debt. Such people need to make a rapid return on this investment.

A million candidates

Even in Europe, where the investment will be less, MBA graduates are generally midcareer and looking for more than the administrative and report-reading duties that agencies typically offer their entry-level recruits. In the short term, during which the agency cannot afford to compete on salaries, it needs to look to other ways to add value to an offer of agency employment. What truly distinguishes a consultancy from an agency in terms of the talent wars is the single-minded competitive focus of consultants on talent recruitment. In a conversation about competition, a top management consultancy typically refers, and is evaluated, in terms of its ability to recruit staff. Every employee is involved in recruiting; it is seen, rightly, as the lifeblood of the business. Andersen Consulting (now Accenture) once boasted that they screen nearly a million candidates to fulfill their worldwide recruiting needs each year!

Concomitant with this emphasis on recruitment is a similar emphasis on training and development. New recruits typically undertake significant training in the way of the firm before being allowed to join a team that is actually working on a client assignment. Once on an assignment, they are given clear areas of responsibility and allowed to develop knowledge power within the team. From time to time, they are assigned to internal knowledge creation projects, which gives them the opportunity to use cutting-edge thinking and offers them exposure to the top managers in the firm. And the training regimen continues throughout a consultant's career.

We are perhaps painting an overly rosy picture. The hours are long and often the work is unglamorous and unrelenting. Most such firms have a fairly rigid hierarchy, and promotion is on an up-and-out system. But, at least as consultants, they are regularly assessed and generally know where they stand and what to expect.

There are a number of pointers here for how agencies should compete for talent. First, we should not compete for postgraduates but concentrate on graduates, whereby the differences between salary levels will be less pronounced. However, agencies should certainly compete in terms of training and development. New recruits to the agency should feel that their experience in the agency is adding value in terms of their career and know the future options that are available to them.

Agencies should target a distinctive, less conventional type of graduate. Agencies are anarchic but sexy places to work; they can compete with consultancies in terms of lifestyle. To quote Jean-Marie Dru, agencies are "fluid spaces in which there is room for everyone to perform to his or her best." By rotating people around the network, agencies can give their employees invaluable professional and life experiences, while in the process strengthening the network immeasurably.

Convention Agencies cannot compete with the banks, law firms, and consultancy companies for the top talent.

Disruption What in the short term we cannot afford in money, we can cost-effectively make up in experiences.

Vision An agency that is repopulated by unconventionally brilliant people, in a coherent global network.

Toward Reinvention

So, what are we doing in order to achieve our vision for disrupting industry conventions? Around the world, we work in a horizontally integrated structure — that is, a full suite of communications services organized under common ownership and management, also known as "integrated" services. Of course, there is nothing new in this. The concept of total communications services has been around since the 1970s.

The marketplace does, however, increasingly require agencies to operate on the basis of this model. As marketing becomes more complex, the lines between disciplines continue to blur. Because of this, clients increasingly demand broader service delivery from their advertising agencies. Working in a broader context also enables us to have the scale to invest in the talent needed to provide the quality of advice our clients need.

But pulling together a collection of marketing services is not enough. It does not add much. Clients can perform the task of integration themselves. And they do. *Integration*, from the Latin root *integrare*, simply means to make separate things whole. Therefore, integration, by definition, happens after the fact. Making the direct-mail piece and the web site look like the ads is really not very interesting. Of course, coordination is important, but it is not transformational.

From media neutral to solutions neutral

There is a further, more important, problem with conventional approaches to integration. In most approaches, the world continues to revolve around advertising. We believe this is fundamentally wrong, and we believe this is a reflection of 1950s thinking. Advertising is simply one of several means — albeit important and potentially powerful — of delivering and executing ideas. Many integrated offerings propose media-neutral approaches. We aim to go beyond media, to a solutions-neutral approach. Why presuppose the use of media? In reinventing itself, Bilbao could have launched a tourism campaign in large tourist markets. Instead, they hired Frank Gehry to create a building, a landmark, an icon, to represent a renewed Bilbao to the world.

Clients need ideas, strategies, and advice to help them in an increasingly complex world. Clients need ideas, strategies, and advice that transcend marketing disciplines, transcend media, and transcend marketing. More important, they need ideas that create economic value and competitive advantage. Within our ranks, we have some of the greatest creative minds in the business world. We are unleashing their talents on a much broader canvas. Why limit them to making ads?

We have also bolstered our strategic capabilities in the past year with the creation of Connect, our communications strategy function, and the creation of Brand Architecture International, a brand strategy consultancy. In building strategic capabilities, we should be clear that we are not attempting to compete with management consultancies. In fact, we strive to collaborate with our clients' consulting advisers, instead of attempting to compete with consultants. Consultants benefit, just as they benefit from spending more time with their clients' line managers. And agencies certainly learn from working more closely with consultants. Clients deserve to have their professional services partners collaborating.

Nor do we seek to replace our brightest strategic thinkers, our planners, with new strategic resources. We are adding, not substituting or re-creating, in this area. We are simply ensuring that we provide our clients with much-needed advice in our core areas — branding and communications.

And, finally, we remain true to what has made us great all of these years — creativity. Creativity in the broadest sense: creation of ideas that create economic value, whether that be through branded communications (including brilliant 30-second advertisements), a new approach to customer service, a new product concept, or hiring the world's most famous architect to create a building. And, whether our experience comes from advertising, direct marketing, interactive marketing, public relations, or brand architecture consulting, we rely on Disruption for inspiration in creating ideas.

1984

2002

Scores of ideas and opinions have been expressed throughout this book. By way of a conclusion, I would like to take a moment to deliver a few of my own. First, I would emphasize how firmly Disruption is rooted in life itself. Life's essence lies in accidents and interruptions, in conflicts and tensions, rather than in a form of linear or static continuity. The same is true of the thought process. Thinking, to a great extent, means breaking away from our certainties. Changing our convictions. Disrupting our well-ordered opinions. Brands have to understand this. To reinvent themselves over and over again, they must question themselves, shake themselves up. That is why we in the advertising industry like to see brands take initiatives, accept risks, create discontinuity. I say this, but I still occasionally find myself guilty of relying on past experience and reproducing a too-familiar model — one that is tried and true...and often worn out. Disruption safeguards against that. It prevents me from falling into this trap. I would like it to do the same for you.

Next, Disruption helps us see the world as it is, not as we want it to be. We would like things to be simple, yet they are often complex. By forcing us not to settle for ready-made solutions, by pushing us to identify conventions and uncover the reality underneath, Disruption opens our eyes: to the complexity of the world, for example, and to the foolishness of claiming the world is simple. Deluding ourselves that the world is easy to apprehend leads us to create pat remedies. That is a hazardous approach. We cannot get away with providing easy answers to questions that have barely been formulated. Resolving a brand's issues demands investment and reflection, which in turn require time and, usually, money. You do not get anything for nothing — except hackneyed formulas that will soon prove worthless. That is why Disruption, while not rejecting simplicity (far from it), flushes out and fights the growing tendency toward oversimplification.

I would also point out that Disruption is meant to be an agent of growth. It should be seen as a simple method that aims to sell more under the same brand name. Simply stated, it makes it possible to do more with less, to give more meaning and substance to something that already exists, to achieve higher sales, because the brand or company has succeeded in making itself more appealing. You have seen it throughout the chapters of this book, Disruption generates growth. Following the recent frenzy of mergers and acquisitions, company executives will again have to respond to the growing need for natural growth —that is, organic growth. The only real kind of growth, all things considered. This is easier said than done: any company can seek to grow by 5, even 10 percent — but how do you strive for a higher percentage without resorting to external growth? It takes both discipline and imagination. And I believe Disruption unites the two.

Being "Both"

Centralized or decentralized? Specialist or generalist? Companies are always expected to align themselves with one of two opposites. It is true within our profession, too. An agency is supposed to have either a strategic *or* a creative vocation. In a sense, we are ordered to choose. It is as if we cannot, alternatively or simultaneously, be both one and the other. This rather harsh restriction brings me back to the *Tyranny of the Or*, which I mentioned in the introduction. I think that in most cases, one must decide not to choose.

Many clients' companies view their advertising agency as a distribution network, a set of tubes designed to disseminate globally an idea that was conceived centrally. They might agree to add a bit of local color, inject a touch of exoticism for good measure, without really believing that it is necessary. They do not see that more and more, the local angle is taking precedence everywhere. They forget that any brand — all the more so if it is a worldwide one — must take care to become part of the fabric of the society in which it is trying to establish itself. Furthermore, uniformity, another pernicious result of oversimplification, does not make something intelligible to all, any more than it inspires creativity.

In a word, networks like ours must manage differences, then try to create points of convergence. The task is complex, but it is achievable — on condition once again that we refuse so-called foolproof formulas.

This artificial global-versus-local dichotomy is evidenced in the way people regard major advertising networks. According to the commonly held view, there are the longstanding, highly centralized agencies on one side and, on the other, the more recent creative ones, like ours, perceived as loosely connected federations. Here, again, it is as though one cannot be good at both the global and the local level! Wrong. A single advertising network can comprise many excellent local agencies that are still run by the local entrepreneurs who created them — sort of first-generation agencies — and, at the same time, ensure that these agencies are united by practices and language as structured as "Disruption" and "Connections." The strength of the central concept makes diversity possible at the local level. Better yet, the more unifying the central concept is, the more cultural differences can be taken into account.

One more opposition that is purely theoretical: the idea that one cannot be both a specialist and a generalist. A communications group must consist of a set of specialist agencies that are just as capable of finding a transversal idea that cuts through all disciplines as a generalist. In "Connections," we saw that we cannot settle for ready-to-use solutions, like "TV only." We have to make the most of every point of contact with the consumer, whether we do that through direct marketing, sponsoring, or any other avenue. Some will then rush to the conclusion that all the time spent optimizing these interactions will distract us from our main objective of investing brands with powerful ideas.

But here, too, we should be suspicious of overly simplistic conclusions. Take television commercials. In fact, nothing is more effective at communicating a brand than TV. Over the past 50 years, ad agencies have developed unparalleled savoir faire in the art of communicating an entire brand identity in a matter of seconds. The advertising industry is master of the condensed message. It is absurd to say that the 30-second spot will eventually die. On the other hand, the breadth and complexity of the consumer's experience cannot be adequately addressed by systematically handing the job over to only advertising. Each discipline has its special, and complementary, area of intervention. We must stop building the reputation of one discipline out of the so-called weaknesses of another. We must understand that the rise in power of each one enriches the whole.

Preconceptions, conventions, presumptions: Our profession, like many others, is crippled by them. And yet, ironically or paradoxically, advertising's reason for being lies at the opposite end of the spectrum. Our supposed job consists in putting forward "new" ideas.

Brave Thinking

An enlightened humanist, Benjamin Franklin is well loved on both sides of the Atlantic. He said: "there are many ways not to succeed, but the most certain is never to take risks." It is hard to imagine that this great individual invented the lightning rod or took part in America's War of Independence against the British crown without some degree of personal risk. This same man observed that humanity can be divided into three groups: those who cannot act, those who can act but choose not to, and those who act. Read: success and glory await those who dare to act!

In any war of position, he or she who does not move is doomed. This is true both for companies and for brands. The moment they find reasons not to move, they start to lose ground. A brand that will not change or constantly question itself quickly becomes out of step with the times. Brands must envision a future for themselves, all the while knowing that the future cannot be predicted, just imagined. This has led us to a thought process that steers clear of seeking gradual or incremental change and, instead, encourages discontinuous thinking, leaps into the future. Leaps into the unknown.

This requires brave thinking. Bravery is a behavioral trait; it manifests itself through action. But we like to apply it to the thought process. Brave thinking rejects the laziness and resignation that characterize conventional thinking. It exalts the unexpected and welcomes change.

Brave thinking creates brave brands. Think of Apple, Danone, and Sony. Think of Nordstrom, Southwest, and Starbucks. These brands have adopted bold stances, ambitious visions, and courageous points of view. They never settle for less. They have perspective, and therefore have gone beyond the limits of the marketplace. They are constantly fighting for a larger share of the future.

Do the same with the brand you are in charge of. Try to take it beyond what is expected or known. Do not favor discernment at the expense of audacity. Do not favor thoroughness at the expense of being bold. Be both. Be brave.

You have no choice.

In Order of Appearance

Cindy Scott Director of Business Strategy, Los Angeles

Tom Carroll President of the Americas, New York

Anne Charbonneau Strategic Planning Director, Amsterdam

David Hackworthy Executive Planning Director, New York

Ian Leslie Senior Strategic Planner, New York

Neil Dawson Executive Planning Director, London

John Hunt Co-Chairman & Executive Creative Director, South Africa

Marie Jamieson Strategic Planning Director, Johannesburg

Fiona Clancy Worldwide Strategic Planner, London

Alastair Maclean Senior Strategic Planner, Paris

Gavin Hilton Strategic Planning Director, London

Richard Lewis Worldwide Account Director, New York

Louis Gavin Chief Executive Officer and Creative Director, Johannesburg

Heather Albrecht eMarketing Specialist & Digital Trainer,

One Brand Development Group, Sydney

Neil Lawrence Chief Executive Officer & Creative Director, Sydney

Paul Worboys Managing Director, Sydney

Laurie Coots Chief Marketing Officer, Worldwide, New York

Monica Karo Chief Media Officer, Worldwide, Los Angeles

Trevor Beattie Chairman & Creative Director, London

Rob Alexander Strategic Planner, London

Gavin Heron Regional Planning Director, Hong Kong

Sandip Mahapatra Head of Strategic Planning, India

Adam Stagliano Founding Director/Principal Brand Architect

Brand Architecture International, New York

Richard Monturo Executive Planning Director, Los Angeles

Nick McLean Executive Director, Connections, New York

Robert Birge Chief Operating Officer, New York

Damian O'Malley Director/Principal Brand Architect

Brand Architecture International, Dublin

disruption.com

As you have traveled these pages with us, we hope that you have seen the potential for Disruption in advancing your business vision.

We would like to invite you to join us as we continue the dialog at www.disruption.com. This interactive environment and community is where you will find out more about the cases described in this book, as well as entirely new Disruption stories. You can learn more about the tools and their best practices and, most important, you can become part of the story as a participant in ongoing forums and discussion groups. We hope the site will be one that you bookmark and visit often.

A collective book.

Thanks first and foremost to all the authors who so generously gave us their thoughts in each chapter. Without them, and without all the collaborators in our company who practice Disruption, this book would never have existed. The names of the authors are listed on the page entitled "in order of appearance."

This book is about business in general, as well as about advertising and marketing. As John Hunt puts it, disruptive thinking at a business or marketing level must be reflected in unexpected advertising. So, I would like to pay special tribute to all the great creative minds in our company who give life to our strategic ideas: Lee Clow, our Chairman and Worldwide Creative Director; Marie-Catherine Dupuy; Trevor Beattie; John Hunt; Chuck McBride; Béla Stamenkovits. . .and all our great creative directors all over the world.

I would also like to thank those people who, while not credited with a specific chapter in the book, make it their mission to constantly enrich and advance the Disruption concept: Corinne Malsert, Emmanuelle Guillon, Valerie Hénaff, Hervé Brunette, Rod Wright, Ugo Ceria, and Anne Robert.

A collective book is a very complicated project for the person responsible for centralizing it. I would particularly like to thank Emma Boyce for her assiduous work on the manuscript. With the help of Michele Spencer in New York and Nicole Cooper in Paris, who also worked extremely hard on this project, Emma acted as an internal editor of the book, assisting and guiding each author, and enabling *Beyond Disruption* to see the light. In looking for a visual for the cover, Doug Jaeger equipped us with a perfect symbol for the three Disruption phases. Thanks go to him. The very talented Philippe Ghielmetti was responsible for the artistic direction of the book and, Serge Robert, Jean-Christophe Aussel and Sandrine Chattey from Question d'Edition for the photo-engraving. Their work was co-ordinated by Nathalie Ollivier.

I would also like to thank all the people who in one way or another contributed to this book: Amy Moorman, Laura Langdon, Larry Gies, Mick McCabe, Benjamin Bittman, Harriet Rubin, Michael Sharp, Vanessa Barbel, Sarah Baldwin, Louise Blything, Nicolas Bordas, Djazia Boukhelif, Pascal Dupont, Denis Quénard, Arthur Sadoun, as well as my friends from Hakuhodo: Akira Miyachi, Takaki Nakamura, Ichiro Zama, and Ayami Nakao. The Connections team in New York: Dan Ng, Francis Anderson, Joseph Jaffe, and Stephanie Zufle.

And the members of our Worldwide Operating Group: Paul Bainsfair, Nick Baum, Tom Carroll, Carl Johnson, Reg Lascaris, Jonathan Ramsden, Rob Rosenthal, Keith Smith, Denis Streiff, and Perry Valkenburg.

I am also very grateful to Airié Dekidjiev, her assistant Jessica Noyes, as well as Maureen Drexel and Linda Witzling from John Wiley & Sons, Inc. for their constant support, their professionalism, and patience.

Finally, I cannot finish without expressing my profound gratitude to Andrew Jaffe who initiated the John Wiley ADWEEK series, for which *Disruption* was the first work. It is to Andrew that I owe the publication of *Disruption* and *Beyond Disruption*.

JMD

Exhibit A
More on Disruptive South Africa

South Africa is a relatively small market — about 42 million people. Yet, it is one of the most diverse in the world. There are 11 official languages and a baffling array of cultures: traditional African, urban African, Indian, Cape Malay, European, to name a few.

South Africa *was* the land of apartheid. Since 1994 it has been a modern, multiparty democracy with a constitution that protects all cultural rights, all religious beliefs, and all sexual persuasions.

It is the African meeting point of the first and third worlds. Some still live in thatched huts. But there just might be a TV satellite dish on top. It is a land of conspicuous consumption. A new middle class is leaving previously disadvantaged communities for leafy suburbs, custom kitchens, and private swimming pools. It is also a land of poverty (unemployment officially hovers around 30 percent).

There are high levels of adult illiteracy, too. Yet South Africans create technology that often astounds the western world — producing everything from pebble-bed nuclear reactors to leading-edge e-commerce software.

This land is troubled by crime and violence. But its peoples are famed for their friendliness and hospitality. South Africa is also the only country in the world to voluntarily give up its nuclear weapons.

South Africa generates and consumes more electricity than the rest of Africa put together. Its people have more personal computers and telephones than the rest of Africa. It has more tarred road than the rest of the continent, the best harbors, the most modern airports, and the most efficient railways.

It boasts the most highly developed private-sector health system in Africa. A higher percentage of caesarian sections are reportedly performed in Greater Johannesburg than in Los Angeles. Christiaan Barnard performed the world's first heart transplant here. Yet it is also the country with the world's highest HIV/AIDS prevalence.

It is a land of oddities. Police stations have been known to hire private security firms to protect them. An investigation at the Beitbridge border post in 2001 revealed that five immigration officials were themselves illegal immigrants. Its engineers performed a modern miracle, bringing the pure mountain waters of Lesotho 500 miles to South Africa's industrial heartland. Yet 50 percent of domestic water supply in Soweto goes to waste because of leaking pipes.

Efforts to bring electricity and tap water to the poor are being fast-tracked. Yet scores can still die in cholera outbreaks. Millions live in urban shacks, while the democratically elected government carries out a housing program without parallel anywhere in the world, building more than 150,000 subsidized start-up homes a year, while teaching unsophisticated people how to budget for home loan repayments.

South Africa's peoples are impatient for a better life. Yet they show forbearance and restraint when early hopes are dashed. They have an offbeat sense of humor and enjoy the absurdities of life. Their unique capacity for forgiveness and reconciliation made possible a national healing process in the 1990s that astounded a world braced for a South African race war.

This is a land of song and sport. South Africa won the rugby world cup in 1995 (Nelson Mandela wore the Springbok No. 6 shirt at the presentations). It was one of the first African nations to qualify for the soccer world cup of 2002. String quartets from Soweto perform African interpretations of Bach, while Johnny Clegg, the White Zulu, redefines what it is to be a song-and-dance man.

Media cover the full spectrum. Upper income groups have a choice of more than 60 local and global TV channels. International and local brands battle for shelf space in huge supermarkets or in township spaza shops where retailing was a criminal activity until a few years ago (apartheid laws prevented black people from owning and running their own stores).

With a past like that, is it any wonder Disruption has so much contemporary appeal? South Africans of the transformation years are uniquely receptive to the notion that established precedents are there to be overturned, not honored in perpetuity.

So, just maybe, if Disruption as a philosophy and a methodology continues to take root in South Africa, it could change the country, the continent, even the world. There is so much global pessimism and uncertainty right now. Yet there are also the first stirrings of an African Renaissance. If it is not to be stillborn, we will have to quantum-leap into the future, not tiptoe toward it. Africa can no longer go to the West and say, "It's about our future. We'd like to have one."

We will have to be optimistic and think out of the box that was previously labeled "Africa." We have one successful precedent. South Africa's leap into democracy and shared nationhood after the barren years of apartheid.

If we can disrupt that convention, we can disrupt anything.

Exhibit B
Five Major Value Shifts Common to Youth in Japan, China, Hong Kong, Singapore, and Malaysia
From Modesty to Confidence

Asian youth are more confident about themselves. Exposed and supported by increasing wealth, better education, and greater access to information, they believe they can perform as well as (or even better than) their elders. Rising material wealth has also established higher aspirations. And reinforced their belief in their ability to change things.

From Listening to Speaking

Traditionally, communication was one way. In the past, Asian youth were taught to obey and listen. And never to argue back. The Confucian ethic established a "do as you are told" mode of communication between generations and levels in society. Today's youth have been given the freedom to express themselves (although still in socially acceptable ways).

From Identical to Identifiable

With this shift from a communal to an individual ethic, Asian youth are struggling to find the balance between "we and me." On one hand, they want to stand out from the crowd, but on the other hand, they want to be assured that their peers will accept them. They do not want to be unique, but neither do they want to be identical. Coupled with rising confidence, a balance has been struck: to be a nonconventional conformist. This value shift has been the key driver behind the lightning-fast adoption and rejection of youth fashion in major Asian cities.

From Thinking to Feeling

On the surface, Asian culture tends to be rational. Emotions are very seldom publicly expressed. Do not shout in public. Do not fight. Do not engage in intimate behavior in public. Be cool. Do not show your heart. There has been a strong shift toward public expression. Asian youth have become, and are becoming, much more expressive. While IQ is still vital in these markets, EQ is becoming an important part of social life.

From Spoon-fed to Exploring Life

Traditional learning is by rote. Confucian culture places educators, bureaucrats, and parents on a pedestal. Learn by copying. Repeat after me. Over and over.

We have seen a radical shift in this mode of instruction, primarily driven by an opening up of markets to Western education and the increasing number of influencers studying in the United States, United Kingdom, Australia, and Europe.

In addition, particularly in China, the thirst for knowledge is evidenced by strong desire to travel within and out of China. The rising popularity of TV stations such as the Discovery Channel and shows presented by *National Geographic* also reflects this value shift.

Today, Asian youth are taking the Chinese idiom, "You shouldn't only sit in one tree until you die," to heart.